Hardware Implementation
of Intelligent Systems

Studies in Fuzziness and Soft Computing

Editor-in-chief
Prof. Janusz Kacprzyk
Systems Research Institute
Polish Academy of Sciences
ul. Newelska 6
01-447 Warsaw, Poland
E-mail: kacprzyk@ibspan.waw.pl
http://www.springer.de/cgi-bin/search_book.pl?series=2941

Horia-Nicolai Teodorescu
Lakhmi C. Jain · Abraham Kandel
Editors

Hardware Implementation of Intelligent Systems

With 105 Figures
and 6 Tables

Physica-Verlag

A Springer-Verlag Company

Prof. Horia-Nicolai Teodorescu
Romanian Academy
Calea Victoriei 125
Bucharest
Romania
hteodor@etc.tuiasi.ro

Prof. Lakhmi C. Jain
University of South Australia
Knowledge-Based Intelligent
Engineering Systems Centre
Adelaide, Mawson Lakes
South Australia 5095
Lakhmi.Jain@unisa.edu.au

Prof. Abraham Kandel
University of South Florida
Computer Science and Engineering
4202 E. Fowler Ave., ENB 118
Tampa, Florida 33620
USA
kandel@csee.usf.edu

ISSN 1434-9922
ISBN 978-3-7908-2491-9   e-ISBN 978-3-7908-1816-1

Cataloging-in-Publication Data applied for
Die Deutsche Bibliothek – CIP-Einheitsaufnahme
Hardware implementation of intelligent systems: with 6 tables / Horia-Nicolai Teodorescu ... ed. – Heidel-
berg; New York: Physica-Verl., 2001
    (Studies in fuzziness and soft computing; Vol. 74)

Physica-Verlag Heidelberg New York
a member of BertelsmannSpringer Science+Business Media GmbH

© Physica-Verlag Heidelberg 2010
Printed in Germany

Hardcover Design: Erich Kirchner, Heidelberg

Preface

Intelligent systems are now being used more commonly than in the past. These involve cognitive, evolving and artificial-life, robotic, and decision-making systems, to name a few. Due to the tremendous speed of development, on both fundamental and technological levels, it is virtually impossible to offer an up-to-date, yet comprehensive overview of this field. Nevertheless, the need for a volume presenting recent developments and trends in this domain is huge, and the demand for such a volume is continually increasing in industrial and academic engineering communities. Although there are a few volumes devoted to similar issues[1], none offer a comprehensive coverage of the field; moreover they risk rapidly becoming obsolete. The editors of this volume cannot pretend to fill such a large gap. However, it is the editors' intention to fill a significant part of this gap.

A comprehensive coverage of the field should include topics such as neural networks, fuzzy systems, neuro-fuzzy systems, genetic algorithms, evolvable hardware, cellular automata-based systems, and various types of artificial life-system implementations, including autonomous robots. In this volume, we have focused on the first five topics listed above.

The volume is composed of four parts, each part being divided into chapters, with the exception of part 4. In Part 1, the topics of "Evolvable Hardware and GAs" are addressed. In Chapter 1, "Automated Design Synthesis and Partitioning for Adaptive Reconfigurable Hardware", Ranga Vemuri and co-authors present state-of-the-art adaptive architectures, their classification, and their applications. Efficient and retargetable design synthesis techniques that effectively exploit adaptive architectures are discussed. The authors provide a description of a collection of synthesis and partitioning techniques and their embodiment in a synthesis system.

In Chapter 2, the authors present a GA specifically conceived for efficient hardware implementation. Based on this algorithm, a pipelined genetic algorithm processor is presented that can generate one new chromosome per machine cycle. The functions of parent selection, crossover, mutation, evaluation, and survival are implemented in hardware

---

[1]For example the volume *Kandel, A. & Langholz G. (Eds.): Fuzzy Hardware. Architectures and Applications, Kluwer, 1998*

in such a manner that each function can be executed in a single machine cycle. A linear pipeline architecture is introduced connecting the function blocks. The GA machine prototype runs at 1 MHz and generates one million new chromosomes per second.

The second section of the volume, "Fuzzy Logic Hardware Implementations" includes three chapters. Chapter 3, "Hardware Implementation of Intelligent Systems" represents an introductory overview of several issues related to the implementation of fuzzy logic systems and neural networks. The author emphasizes the hardware specifications issues specific to intelligent systems. The architectural specifications, technological specifications, and performance specifications are discussed. Various VLSI digital and analog implementations of intelligent systems are reviewed.

In Chapter 4, "High Performance Fuzzy Processors", methodologies for developing both fuzzy hardware architectures for general purpose, and task oriented fuzzy architectures are presented. An architecture exploiting specific properties of fuzzy processing, which simplifies and speeds up operation is examined. Technological issues and experimental results are presented. In Chapter 5, the authors introduce two versions of a digital fuzzy processor for fuzzy-rule-based systems designed for high speed. The hardware implementation issues are discussed in detail and implementation results are presented.

The third section of the volume is devoted to "Neural Networks Hardware Implementations". In Chapter 6, the application of the mean field annealing neural networks for optimum multiuser detection for CDMA systems is addressed and the analog VLSI hardware implementation of the application is discussed. In Chapter 7, "Analog VLSI Hardware Implementation of a Supervised Learning Algorithm", the authors present an analog chip hosting a self–learning neural network with local learning rate adaptation. Experimental results on two learning tasks and simulation results on handwritten character recognition are described. Several technological issues are also discussed.

In Chapter 8, "pRAM: the Probabilistic RAM Neural Processor", the author discusses the implementation of the pRAM as a VLSI processor incorporating 256 neurons with on-chip learning, with the capability of interconnection to form larger networks. Interestingly enough, the pRAM has originally been conceived to model the noisy release of neurotransmitter vesicles in synaptic connections, moreover, the reinforcement training used is also biologically realistic. Several applications, including thermal image processing systems, object identification, character recognition, biometric image analysis, and ATM network control are examined.

The volume also includes a section on advanced algorithms, "Part 4: Algorithms for Parallel Machines". In this section, a single chapter illustrates advances in graph algorithms – a field having applications in virtually all domains of AI and intelligent systems, including hardware design and communications. The topics dealt with by the authors are subgraph isomorphisms problems and applications. Complexity and parallelization issues and applications are discussed.

In all chapters the authors go beyond reviewing the state of the art in the field. Indeed, the contributors introduce developments on the leading edge of cognitive science and technology.

The editors have aimed to present key aspects in this book. These include:

- offering an overview of a large spectrum of implementations for the computational intelligence based on neuro-fuzzy and evolvable systems
- up-to-date references providing insights into several challenging interdisciplinary research issues
- detailed explanations aimed at explaining the hardware implementation aspects of the new computational intelligence paradigms.

The editors hope that the book will be of great value to the researchers and practicing engineers alike. Doctoral students and researchers involved in the design, manufacturing, and use of hardware for intelligent systems, and engineers from high-tech industries, universities, and research institutes will find this volume a must for their reference libraries. Graduate students in the following fields may also find the volume an essential supplementary reading:

- computer engineering
- computer science
- electronic engineering, especially those active in solid-state circuit implementation
- cognition scientists interested in implementations
- microsystems / microtechnology.

This is a multidisciplinary book which may interest Ph.D. students and scientists in areas connected with the above-mentioned fields. We hope that the bio medical engineers, applied physicists, and biologists utilizing intelligent systems or looking for hardware models for processes in their fields will find issues of interest in this volume.

We have tested part of this volume as a textbook for graduate classes with excellent results. Teachers wishing to adopt this book as an additional reading for their classes are invited to contact the first Editor for additional material (in electronic format) supplementing the volume. The editors also intend to provide a web page with teaching material.

Acknowledgments

We are grateful to all those who have helped us in building up this volume. In the first place, we kindly thank all contributors for endeavoring the trying and time consuming task of writing and revising chapters several times. We also thank them for their patience during the refereeing process and the overall editing process.

We are particularly grateful to colleagues and contributors who helped revise this volume. Dr. Srinivas Katkoori (University of South Florida), Dr. Barry Shacklefield (Hewlett Packard), Mr. Scott Dock (University of South Florida), and Mr. Dan-Marius Dobrea (Technical University of Iasi) helped reviewing a large number of chapters. Dr. Katkoori was extremely helpful in recommending a new chapter for inclusion. Other colleagues, namely Prof. Daniel Mlynek and Mr. Xavier Peillon (Swiss Institute of Technology of Lausanne), Dr. Adrian Brezulianu (Technical University of Iasi) and Dr. Cristian Bonciu (Montreal, Canada) have reviewed one chapter each. Thanks are due to R. Corban and I.V. Pletea for correcting some of the chapters. Finally, we wish to express our sincere gratitude to Berend-Jan van der Zwaag, Bill Daniels and Ajita Jain for their help in the preparation of the manuscript.

We have been distinctly delighted to see the keen interest shown by Prof. Janusz Kacprzyk, the Book Series Editor, and we thank him for his kind invitation to publish with Springer Verlag.

We wish to thank the staff at Springer-Verlag, particularly Gabriele Keidel and Martina Bihn, for their excellent professional work in the production of this volume.

Horia-Nicolai L. Teodorescu
Lakhmi C. Jain
Abraham Kandel

Table of Contents

Part 1: Evolvable Hardware and GA

Chapter 1. Automated design synthesis and partitioning
for adaptive reconfigurable hardware 3
Ranga Vemuri, Sriram Govindarajan, Iyad Ouaiss, Meenakshi Kaul,
Vinoo Srinivasan, Shankar Radhakrishnan, Sujatha Sundaraman,
Satish Ganesan, Awartika Pandey, and Preetham Lakshmikathan

**Chapter 2. High-performance hardware design and
implementation of genetic algorithms 53**
*Barry Shackleford, Etsuko Okushi, Mitsuhiro Yasuda, Hisao Koizumi,
Katsuhiko Seo, Takahashi Iwamoto, and Hiroto Yasuura*

Part 2: Fuzzy Logic Hardware Implementations

Chapter 3. Hardware implementation of intelligent systems   91
Marco Russo and Luigi Caponetto

Part 3: Neural Networks Hardware Implementations

Part 4: Algorithms for Parallel Machines

Part 1

Evolvable Hardware and GA

Chapter 1

Automated Design Synthesis and Partitioning for Adaptive Reconfigurable Hardware

Ranga Vemuri, Sriram Govindarajan, Iyad Ouaiss, Meenakshi Kaul, Vinoo Srinivasan, Shankar Radhakrishnan, Sujatha Sundaraman, Satish Ganesan, Awartika Pandey, Preetham Lakshmikanthan

Digital Design Environments Laboratory, ECECS Department, ML 0030, University of Cincinnati, Cincinnati, OH 45221-0030, USA

The advent of reconfigurable logic arrays facilitates the development of adaptive architectures that have wide applicability as stand-alone intelligent systems. The hardware structure of such architectures can be rapidly altered to suit the changing computational needs of an application during its execution. The power of adaptive architectures has been demonstrated primarily in image processing, digital signal processing, and other areas such as neural networks and genetic algorithms. This chapter discusses the state-of-the-art adaptive architectures, their classification, and their applications.

In order to effectively exploit adaptive architectures, efficient and retargetable design synthesis techniques are necessary. Further, the synthesis techniques must be fully integrated with design partitioning methods to make use of the multiplicity of reconfigurable devices provided by adaptive architectures. This chapter provides a description of a collection of synthesis and partitioning techniques and their embodiment in the SPARCS (Synthesis and Partitioning for Adaptive Reconfigurable Computing Systems) system.

1
Introduction

With the advancement of the *Integrated Circuit* (IC) technology, the design of digital systems starting at the transistor-level or the gate-level is no longer viable. On the other hand, at higher levels of abstraction the design functionality and tradeoffs can be clearly stated. Therefore, use of automation from conceptualization to silicon became an integral part of the design cycle. This encouraged the development of Computer-Aided Design (CAD) automation tools that can handle the increasing complexity of the VLSI technology. In addition, CAD algorithms have the ability to perform a thorough search of the design space, i.e. contemplate several design possibilities, in order to generate high quality designs.

Currently, designers follow a top-down methodology where they describe the intent of the design and let CAD tools add detailed physical structure to it. This method of synthesizing systems from a design description suits the design of large systems. Thus, the design process could handle the increasing demands on the system complexity as well as the time-to-market. High-Level Synthesis (HLS) [1], in particular, is the process of generating a structural implementation from the behavioral specification (functionality) of a design. At this point of evolution, VLSI technology has reached a stage where high-level synthesis of VLSI chips and electronic systems is becoming more cost effective and less time consuming than being manually handcrafted.

The field-programmable logic arrays led to the development of reconfigurable devices. Reconfigurable devices such as the *Field-Programmable Gate Arrays* (FPGAs) consisting of a sea of uncommitted logic devices offer the same performance advantages as that of the custom VLSI chips while retaining the flexibility of general-purpose processors. It is predicted that in the near future, reconfigurable devices will offer 100× performance improvement over contemporary microprocessors, 20× progress in density (gate-count), 10-100× reduction in power gate, and 1,000,000× reduction in reconfiguration time compared to the current devices [2]. The advancement of the reconfigurable device technology facilitated the development of *adaptive architectures* that can dynamically change during the execution of an application. Such adaptive hardware architectures are at the heart of *Reconfigurable Computers* (RCs). An RC typically consists of one or more re-programmable processing elements, memory banks, interconnection network across these devices, and interface hardware to the external environment. The wide variety of RC resources enables RCs to act as stand-alone intelligent systems.

Research in the field of CAD for RCs is still in its nascent stages. In order to demonstrate a performance improvement over conventional microprocessors, most of the applications are handcrafted for a specific RC architecture [3]. Typically, the handcrafted applications are small, requiring little hardware design and the RC architectures are simple, most often having a single reconfigurable device. The designers primarily rely on application-level parallelism to obtain speed-up. Whereas many large-scale applications that have inherent computation-level, instruction-level, word-level, and bit-level parallelism have not been exploited.

A wide variety of RCs available in the market today offer tremendous reconfigurable computing power, and may be used for realizing implementations of computation intensive applications. In order to effectively exploit the RC architectures, efficient and retargetable design synthesis techniques are necessary. Further, the synthesis techniques must be fully integrated with design partitioning methods to make use of the multiplicity of reconfigurable devices provided by RC architectures. Synthesis and partitioning techniques need to mature to be able to fully utilize the computing power of RCs and handle challenging applications.

This chapter is organized as follows. Section 2 provides a description of RC architectures, a survey of RC application domains, and a classification of currently available RCs. Section 3 describes a typical RC design flow and the fundamental problems in the design automation of RCs. Section 4 provides an overview of the SPARCS synthesis and partitioning environment. Section 5 introduces the computational models used to capture the design specification in SPARCS.

Sections 6 and 7 describe techniques used to solve the temporal and spatial partitioning problems, respectively. In Section 8, we describe the techniques for solving the interconnection synthesis problem. Finally, in Section 9, we provide insight into techniques used to solve some primary issues in design synthesis for RCs.

2
Adaptive Reconfigurable Hardware Systems

A generic adaptive reconfigurable hardware system, or a reconfigurable computer, is shown in Figure 1. An RC typically consists of the following components:

Reconfigurable devices: Although the capacities of a configurable device, such as a Field Programmable Gate Array (FPGA) [4], have been increasing rapidly, they are nowhere close to the gate-capacity of the full-custom or semi-custom ASICs. Therefore, it is common to design large-scale RC systems using multiple reconfigurable devices such as FPGAs or special-purpose processors, on a single printed circuit board.

Memory banks: These are usually based on RAMs (Random - Access Memory) that provide data storage space for computation. They also provide means of data communication between the external environment and the reconfigurable devices. Memory banks can be viewed as either being *shared* between multiple reconfigurable devices or *local* to a single reconfigurable device.

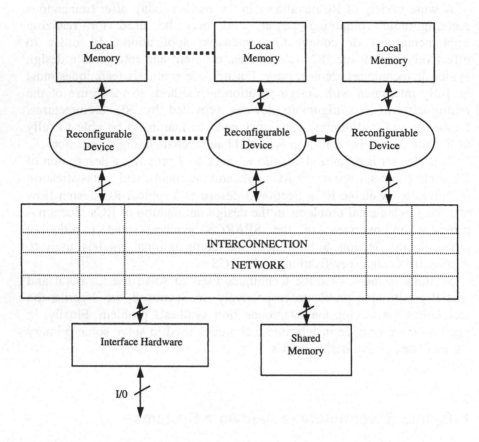

Fig. 1. A Generic Reconfigurable Computer Model

Interconnection network: Interconnection network is a collection of *dedicated* or *programmable* connections between the components of the RC. A programmable interconnection network can be configured to provide a desired set of connections, whereas a dedicated network offers fixed hardware connections.

Interface hardware: The interface consists of a variety of application-specific I/O connectors such as PCI ports, and/or extension ports to expand the RC hardware. The interface is used for downloading input data to the RC, controlling its reconfiguration, and monitoring its execution.

2.1
Reconfigurable Computer Applications

The application domain suitable for RCs usually covers problems that are computationally intensive and exhibit parallelism. These include digital signal processing algorithms [5] [6], image processing [7], database search algorithms [7], multimedia algorithms [8], genetic algorithms [9], and neural network applications [10].

Table 1 lists a collection of design examples from various application domains. The designs have been primarily handcrafted for various RC architectures and the results published. These examples are *Genetic Partitioning* [11], *Boolean Satisfiability* [12], *Neural Networks* [13], *Image Correlation* [14], and *Mean Filter* [15]. An important feature is that all these systems have inherent data parallelism at different levels of abstraction. Most of the examples used little inter-device communication. Similarly, the usage of the RC memory is very little, with data mostly being hard-wired of self-generated. Speed-up in the examples using *Xilinx 4000* devices, required multiple FPGA devices without using host-to-device communication and using only self-generated data. Speed-up in the examples using *Xilinx 6200* devices required the data to be distributed within each device using the feature of direct addressability of logic cells. Also, these design examples were carefully synthesized into parallel and pipelined structures.

Table 1: Comparative study of designs implemented on RCs

Feature	Genetic Partition	Boolean Satisfiability	Neural Networks	Image Correlation	Mean Filter
FPGA Type	XC6200	XC4000	XC3000	XC62000	XC6200
# FPGAs	1	64	4	1	1
Run-time Reconfig.	yes (partial reconfig.)	no	yes	yes (partial reconfig.)	no
Data Communic.	Self-generated	Self-generated	local memory (1 or 4)	memory mapped + hard wired	memory mapped from host
Level of Parallelism	block-level	algorithm-level	word-level	bit-level	word-level
Published Results	(20 Mhz 2 parallel 87 stage pipelines)	8× speed-up		projected 2× speed-up (more than 23 FPGAs)	50× speed-up (10mhz, 32 stage pipeline)	10× speed-up

Goldstein and Schmit [3] have compiled a similar variety of design examples that demonstrate a 10× speed-up when using an RC over a conventional microprocessor.

2.2
Classification of Reconfigurable Computers

Over the last decade, several RC architectures have emerged in order to meet the increasing computational demands of various application domains. Most RCs that are available currently can be classified based on the type of reconfigurable devices used:

Field-Programmable Gate Array: The FPGA [4] [16] is usually a stream-reprogrammable device that can be reconfigured by serially loading the entire configuration bit-stream into a logical program register. For such devices, the reconfiguration time is sufficiently high (in the order of milliseconds [4]) since the entire bit-stream needs to be reloaded. An RC architecture may be based on one or more FPGA devices. The *Xilinx Demo Board* [4] is an RC with a single FPGA device. Examples of multi-FPGA RCs are *Wildforce* [17], *GigaOps* [18], and *Garp* [19].

Reconfigurable Processor Array: The FPGA consists of an array of fine-grained programmable elements called CLBs (Configurable Logic Blocks) [4]; whereas, the reconfigurable processor array is a device consisting of an array of coarse-grained processing elements. The REMARC [20] is such a device consisting of an array of 64 16-bit reconfigurable processing elements and a global control unit. The REMARC device, unlike an FPGA, uses *instruction words* to control the configuration of the processing elements as well as interconnection network. An RC architecture based on the REMARC reconfigurable device is presented in [8] and another RC architecture based on a reconfigurable processor array is the *Raw microprocessor* [21].

Partially Reconfigurable FPGA: The recently introduced bit-reprogrammable FPGAs, the *6200 series from Xilinx* [22] make it possible to reconfigure selected portions of the device without having to reload the entire bit-stream. In these architectures, the reconfigurable logic is fully accessible such that specific logic cells can be addressed, or *memory-mapped*, and reconfigured as desired. Bit-reprogrammable devices reduce the reconfiguration time by a factor of 1,000,000×, from milliseconds to nanoseconds. These devices are quite conductive to permit reconfiguration mid-way through an application execution. The *Firefly* [23] and *Virtual Workbench* [24] are examples of RCs based on a single partially reconfigurable FPGA. The *ACE Card* [25] and *Wildstar* [26] are examples of RCs based on multiple partially reconfigurable FPGAs.

Context-Switching FPGA: This is an enhancement that allows complete reconfiguration of an FPGA at a rate far better than that of the standard FPGA. A context-switching FPGA device has the ability to store multiple configurations (or *contexts*) and switch between them on a clock-cycle basis. Also, a new configuration can be loaded while another configuration is active (or in execution). The *Time-Multiplexed* FPGA [27], from *Xilinx Corporation* can store up to seven context and switch between them through an internal controller. The *Context-Switching* FPGA [28] from *Sanders − A Lockheed Martin Company*, can store four contexts and has a powerful cross-context data sharing mechanism implemented within the device.

Hybrid Processor: This type of hybrid architecture comprises of a main processor that is tightly coupled with a Reconfigurable Logic Array (RLA). A portion of the device area is devoted for conventional microprocessor architecture and the remaining for an RLA. NAPA [29] is such a hybrid processor consisting of an *Adaptive Logic Processor* resource combined with a general-purpose scalar processor called the *Fixed Instruction processor*. An RC architecture based on the NAPA processor is also presented in [29]. The *MorphoSys* [30] is another RC architecture that has a coarse-grained reconfigurable logic array and a MIPS-like RISC processor.

From a different perspective, the RCs can also be classified based on their usage:

Coprocessor: RC coprocessors are subservient to a host processor. The host processor executes the application, occasionally configuring the coprocessor to perform a special function and delegating portions of the application, that needs a special function, to the coprocessor. The host maintains the set of permissible coprocessor configurations as a library of "hardware functions". If the host is a high-end workstation computer, it is possible to keep a large number of configurations on the hard disk. If the host is a small DSP-style motherboard, then it is possible to store only a small number of configurations in the RAM. This number of configurations that can be stored in the system impacts the synthesis process. Often coprocessor applications attempt to absorb the reconfiguration overhead through parallel execution of the host processor and the coprocessor.

Embedded Processor: One can view the RC as an embedded processor when it is not attached to any host processor. Embedded RC architectures contain a finite number of alternative configurations stored on ROMs (Read - Only Memory) on-board. A micro-operation system, also loaded in an on-board ROM, controls the loading of these configurations.

Statically / Dynamically Reconfigurable Processor: During the course of execution of an application, the RC may be reconfigured only once to act as a *statically* reconfigurable processor, or several times to act as a *dynamically* reconfigurable processor. From an application perspective, statically reconfigurable RCs offer a finite set of hardware resources that can be configured to execute the application. On the other hand, dynamically reconfigurable RCs offer an infinite set of hardware resources, only a finite number of which can be used at any time during the execution of the application.

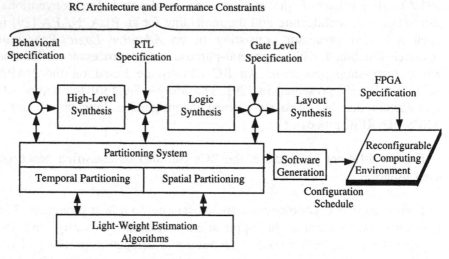

Fig. 2. Design Automation for Reconfigurable Computers

In this section, we described the generic RC architecture model, provided references to number of RC architectures, and classified them according to the reconfigurable device type and usage. In the following section, we will describe design automation techniques for RCs.

3
Design Automation for Reconfigurable Computers

The design automation techniques for RCs are shown in Figure 2. The design process generates *bit-streams* for configuring the hardware and a *configuration schedule*, which controls loading of the bit-streams on the hardware. The configuration schedule is either a software program running on a host-computer attached to the co-processor, or a controller program that is loaded on a ROM and running from within the embedded processor. This chapter will cover design automation techniques for the generation of configuration bit-streams such that the hardware resources on the RC are efficiently utilized.

The design automation process involves *synthesis and partitioning* of a given design specification. The design flow can start from any of the three levels of abstraction, behavioral level, Register-Transfer Level (RTL), and gate level. At each level, the RC architecture and the performance constraints are provided. The design is specified at behavioral level as an algorithmic description, at RT level as a structural net-list of components, and at the gate level as a set of boolean equations. As we move top-down, from behavior-level to gate-level, the design specification embodies structural details.

At the RTL and gate level, since the design structure has already been decided, synthesis and partitioning of designs either lead to poor utilization of the RC resources, or have higher chances of failure. Moreover, it is almost impossible for the designer to consider all RC architectural constraints while specifying a design at the RTL or gate level. Vahid et al. [31] have shown the advantages of functional partitioning over structural partitioning approaches. Although few special-purpose systems have a design entry at the gate/logic level [27], [28], the focus of the state-of-the-art RC research is on automating the process of High-Level Synthesis (HLS) and behavioral partitioning of specifications, starting at a high-level of abstraction.

Further research is required in the area of HLS [32] [33] before these algorithms become practical and applicable to the RC design flow. On the other hand, logic and layout synthesis algorithms [32] [34] [35] introduced two decades ago, are well established, with sound mathematical models for optimization. At the expense of computing time, logic and layout synthesis algorithms perform a near-exhaustive search, and are capable of producing good quality designs. Although quite mature, logic and layout synthesis algorithms have not been able to efficiently control the area-speed tradeoffs for large-scale designs, the main drawbacks being poor device utilization and poor performance for high-density designs. This inability to handle large designs is compensated by allowing the HLS to explore tradeoffs at a higher level of abstraction. High-level synthesis techniques that perform efficient search of the design space are still emerging.

Behavioral partitioning for RCs can be classified into two sub-problems, *temporal partitioning* and *spatial partitioning*, explained in the following sections. Behavioral partitioning algorithms need to obtain estimates about the design that is being partitioned. To synthesize designs that efficiently utilize the RC resources, the partitioning algorithms need to closely interact with lightweight (fast) estimation algorithms that predict the outcome of synthesis.

The following sections will provide an informal overview of the fundamental problems involved in the design automation of RCs. For further details, interested readers can refer to the rich set of literature available in the proceedings of the FCCM [36] and the FPGA [37] conferences.

3.1
Design Specification Model

The design specified in a Hardware Description Language (HDL), such as VHDL [38], is usually captured into an intermediate *computational model* and used for partitioning and synthesis. The computational model is typically a graph-based representation, with nodes representing elements of computation and edges representing the flow of data and control. Some well-known computational models are communicating sequential processes [38] [39], synchronous dataflow [40], program-state machines [41], and CDFGs [42] [43].

For the design automation process to effectively utilize the rich set of resources on an RC, the computational model of the specification should support the following features:

  (i)   Explicit capture of *parallelism* at the fine-grain (e.g. statement-level in VHDL) and coarse-grain (e.g. process-level in VHDL) levels;
  (ii) Allow contiguous *data storage* (arrays) that can be mapped to the physical memory banks;
  (iii) Capture of *data communication* at the coarse-grain level (e.g. across computations among different processes in VHDL);
  (iv) Provide *synchronization* mechanism for computations at the coarse-grain level of parallelism;
  (v)   *Capture computations* at the fine-grain level of parallelism, using representation such as a Data Flow Graph (DFG).

For these features, the model should provide well-defined *synthesis semantics* that are precisely interpreted by the design automation tools.

3.2
Temporal Partitioning

A behavioral specification that is reasonably large – does not fit within the given RC hardware – can be partitioned *over time* into a sequence of temporal segments. A *temporal segment* is a subgraph of the given computational model of the behavior. Every synthesized temporal segment is allowed to utilize all the resources in the RC. In order to execute the design, the RC is configured to execute each synthesized temporal segment, one at a time, in the sequence of temporal steps generated by temporal partitioning. Thus, the RC is *dynamically reconfigured* several times during the execution of an application. The key issues in temporal partitioning are: (1) the time taken to reconfigure the RC; (2) the memory space required to store the live data between temporal segments; and (3) the estimation of the hardware requirements of a synthesized temporal segment.

Typically, a temporal partitioner attempts to minimize reconfiguration overhead. The partitioner also ensures that the amount of live data between temporal segments fits within the available memory space by assuming a lumped model of data communication. More importantly, the partitioner has to ensure that the estimates about the hardware requirements have to be close to the actual synthesized values. Otherwise, it could lead to failure later in the design process. Therefore, it is imperative that temporal partitioning obtains these estimates through some lightweight high-level synthesis process.

3.3
Spatial Partitioning

Spatial partitioning involves partitioning each temporal segment into as many spatial segments as the number of reconfigurable devices on the RC. A *spatial segment* is a subgraph of a given temporal segment and a *spatial partition* of the temporal segment is the collection of all mutually exclusive spatial segments generated by spatial partitioning. The primary issues in spatial partitioning are: (1) estimating the area requirements of the spatial partition, such that each spatial segment when synthesized fits in the FPGA, (2) partitioning the memory requirements across the available memory banks, and (3) estimating the interconnect requirements between the spatial segments.

The estimation of partition areas is complicated, especially in the presence of performance constraints such as latency of the temporal segment. This is because spatial partitioning of a behavior needs to make efficient area-speed tradeoffs in order to produce high quality designs. Furthermore, spatial partitioning usually performs memory partitioning along with the partitioning of computations. These problems can be efficiently solved only through a well-defined interaction with high-level exploration and synthesis. Finally, spatial partitioning is typically integrated with interconnection estimation, in order to determine the interconnection feasibility.

3.4
Interconnection Synthesis

Many RC architectures [17] [18] [23] [24] [25] [26] provide the flexibility of programmable interconnection networks in order to realize different connectivity patterns among the RC resources. This poses a severe constraint on the partitioner in estimating the routability of signals across the contemplated partition segments. The effort required in modifying existing CAD tools to handle a new RC interconnect architecture is often comparable to that of developing a new CAD algorithm specific to that interconnect architecture. An ideal multi-device partitioning tool must be able to support a generic interconnection model.

It is essential for any partitioning algorithm targeting multi-device boards to appropriately assign logic signals to the device I/0 pins. This is due to the fact that pins of a device are not functionally identical in establishing the same connection pattern between the processing elements. The viability of routing connections between devices is contingent on the correct assignment of the logic signals to the pins. This problem is referred to as *pin assignment* and directly impacts the functionality of the programmable interconnection. The *interconnection synthesis* problem for RC architectures is the unified problem of generating a pin assignment and synthesizing the appropriate configuration stream for the programmable interconnection network, such that a given interconnection requirement is met.

3.5
Design Synthesis

High-Level Synthesis (HLS) [1] [32] [33] [42] is the process of generating a structural implementation from a behavioral specification, so that the design constraints such as area, latency, clock period, power, etc. are best satisfied. The behavioral specification is typically algorithmic in nature, without any architectural details. The structural implementation is usually at the register-transfer level of abstraction consisting of a *datapath* and a *controller*. The datapath is a structural net-list of components, such as ALUs, registers, and multiplexers, and the controller is a finite state machine that sequences the execution of datapath components.

Given a behavioral specification, there are many different structures that can realize the behavior. Each such structural implementation denotes a *design point* and the set of all possible design points determines the *design space* of the specification. One of the most compelling reasons for developing HLS systems [32] [44] is the desire to quickly explore a wide range of design points. The goal of *design space exploration* is to identify possible implementation alternatives from the design space of a behavioral specification, such that the design constraints are satisfied. In the following section, we will describe some basic issues that have to be addressed in design synthesis for RCs.

Synthesis with Partitioning

Design automation involving HLS and partitioning can be broadly classified into the *vertical* and the *integrated* design flows. There are two approaches to the vertical design flow, namely: (1) HLS followed by structural partitioning, and (2) behavioral partitioning followed by HLS. The primary disadvantage of the first approach [45] [46] is that structural partitioning is done on a pre-synthesized design and could fail most often due to I/0 pin shortage. The second approach [31] [47] [48] is more efficient since behavioral partitioning contemplates several partition solutions prior to HLS. However, this approach relies heavily on pre-synthesized design points that limit the exploration process.

On the other hand, researchers [31] [49] [50] developed the *integrated* design flow where the design space exploration is performed in conjunction with partitioning. Partitioning algorithms are typically based on global search techniques such as Genetic Algorithm (GA) or Simulated Annealing (SA), and hence contemplate millions of partitions during the search. It would be imprudent to apply exploration techniques based on either *exact models* [51] [52] [53] or *simultaneous scheduling and binding* [54] [55] [56], since it would take an impractical amount of time for partitioning with dynamic exploration. Hence, we require heuristic exploration techniques that primarily perform the *scheduling* phase of HLS along with design estimation. More importantly, the exploration technique should have the ability to *simultaneously explore multiple spatial segments* to effectively satisfy global constraints such as design latency.

Arbiter Synthesis

Another issue in design synthesis is resource sharing. After partitioning, a physical resource on the RC might be shared between parallel execution threads, thereby requiring arbitration. RCs offer a varying number of physical resources. For instance, a RC board can have a variable number of physical memory segments or a variable number of interconnection pins. To support architecture independence, the synthesis tool must be able to synthesize the same design for different boards.

If the design makes use of L resources (e.g. logical memory segments) and the board only has P such resources (e.g. physical memory segments), then two cases arise: when L is less than or equal to P, and when L is greater than P. Obviously, if L is less than or equal to P, then the mapping is straightforward: each design resource is mapped to an individual physical resource. On the other hand, when L is greater than P, there are more used resources in the design than there are physical resources on the multi-FPGA board. In this case, the mapping becomes difficult since more than one design resource has to be mapped to the same physical resource. This mapping might introduce resource access conflicts since different process might be accessing the different design resources.

It would be advantageous to have a mechanism that would resolve resource access conflicts thereby providing the flexibility of freely scheduling resource access during HLS. At the same time, this mechanism should not introduce complexity to the partitioning process.

Integrating Logic Synthesis with HLS

The traditional HLS process synthesizes operations in a behavior to components picked from a given RTL library. This library is pre-characterized so that the HLS can predict the area and performance of the design that is being synthesized. For the reconfigurable device technology, the pre-characterized component data is highly dependent on the specific layout of the component. Therefore, an HLS tool accepts a *macro-library* consisting of pre-synthesized macro components that have layout specific shape information [54]. The use of such macro components enables HLS to make better estimates about the design. However, during logic synthesis, these macro components are treated as black boxes thereby preventing any kind of logic optimization across macros that would otherwise be achieved by fully flattened logic synthesis.

The RTL design is a sequential circuit consisting of combinational blocks separated by registers. The HLS process can be viewed as making optimization decisions that result in the insertion of registers and the formation of the combination blocks. Once the RTL design is generated, logic optimization is typically limited to within a combinational block. Therefore, it is necessary to come up with an efficient RTL design that maximizes logic optimization. This requires effective integration of logic synthesis with HLS.

The macro library is usually a one-time pre-characterized set of components that support only basic operation types in the input specification. This is insufficient since it restricts HLS design decisions that select the combinational blocks of the RTL design. On the other hand, HLS would highly benefit if the library were populated with efficient logic optimized macros.

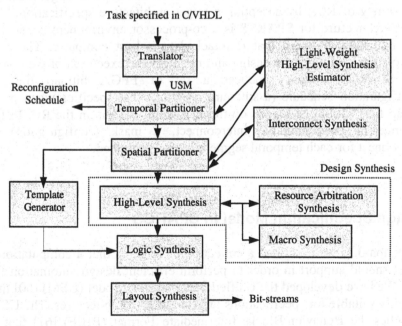

Fig. 3. SPARCS System

4
The SPARCS System: An Overview

The SPARCS system [57] [58] [59] (Synthesis and Partitioning for Adaptive Reconfigurable Computing Systems) is an integrated design system for automatically partitioning and synthesizing designs for reconfigurable boards with multiple devices (FPGAs). The SPARCS system (see Figure 3) accepts behavioral design specifications in VHDL [38] and compiles a *task graph* model called the Unified Specification Model (USM) (explained in the following section). The SPARCS system contains a temporal partitioning tool to temporally divide and schedule the tasks on the reconfigurable architecture, a spatial partitioning tool to map the tasks to individual FPGAs, and a collection of design synthesis tools to synthesize efficient register-transfer level designs for each set of tasks destined to be downloaded on each FPGA. Commercial logic and layout synthesis tools are used to complete logic synthesis, placement, and routing for each FPGA design segment. A distinguishing feature of the SPARCS system is the tight integration of the partitioning and synthesis tools to accurately predict and control design performance and resources utilization.

Another important feature of SPARCS is its ability to re-target a design to a variety of RCs, by accepting a target architecture specification. The target architecture for SPARCS is a co-processor environment consisting of a multi-FPGA board that is attached to a host computer. The host controls the loading of the design and monitors the execution of the board. The SPARCS system produces a set of FPGA bitmap files, a reconfiguration schedule (a software program) that specifies when these bitmap files should be loaded on the individual FPGAs in the RC. In the presence of programmable interconnect, a mask (configuration) of interconnect for each temporal segment is also generated.

5
Design Specification Model in SPARCS

In Section 3.1, we described a collection of features that a computational model should support in order to perform efficient design automation for RCs. We have developed the Unified Specification Model (USM) [60] that is highly suitable for specifications targeted to RC architectures. The USM embodies the Behavior Blocks Intermediate Format (BBIF) [61] that is well suited for high-level synthesis. In this section, we provide a short description of these computational models and further details may be obtained from [60] [61].

5.1
The Unified Specification Model

The USM is a hierarchical representation for capturing the behavior of a design. It is also possible to capture the behavior of the environment with which the design is supposed to interact. There are two levels in the hierarchy, the top level comprising of coarse-grain design objects and the lower-level describing the behavior of these objects. An example of the USM is shown in Figure 4. There are two types of design objects at the top-level, a design *task* (an ellipse in the figure) and a logical *memory segment* (a box in the figure). Tasks in the USM represent elements of computation and memory segments represents elements of data storage. In order to capture computations of a task, the BBIF model is used. The memory segments are *logical* since the user has the flexibility to specify as many as required, irrespective of the number of physical memories available on the RC. The tasks are further classified into *design tasks* and *environment tasks*. Design tasks are those that need to be synthesized onto the RC and environment tasks are used to extract information about the I/O interface of the complete design and the protocol.

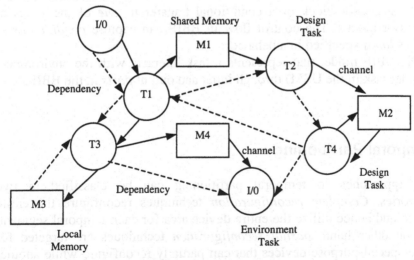

Fig. 4. An example of the Unified Specification Model

The implicit execution semantics of the USM can be described as follows. All tasks, as well as memory segments, are said to be *simultaneously alive* during execution. This captures the parallelism at the coarse-grain level of abstraction. The synchronization mechanism between tasks is established using *dependencies* and the data communication is established using *channels*. Through dependencies, a task may *wait* for an initiation signal from other tasks. The *execution cycle* for a USM model finishes when all the tasks are indefinitely waiting. The model assumes an indefinite wait at the end of each task to denote the completion of the task.

5.2
The Behavior Blocks Intermediate Format

The BBIF model is used to capture the behavior at the fine-grain level of parallelism. The BBIF[1] is a hierarchical CDFG [42] [32] representation with features well suited for *formally verified* HLS [61]. The BBIF model represents a behavioral *task* with a single thread of control. The BBIF is a graph with *behavior block* Nodes and *control flow* edges where each block contains a DFG [42] [32]. Thus, data flow and computations are captured within each behavior block, while the control flow is captured between the blocks. The control flow starts as the *root* block and transfers from one block to another through the *branch* construct provided at the end of each block. The branch construct specifies either an unconditional transfer to a single successor block or a conditional transfer to *one* of the series of successor blocks. The control flow in BBIF can capture *conditionals* as well as *loops* specified in a behavior.

The BBIF model that represents a task interacts with the environment (another task in the USM) through input and output *ports* in the BBIF.

6
Temporal Partitioning

The approaches to temporal partitioning can be classified in two categories. *Complete reconfiguration* techniques reconfigure the entire device and hence utilize the entire device area for each temporal segment. On the other hand, *partial reconfiguration* techniques are targeted for those special-purpose devices that can partially reconfigure while another

---

[1] The BBIF model is used in *Asserta*, an HLS system developed at the University of Cincinnati [61]

portion is executing. In the following sections we provide a survey of techniques in these categories and an overview of the temporal partitioning techniques developed for SPARCS.

6.1
Temporal Partitioning for Complete Reconfiguration

In the past, researchers have proposed temporal partitioning for designs at the logic-level or circuit-level. Spillane and Owen [62] perform temporal partitioning on gate level designs. The algorithm first performs a cone based clustering followed by a mapping of the clusters onto temporal segments. The entire gate level design is transformed into a number of clusters that are then scheduled on a XC6000 family FPGA. Chang and Marek-Sadowska [63] perform an exchanged Force Scheduling (FDS) [64] on gate level sequential circuits for the time-multiplexed FPGA [65]. The enhanced FDS algorithm produces a design that reduces the amount of data transfer required between temporal segments. Trimberger [27] takes post logic synthesis and technology mapped designs and again uses list based scheduling and its variations to perform temporal partitioning for the time-multiplexed FPGA [65].

Researchers have also proposed temporal partitioning techniques at a higher level of abstraction using operation-level data flow graph (DFG) as in traditional HLS. Vasilko and Ait-Boudaoud [66] have extended the static list-based scheduling technique of high-level synthesis for producing temporal segments. No functional unit sharing is performed and the area overhead due to registers needed to store data values between control steps is not taken into account. Gajjalapurna and Bhatia [67] perform a topological sort of the nodes in the DFG. Each node uses a distinct functional unit (from an RTL library), without any sharing. In their approach, each temporal segment is similar to a control step where registers are placed at the input and output of the temporal segment and operations are chained within each temporal segment. Gajjalapurna and Bhatia [68] also perform a depth first assignment of nodes to temporal segments such that the memory transfer required between temporal segments is smaller compared to their earlier approach [67]. Cardoso and Neto [69] extend [67] by providing a priority function based on reducing the critical path length of the partitioned graph. For each node in the DFG, pre-synthesized macro components are present and no sharing of the macro components or register insertion occurs during the process of temporal partitioning.

Optimal Temporal Partitioning in SPARCS

Design space exploration: A shortcoming of current automated temporal partitioning techniques is the selection of an implementation of the components of their design prior to partitioning. Since there are multiple implementations of the components with varying area/delay values, it would be more effective to choose the design implementation while partitioning the design by dynamically performing *design space exploration*. Temporal partitioning in SPARCS uses the USM as the input model. For each task in the USM, different *design points* (or Pareto points [32]) are derived from its design space. Depending on the resource/area constraint for the design, different implementations of the same task, which represent different area-time tradeoffs, are contemplated while performing temporal partitioning.

Block Processing: In many application domains such as Digital Signal Processing, computations are defined on very long streams of input data. In such applications, an approach known as *block processing* is used to increase the throughput of a system through the use of parallelism and pipelining (refer to parallel compilers [70] and VLSI processors [71]). Block processing is not only beneficial in parallelizing/pipelining applications, but in all cases where the net cost of processing k samples of data individually is higher than the net cost of processing k samples simultaneously. Most DSP applications, such as image processing, template matching and encryption algorithm, fall in this category.

Integrated design-space exploration and block processing: When the reconfiguration overhead is very large compared to the execution time of the task, it is clear that minimizing the number of the temporal partitions will achieve the *smallest latency* for the overall design. In the resultant solution, each task will usually be mapped to the smallest area design point for a task. However, it is *not necessary* that the minimum latency design is the best solution. We illustrate this idea with an example. In figure 5(a), two tasks are shown. Each task has two different design points on which it can be mapped. Two different solutions (b) and (c) are shown. If minimum latency solution is required, then solution (b) will be chosen over solution (c) because the latency of (b) is 500.3 μsec and latency of (c) is 1000.12 μsec. Now, if we use (b) and (c) in the block processing framework to process 5000 computations on each temporal partition, then the execution time for solution (b) is 2000 μseconds and for solution (c) is 1600 μseconds. Therefore, if we can integrate the knowledge about block processing while design space exploration is being done, then it is possible to choose more appropriate solutions. The price paid for block processing is the higher memory requirements for the reconfigured design. We call the number of data samples or inputs to be processed in each temporal partition, the *block processing factor, k* [72]. This is given by the user and is the minimum number of input data computations that this design will execute for typical runs of the application. The amount of block processing is limited by the amount of memory available to store the intermediate results.

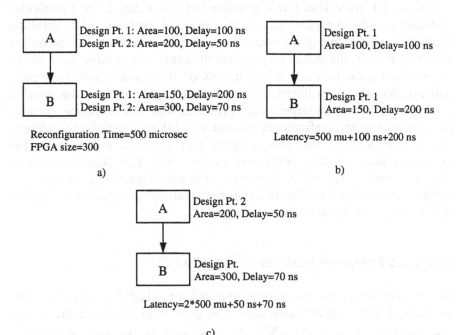

a)

b)

c)

Fig. 5. Design space exploration with block processing

Optimal Temporal Partitioning: The temporal partitioning and design space exploration problem can be formulated as an integer linear programming model. We will provide an overview of this model here, and interested readers may refer to [72] for the ILP equations and exact solution methods. This model can be informally stated as follows: *Minimize the design execution time such that the following constraints are satisfied*: 1. Each task is mapped to a temporal partition; 2. Each task is mapped to a design point; 3. The dependencies among the tasks are maintained; 4. The area constraint of each temporal partition is met; 5. The memory constraint is met.

For a given partition bound, the ILP model corresponding to the temporal partitioning problem is formed and solved. The partition bound is the number of partitions for which the current model has been formed and a solution is being explored. The solution for the current partition bound is the best solution when the given task graph is partitioned over the given partitions. The optimization goal takes into account the reconfiguration overhead of the design and the actual design execution time. Therefore, as the design space is explored, each task gets mapped to an appropriate design point for which the overall design execution time will be least, while satisfying the dependency, area, and memory constraints.

The model given above will generate the best solution for a particular partition bound. To explore the solution space of the temporal partitioning problem, we need to explore more than one partition bound. Based on the design points for the tasks, we generate the range of partitions over which the solution must be explored. Solutions of ILP models with increasing partition bounds are explored until no further improvement in the solution is observed. To handle large design problems with our technique, we also present an iterative refinement procedure [73] that iteratively explores different regions of the design space and leads to reduction in the execution time of the partitioned design. The ILP based integrated temporal partitioning and design space exploration technique forms a core solution method that is used in a constraint satisfying approach to explore different regions of the design space.

Heuristic Temporal Partitioning in SPARCS

In this approach, temporal partitioning and the scheduling phase of HLS are solved in a simultaneous step. The goal is to minimize the *design latency* defined as $k \cdot C_T + \sum_{i=1}^{k} d_p$, where k is the total number of temporal segments, C_T is the reconfiguration overhead of the RC, and d_p is the schedule length of each segment. This section provides an overview of our approach, and more details can be obtained from [74] [75]. We will use the term *segment* to mean a temporal segment and the term *control step* to mean a clock step (or RTL state) introduced by scheduling.

We have enhanced the Force Directed List Scheduling (FDLS) [64] algorithm to perform temporal partitioning and scheduling. FDLS is a resource constrained scheduling algorithm that finds a schedule with near-minimal control steps for a given resource set. The enhanced FDLS algorithm interacts with an estimation engine to estimate the RTL design cost while scheduling. If the RTL design cost of the scheduled specifications exceeds the device area, a new segment is formed by selecting a new resource set. The number of operations scheduled in a segment and the latency of each segment is decided by the resource set chosen.

The algorithm generates a resource set for each segment. The resource set determines the schedule for that segment. Initially, a *minimal* resource set (one resource for each operation type) is selected to generate the initial *solution* (schedules for all segments). The cost of the initial solution is evaluated in terms of the overall design latency. The initial solution has maximum design latency, since the resource set is minimal. The algorithm then, tries to improve the overall latency of the initial solution by exploring different resource sets for each segment iteratively. This could be achieved in two ways, either by reducing the latency of each segment, or by reducing the total number of segments. Both strategies are incorporated in the algorithm.

For each segment, the algorithm iteratively explores various resource sets thereby exploring different possible schedules. For each segment, the resource set is incrementally enlarged, until either the resulting schedule does not improve the overall design latency or the segment area exceeds the device area constraint. At this point, the algorithm attempts to maximize the resource sharing which could lead to a solution with smaller number of temporal segments. The current resource set represents the best solution (least design latency) obtained so far. Therefore, the current segment is scheduled with the current resource set. The algorithm moves to the next temporal segment and performs the resource set exploration again. This process terminates when all nodes in the DFG have been assigned to temporal segments.

6.2
Temporal Partitioning for Partial Reconfiguration

Other automated techniques for temporal partitioning focus on identifying and mapping partially reconfigurable regions to reduce reconfiguration delay. Luk et al. [76] take advantage of the partial reconfiguration capability of FPGAs and automate techniques of identifying and mapping reconfigurable regions from pre-temporally partitioned circuits. They represent successive temporal segments as weighted bipartite graphs to which matching algorithms are applied to determine common components. Schwabe et al. [77] take advantage of some of the feature of the Xilinx XC6200 family of FPGAs to reduce the reconfiguration time overhead by compression of the configuration bit streams. They have developed an algorithm that compresses the bit stream that is decompressed by the embedded hardware on the FPGA. Lechner and Guccione [78] provide a

Java based application-programming interface into the bit stream of the Xilinx 6200 family of FPGAs. A similar facility is provided by Guccione and Levi [79] for the Xilinx XC4000 family of devices. These interfaces provide a capability of designing, modifying and dynamically modifying the circuits for the FPGAs by operating on the FPGA bit streams.

Partial Reconfiguration Technique in SPARCS

Another approach to efficiently utilize reconfiguration feature of a device is to *overlap* execution of portions of the design with reconfiguration of other portions of the design. This can lead to partial, if not complete, amortization of the reconfiguration overhead posed by the device. We provide an overview of this approach, and more details can be obtained from [80], [81].

Figure 6 depicts the overview of our approach. The first phase involves *partitioning* the design into a sequence of temporal partitions. This is followed by a *pipelining* phase, where the execution of each temporal partition is pipelined with the reconfiguration of the following partition. Referring to Figure 6, at the ith instant, TP_i executes and TP_{i+1} reconfigures on the devices. Reconfiguration time of partition TP_{i+1} is reduced due to the overlap with execution of TP_i. Similarly, the $(i + 1)^{th}$ instant involves overlap of execution of TP_{i+1} and reconfiguration of TP_{i+2}. The *overlapped load and execute* cycle is repeated until all the temporal segments have been loaded and executed.

The proposed approach can be explained as follows. Let R_i be the reconfiguration time and E_i be the execution time of the ith segment. The total latency of the design using partial reconfiguration is:

$$Lat_n = R_1 + \sum_{i=1}^{n-1} \max(R_{i+1}, E_i) + E_n \tag{1}$$

Therefore, when $R_{i+1} - E_i \leq 0, \forall i \ 1 \leq i \leq n-1$ there is complete amortization of the reconfiguration overhead using partial reconfiguration. Hence, it is clear that in order to obtain significant improvement in design performance, the reconfiguration time of TP_{i+1} should be comparable to the execution time of TP_i. This allows maximal *overlap* between execution and reconfiguration and results in considerable reduction in reconfiguration overhead.

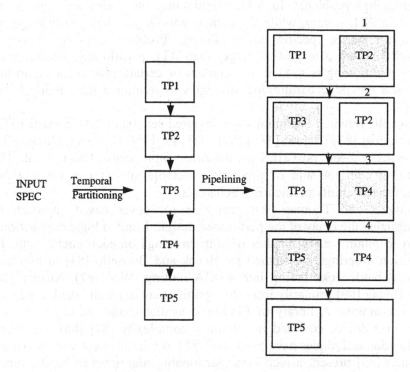

Fig. 6. Partitioning/Pipelining Methodology

When device reconfiguration times are much higher than design execution times, it becomes essential to group computationally intensive structures, e.g. loops, in a single temporal segment to increase E_i and thereby minimize $R_{i+1} - E_i$. The loop structures in the specification can be of two types: the loops are *explicit* when cycles are detected in the input graph; the loops are *implicit* when the entire application is repeated on several sets of input data. The latter type of loops is typically handled by *block processing*. The target architecture model consists of partially reconfigurable devices that are split into two parts, for execution and reconfiguration.

7
Spatial Partitioning

Spatial partitioning of a design may be performed at various levels: behavioral level, RTL, or gate-level. Gate-level and RTL partitioning are both *structural* level partitioning and are conceptually similar (graph partitioning) problems. In RTL partitioning, the nodes are components from an RTL library, while the components in gate-level partitioning are from the target specific device library. Problem sizes for gate-level partitioning are a magnitude larger than RTL partitioning. Usually gate-level partitioning is used in the context of certain placement algorithms that use recursive partitioning strategies to minimize the routing length [82].

The RC research community has invested several efforts in multi-FPGA partitioning [83] [84] [85] [86] [87] [88] [89] [90]. However, almost all of these have been post-HLS partitioning approaches. Chan et al. [83] partition with the aim of producing routable sub-circuits using a pre-partition routability prediction mechanism.

Sawkar and Thomas [90] present a set cover based approach for minimizing the delay of the partitioned design. Limited logic duplication is used to minimize the number of chip-crossings on each circuit path. Bi-partition orderings are studied by Hauck and Borriello [84] to minimize critical bottlenecks during inter-FPGA routing. Woo [87], Kuznar [88], and Haung [89] primarily limit their partitioners to handle device area and pin constraints. A library of FPGAs is available and the objective is to minimize device cost and interconnect complexity [89] [88]. Functional replication techniques have been used [88] to minimize cut size. Neogi and Sechen [85] present a rectilinear partitioning algorithm to handle timing constraints for a specific multi-FPGA system. Fang and Wu [86] present a hierarchical partitioning approach integrated with RTL/logic synthesis.

Behavioral partitioning is a pre-synthesis partitioning often called *functional* partitioning. Various studies [31] [91] [92] comparing behavioral and RTL partitioning show the superiority of the behavioral partitioning for large designs. However, behavioral partitioning must be guided by high-level estimators that make estimates on device area, memory size, I/O performance, and power. These estimations are performed by *high-speed* synthesis estimators. These estimators have to be lightweight because several thousands partition options may be examined. However, being light and accurate at the same time is very difficult. Sophisticated HLS estimation techniques are used to alleviate this difficulty, as described by Vahid [31]. A behaviorally partitioned system may use more gates, since hardware is not shared between partitions. However, since RTL partitions are I/O dominated, the RTL partitions do not tend to under-utilize the device. Thus, this increase in gates is not much of a concern. Behavioral partitioning has been promoted by several system level synthesis groups [31] [91] [92] [93] [94] [95] [96].

7.1
Issues in Spatial Partitioning

Besides *architecture independence* and *integration with synthesis,* the following is a list of issues that need to be addressed.

Utilization of Interconnection Resources: Typically, pins and routing resources are a primary bottleneck in RCs. However, certain behavioral transformations may alleviate such bottlenecks. For example, data transfer between partitions can be time-multiplexed through the same wires or through the use of shared memories.

Utilization of Memory: Memories in RCs have not been effectively used and memory partitioning is an open research area. Only recently, distribution of variables to memories has been discussed [97], but only in a limited scope. The authors do not address the issue of multiple FPGAs accessing a shared memory and the need for arbitration or synchronization. There are few partitioning environments for RCs that integrate both memory and multi-FPGA partitioning in a unified way.

Cost Models: Integrated cost models must be developed to evaluate partitioned designs. Typical cost metrics in RCs are area violation, inter-FPGA routability, critical wire length and clock speed estimation, design latency, and power. Due to the conflicting nature of various cost metrics, aggregate cost functions that optimize different costs are difficult to develop. If not carefully tuned, such functions often tend to work well only for a limited set of applications.

7.2
Spatial Partitioning in SPARCS

This section presents SPADE [96] [98], a system for partitioning designs onto multi-FPGA architectures. The input to SPADE is the Unified Specification Model (USM) [60] that is composed of computational tasks, memory tasks, and the communication and synchronization between tasks. SPADE consists of an iterative partitioning engine, an architectural constraint evaluator, and a throughput optimization and RTL design space exploration heuristic. We show how various architectural constraints can be effectively handled using an iterative partitioning engine.

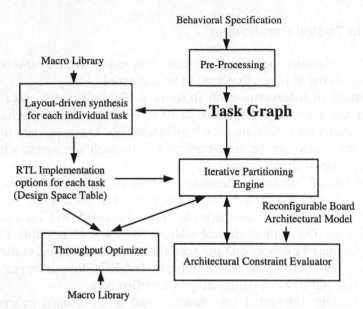

Fig. 7(a). Block Diagram of SPADE

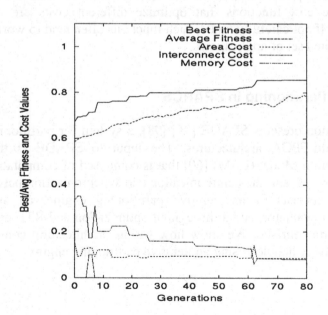

Fig. 7(b). GA Convergence Plot

The SPADE system, shown in Figure 7(a), provides an environment to perform behavioral partitioning with integrated RTL design space exploration for a wide class of multi-FPGA architectures. Prior to partitioning, each task is individually synthesized and various RTL implementation options (design points) are produced using an HLS exploration tool. During partitioning, these options are evaluated and one implementation is selected for each task. The Architectural Constraint Evaluator (ACE) evaluates the constraint satisfaction of a contemplated partition based on the constraints inferred from the reconfigurable board model.

The partitioning engine in figure 7(a) represents any move-based partitioning approach where the partition state changes by moving nodes in the graph from one partition to another and re-evaluating the fitness each time a move is made. Stochastic hill-climbing approaches like simulated annealing [99], genetic algorithms [100], and the Fiduccia-Matteyses (FM) [101] are some well-established move-based partitioning approaches. A detailed analysis and comparative study of these partitioning techniques can be found in [98].

7.3
Architectural Constraint Evaluator

The role of ACE is to evaluate the architectural constraint satisfaction of a contemplated partition of the task graph. ACE returns a fitness measure in the range [0 – 1] depending on how well the various constraints are met. A fitness value of 1 indicates that all constraints are met. ACE considers the following constraints: area, memory, and inter-FPGA routability constraint. The goal of the partitioner is to satisfy multiple conflicting constraints. Accordingly, the cost function that determines the cost of a partition is a combination of the conflicting cost factors. Each cost factor is normalized in the range [0 – 1]:

$$cost = \left(\frac{\sum_{i=0}^{K} \Delta A_i}{\sum_{i=0}^{K} Area(TG_i)} + \frac{\sum_{i=0}^{K} \Delta M_i}{\sum_{i=0}^{K} Mem(TG_i)} \right) + \frac{N_{un}}{N_{tot}}$$

where K is the number of FPGAs/partitions and:

$$\Delta A_i = \begin{cases} 0 & if \ Area(TG_i) \leq Area(F_i) \\ Area(TG_i) - Area(F_i) & otherwise \end{cases}$$

$$\Delta M_i = \begin{cases} 0 & if \ Mem(TG_i) \leq Mem(F_i) \\ Mem(TG_i) - Mem(F_i) & otherwise \end{cases}$$

N_{un}, N_{tot} are unrouted and total inter-FPGA nets. The interconnect evaluator is used to compute the number of unrouted nets. $Area(TG_i)$ is the estimated area of the partition segment, TG_i, when each task in TG_i is mapped to the least area implementation from the available options. An area estimation heuristic that accounts for sharing of resources between tasks that execute at exclusive times is used to estimate the area of the task segment. The area estimation heuristic also accounts for the interconnect resources introduced due to sharing. $Mem(TG_i)$ is the total memory requirement of the partition segment TG_i, and $Mem(F_i)$ is the size of the local memory for the ith FPGA. Fitness of a partition is given by $fitness = \dfrac{1}{1 + cost}$. A fitness of unity implies that all architectural constraints will be satisfied when all tasks are mapped to their respective least area implementations. Further details of the constraint evaluator may be obtained from [96] [98].

7.4
Partitioning Engine

The partitioning engine invokes the throughput optimizer for those partitions whose fitness is one. The throughput optimization process explores the design space for the tasks and selects a faster RTL implementation for critical tasks in the design. Thus, the excess area available in the FPGAs is efficiently utilized to improve the throughput of the partitioned design. The goal of exploration is to minimize the critical path of the design without violating the area constraints.

GA-based Partitioning: GAs work well for multi-modal multi-objective cost functions and unlike heuristic approaches, GAs efficiently move out of local optima and converge towards the global optimum. SPADE has an integer-codes genetic algorithm that is well tuned to optimize the fitness function presented in Section 7.3. Figure 7(b) shows the GA convergence plot for a two-dimensional FFT example partitioned for the Wildforce [17] (four FPGAs, four local memory banks, and partial-crossbar interconnect) architecture. The FFT design has 12 compute tasks,

12 memory tasks and close to 100 interconnections. The plot shows the fitness of the best solution ever and the average fitness of the population with increasing generations. The best fitness increases steadily from 0.67 and converges close to 0.85. The individual cost values (area, interconnect, and memory) of the best solution are also shown in the plot. Further details of this work can be obtained from [98].

FM-based Partitioning: The RC interconnections impose multiple *cutset* constraints that the partitioner has to satisfy. The drawback of using a standard multi-way FM algorithm is that it tries to reduce the sum of all the cutsets. This may not help because each of the cuts has to be minimized individually for pin constraint satisfaction. Therefore, the multi-way FM has to be modified to behave as a constraint-satisfying algorithm rather than an optimizing algorithm. The modified FMPAR algorithm [102] attempts to simultaneously satisfy the individual *pin constraints* (between each pair of devices) and the *device area* constraints (on each partition segment). The algorithm has a collection of different types of moves that can be made given a current partition configuration. The moves are then *prioritized* based on the respective cutset violations. After a move, positive *gains* are assigned to moves that minimize cutset violations, and negative gains are assigned to moves that worsen the cutset. A move is accepted only if it satisfies the area constraints, thereby always moving towards area satisfying solutions. Thus, during each iteration, the algorithm contemplates several moves and accepts the best constraint-satisfying move. The algorithm completes as soon as a constraint-satisfying solution is obtained, or an upper-limit on the number of iterations and moves has been reached. Further details of this work can be obtained from [102].

8
Interconnection Synthesis

Interconnection synthesis is a highly architecture-specific task in any partitioning environment for reconfigurable multi-FPGA architectures. In this section, we will begin by reviewing some related research on inter-FPGA routing in RCs. Then, we will describe the interconnection synthesis in SPARCS.

8.1
Related Research

The problem of pin-assignment and inter-FPGA routing, in the presence of interconnection networks, has been investigated in the past. Hauck and Borriello [103] present a force-directed pin-assignment technique for multi-FPGA systems with fixed routing structure. Mak and Wong [104] present an optimal board-level routing algorithm for emulation systems with multi-FPGAs.

Selvidge et al. [105] present TIERS, a topology independent pipelined routing algorithm for multi-FPGA systems. The interesting feature of TIERS is that it time-multiplexes the interconnection resources thus increasing its utility. However, the limitation is that the interconnection topology has only direct two-terminal nets between FPGAs.

Khalid and Rose [106] present a new interconnection architecture called the HCGP (Hybrid Complete-Graph Partial-Crossbar). They show that HCGP is better than partial crossbar architectures. They present a routing algorithm that is customized for HCGP.

A unique feature of the interconnection synthesis technique [107] employed in SPARCS is that it works for any generic interconnection architecture. Any type of programmable architecture can be specified and the interconnection topology is not fixed prior to partitioning. The necessary configuration information is produced as the result of interconnection synthesis.

8.2
Interconnection Synthesis is SPARCS

Figure 8 shows the components that constitute the interconnect synthesis environment [107] [108] in SPARCS. The shaded region shows the interconnection synthesis tool. The RC interconnection architecture is specified using a hierarchical specification language and the architecture elaborator flattens the hierarchy as and when required. The Interconnection Synthesis Tool (IST) has two components, a symbolic evaluator and a boolean satisfier. The symbolic evaluator can generate various boolean equations representing the set of allowable connections in the interconnection network. The symbolic evaluator is tightly integrated with the boolean satisfier and produces the necessary boolean equations when queried. The set of desired interconnections is presented to the boolean satisfier as a simple boolean expression. The desired nets are generated by the partitioner based on the current partition configuration. The results of interconnection synthesis are: 1) the bits that achieve the desired interconnect configuration, and 2) an interconnection penalty that is fed back to the partitioner.

We have used an RC architecture modeling language,PDL+ [109], to specify interconnect architectures. The PDL+ model of architecture is then elaborated using the ARC system [110]. We use the symbolic evaluation capability in the ARC system to generate a boolean model that represents the given interconnect architecture. The boolean satisfier tool attempts to generate the configuration bits and the pin assignments such that the desired interconnections are routed.

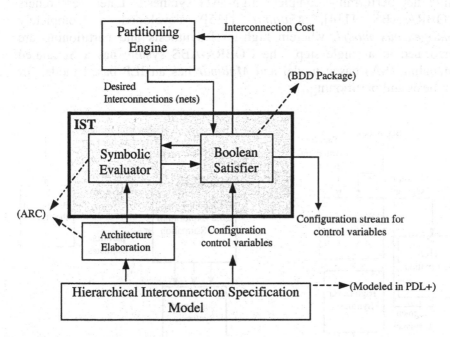

Fig. 8. Interconnect Synthesis Environment

9
Design Synthesis

In this section, we will discuss the three primary issues of design synthesis: (1) interaction between HLS and partitioning, (2) synthesis of arbiters and (3) integrating logic synthesis with HLS. For each of these categories, we will provide a survey and existing techniques and an overview of the technique employed in the SPARCS environment.

9.1
Interaction between HLS and Partitioning

Related Work: In order to perform *hardware design space exploration,* researchers [31], [49], [50] have *integrated* the HLS exploration and estimation phase with partitioning. This led to the traditional heterogeneous *model,* shown in Figure 9(a), where the design area and latency costs of each contemplated partition segment was evaluated by the HLS phase. Several heterogeneous systems, such as *SpecSyn* [111], *Chop* [112], and *Vulcan I* [113], focused on providing good design estimates while not performing complete high-level synthesis. Later, researchers (COBRA-ABS [114], *Multipar* [115]) developed a completely *homogeneous model,* wherein high-level synthesis and partitioning are performed in a single step. The COBRA-ABS system has a Simulated Annealing (SA) based model and *Multipar* has an ILP based model for synthesis and partitioning.

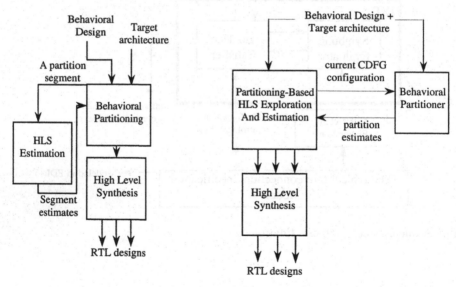

a) Traditional Heterogeneous Model   b) Proposed Heterogeneous Model

Fig. 9. Integrated Synthesis and Partitioning Models

However, unification of partitioning and synthesis into a homogeneous model, adds to the already complex sub-problems of high-level synthesis, leading to a large multi-dimensional design space. Therefore, the cost (design automation time) of having a homogeneous model is very high, i.e.

either the run times are quite high (COBRA-ABS [114]) or the model cannot handle large problem sizes (*Multipar* [115]). The traditional heterogeneous model, although less complex, has a significant drawback of performing exploration on a particular partition segment, which is only a locality of the entire design space.

Dynamic Exploration with Partitioning in SPARCS

We have proposed a new HLS exploration technique [116] that combines the best flavors of both models. In the *proposed heterogeneous model* shown in Figure 9(b), both the partitioner and the HLS exploration engine maintain an identical view of the partitioned behavior, and the partitioner always communicates any change in the partitioned configuration. In the following paragraphs, we will provide an overview of the exploration model and the technique. Further details may be obtained from [116].

Exploration model: The Control Data Flow Graph (CDFG) [117] is a popular representation for a behavioral specification. The CDFG that we use is a *block call graph* (or BBIF [61]) shown in Figure 10(a). It consists of a set of nodes (N_{blocks}) called *blocks*, and edges that represent the flow of data and control across blocks. Each block contains an *operation graph*, which is purely a Data Flow Graph (DFG) [117]. The control *flow* at the end of a block can conditionally branch into one of the mutually exclusive blocks connected to it. The control flow also permits *loops* in the block call graph. The block call graph represents a single thread of control where all blocks are mutually exclusive in time. We define the following terms with respect to our partitioned CDFG model: (1) A *partition* $P_i \subseteq N_{blocks}$, is a subset of blocks in the CDFG. (2) A *configuration* C_{set} is a set of mutually exclusive partitions of all the blocks. (3) A *design point* DP_k is a set of schedules, one for each block in partition P_k. (4) A *design space* of a partition is the set of all possible design points bounded by the fastest (ASAP) and the slowest (smallest resource bag) schedules of all blocks in that partition.

For the partitioned CDFG shown in Figure 10(a), $C_{set} = P_1, P_2$, where $P_1 = \{B_1, B_2\}$ and $P_2 = \{B_3, B_4\}$. Figure 10(b) shows the design points DP_1 and DP_2 corresponding to the partitions. Each partition is synthesized into an RTL design (datapath-controller pair [117]) for the corresponding device in the target multi-device architecture. Therefore, for each design point, an RTL design estimate is maintained as shown in Figure 10(c). In addition, the RTL resource requirement for each individual block is also maintained. Note that blocks belonging to a partition share all the datapath resources and a single finite state machine controller. Interested readers may refer to [50] [118] [119] for RTL design estimation techniques.

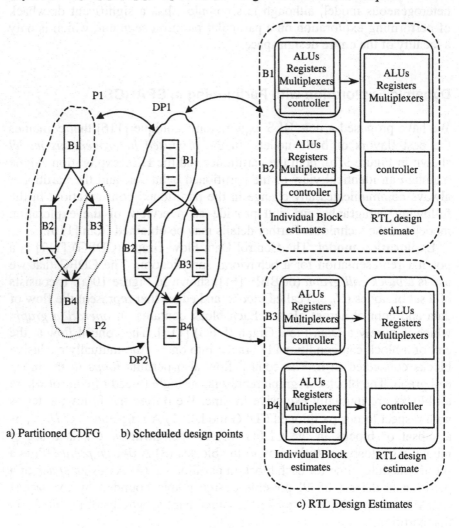

a) Partitioned CDFG   b) Scheduled design points

c) RTL Design Estimates

Fig. 10. Partitioning-based Exploration Model

Exploration Technique: Given a subset of partitions $P_{set} \subseteq C_{set}$, the goal of the exploration technique is to *schedule* a given subset of blocks in $B_{set} = \bigcup_{P_k \in P_{set}} P_k$ such that the constraints, design latency, and individual device areas, are best satisfied. The algorithm performs exploration in a loop where each iteration *relaxes or tightens* the schedule of a block. Relaxing (incrementing) the schedule length of a block could decrease the area of a partition and increase the latency of the entire design and tightening works vice versa. At the core of the exploration algorithm is a collection of four *cost functions* [116] that determine the block to be selected for relaxing/tightening. Each cost function captures an essential aspect of the partitioning-based exploration model and these functions collectively guide the exploration engine in finding a constraint satisfying design. During each iteration, the blocks are scheduled at various possible schedule lengths, thereby distributing the design latency over the blocks in various combinations.

Also, at each iteration, after re-scheduling a block, the corresponding partition area is re-computed, thereby dynamically maintaining the estimated areas of partitions. The exploration algorithm stops when either all the partition area fall within the device area constraints, or none of the blocks can be relaxed or tightened without violating the design latency constraint. At the end of the exploration, if the area constraints are not satisfied, the blocks are reset to the schedules corresponding to the best area satisfying solution obtained so far.

The exploration technique has the following unique features: (1) it has the capability to simultaneously explore the four-dimensional design space of multiple partition segments. Therefore, the technique can generate a constraint satisfying solutions in cases where the traditional heterogeneous model will fail. (2) The technique, unlike in a homogeneous model, uses a low-complexity heuristic instead of an exhaustive search. The effectiveness of the heuristic is demonstrated using an illustrative example in [116]. (3) It is independent of the partitioning algorithm and can be interfaced with any partitioner. The results presented in [116] demonstrate the effectiveness of the integrated exploration and partitioning methodology in generating constraint-satisfying designs.

9.2
Arbiter Synthesis in SPARCS

Related Work: Several mechanisms exist to reuse pins for interconnections; Virtual wires [120] offer a way of overcoming pin limitations in FPGAs by statically scheduling data transfers so that multiple transfers reuse the same set of pins. This comes at the price of statically scheduling accesses. On the other hand, Vahid used functional partitioning and the concepts of *Function Bus* interprocessor bus and *port calling* to reduce the I/O requirements [121]. This solution came at the price of intrusive modifications to the partitioning and synthesis process.

The following paragraphs briefly discuss the arbitration mechanism in SPARCS. Further details may be obtained from [122].

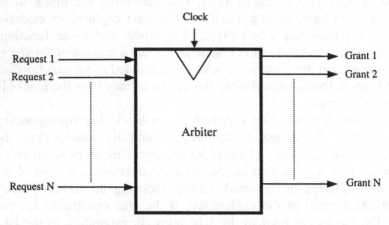

Fig. 11. Generic N–bit arbiter

Generic Arbitration: An arbiter should be introduced for each resource that is to be shared between processes executing in parallel. The size of the arbiter depends on the number of processes accessing that resource; and a general N-bit arbiter is shown in Figure 11. Arbiters are also referred to as mutual-exclusion circuits or interlocks [123].

For each process accessing a shared resource, two wires are introduced –*Request* and *Grant* – between the process and the resource's arbiter. When a process wants to access the shared resource, it asserts its *Request* line and waits until its *Grant* is asserted. Thus, at any given point, the duty of the arbiter is to receive zero or more *Requests* from processes and issue zero or one *Grant*. If there are no requests, then the arbiter should not assert any grants. On the other hand, if there are one or more requests, the arbiter should then assert *exactly* one grant.

In the SPARCS system, arbitration is introduced to solve both memory mapping and pin limitation problems. These problems can be solved with the same technique since they can be both viewed as resource sharing conflicts: multiple data segments are mapped to a single physical memory - the shared resource - and multiple I/O connections are mapped to a single set of I/O pins - the shared resource.

The implementation and functioning of arbiters depend on the environment that they will be in as well as other constraints that the application imposes. For SPARCS, the *round-robin* implementation was selected. This implementation supported fairness, low overhead in terms of area and delay, and ease of insertion and synthesis in this framework.

Memory Arbitration: Consider the case when a task T1 reads/writes from data segment M1 and task T2 reads/writes from data segment M2 (Figure 12(a)). If the two memory segments M1 and M2 are assigned to the same physical memory bank on the RC board, then tasks T1 and T2 are sharing the same address bus, data bus, and read/write mode line of the memory bank. But this creates a conflict since tasks T1 and T2 might be independent from one another (i.e. executing in parallel).

Mutual exclusive access cannot be ensured for the address/data busses as well as the select mode line. So, if T1 is writing to the address bus in clock step c1, T2 cannot be accessing the memory during this step. Moreover, during clock step c1, T2 must tristate its access to the address bus. In conclusion, when two memory accesses are occurring through the same physical memory bank, an arbitration scheme has to be present to avoid any conflicts on the bank. For the example shown in Figure 12(a), an arbiter solution is shown in Figure 12(b).

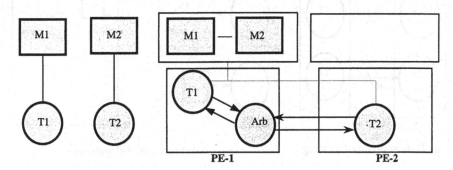

a) Before memory mapping   b) After memory mapping

Fig. 12. Memory access arbitration

Channel Arbitration: Pin limitation between processing elements might cause a practical problem when a design has to be partitioned across several connected processing elements. In actual RC boards, a limited amount of pins is available for interconnection. Typically, a large number of pins on each processing element is already dedicated to accessing a memory bank attached to the processing element. Another set of pins is hardwired to adjacent processing elements. And finally, a limited set of pins might be dedicated to a programmable interconnect network that can connect processing elements with each other or with memory banks. Similar to the memory sharing mechanism described earlier, when the number of physical channels on the board is less than the number of logical connections required, then physical channels can be re-used. A single physical channel can be used by more than one pair of writer/reader, provided that arbitration is introduced to avoid access conflicts.

An example of channel sharing is shown in Figure (13). Two logical channels (k-bit and m-bit wide, with $m < k$) are merged onto one k-bit physical channel. For each receiving end of a shared channel, a register will be introduced whose *enable* originates from the source task (whereas for non-shared channels, a register is introduced at the source end). The reason for having registers at the receiving ends of each transfer is to ensure that data going to one of the targets will not be overwritten by future transfers. In addition, the presence of the registers allows transferred data to be stored and subsequent transfers to take place immediately.

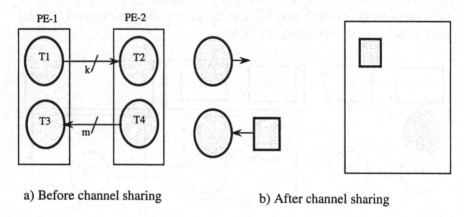

a) Before channel sharing   b) After channel sharing

Fig. 13. Channel arbitration

9.3
Integrating Logic Synthesis and HLS

The traditional HLS process attempts to *predictably* synthesize a design, thereby fails to utilize the power of logic synthesis tools. As explained in Section 3.5, HLS is heavily restricted to select components from a macro-library. We have proposed an approach where macros are dynamically optimized during HLS for area and performance and added to the library. This enables HLS to explore regions of a newly created design space that traditional synthesis tools do not have. We call this the *application-specific macro-based synthesis* where macros are identified for the specific design application.

Related Work: Subgraph matching is used to identify the parts of the design that improve the overall performance when replaced with efficient equivalents. This technique has been used before in [124] and [125]. Cadambi and Goldstein [124] look for certain aspects at the logic-level design such that a logic optimization improves the performance of the design. They build a macro library based on this knowledge and the improvement in the design performance. However, the synthesis of an application is restricted to this macro library. Srinivasa Rao and Kurdahi [125] try to exploit the structural regularity in the DFG of a behavioral specification and perform operation clustering to improve the performance. However, this approach is restricted to graphs that have repeating patterns.

Application Specific Macro-Based Synthesis in SPARCS

To circumvent the problem of having a restricted macro-library, we dynamically populate the library with several macros generated from the given application graph. We characterize each macro by dynamically performing logic and layout synthesis. The characterized information is then used to replace subgraphs of the DFG with macros. This macro-replaced DFG is then taken through HLS to produce performance-optimized designs. The essential aspects of this methodology are explained below, and more details can be obtained from [126].

For *macro generation*, the size (number of nodes) of the macro is used as a limiting factor. The algorithm is a modified depth first search whose terminating condition is satisfied when the number of nodes in the macro is reached. This method exhaustively produces all possible macro subgraphs of the given size from the original DFG. The *macro replacement* technique uses a pattern matcher to identify the parts of the graph where the macros can be replaced. The technique evaluates a gain in performance for replacing a subgraph, by computing the difference in the delays on the *critical path* and the second longest (delay) path. Using this gain value, the technique replaces nodes on the critical path such that the delay is reduced. The matching and replacement procedure is repeated until either there is no gain between two consecutive iterations or the design area exceeds the device area constraint.

10
Conclusions

Adaptive reconfigurable architectures play a central role as intelligent systems. They provide a platform for high-speed designs that can meet the performance requirements of various application domains such as image processing and digital signal processing.

This chapter provided a survey of adaptive architectures and their application domains. These architectures have been classified based on their usage and the type of reconfigurable devices used. A typical design flow for adaptive architectures was presented and the fundamental problems in design automation have been discussed. For each of these problems, a literature survey of CAD techniques is presented. Finally, the chapter provides an insight into the collection of CAD techniques employed in SPARCS [57].

References

[1] M. C. MC Farland, A. C. Parker, R. Camposano: "Tutorial on High-Level Synthesis". In *Proceedings of the 25ʰᵗ ACM/IEEE Design Automation Conference*, pages 330-336, 1988.

[2] R. Parker: "Adaptive Computing Systems: Chameleon". In *Program Overview Foils, DARPA/ITO*, July 1996

[3] S. Goldstein, H. Schmit: "Reconfigurable Computing Seminar". In *Course 15-828/18-847*, http://www.cs.emu.edu/afs/cs.emu.edu/academic/class/15828-s98/www, Spring 1998.

[4] Xilinx, Inc.: *"The Programmable Logic Data Book"*, 1998.

[5] S. Y. Kung, H. J. Whitehouse, T. Kailath: *"VLSI and Modern Signal Processing"*. Prentice-Hall, Inc., 1985.

[6] L. B. Jackson: *"Digital Filters and Signal Processing"*. Kluwer Academic Publishers, second edition, 1989.

[7] S. R. Park, W. Burleson: "Configuration Cloning: Regularity in Dynamic DSP Architectures". In *Proceedings of the ACM Symposium on FPGAs*, pp. 81-89, 1999.

[8] T. Miyamori, K. Olukotun: "A Quantitative Analysis of Reconfigurable Coprocessors for Multimedia Applications". In *IEEE Symposium on Field Programmable Custom Computing Machines*, pp. 2-11, 1998.

[9] D. E. Goldberg: *Genetic Algorithms in Search, Optimization, and Machine Learning*. Addison-Wesley, Reading, MA, 1989.

[10] J. M. Zurada: *"Introduction to Artificial Neural Systems"*. West Publishing Company, 1992.

[11] J. Koza et al.: "Evolving Computer Using Rapidly Reconfigurable Field-Programmable Gate Arrays and Genetic Programming". In *Proceedings of the ACM Sixth International Symposium on Field Programmable Gate Arrays (FPGA)*. ACM Press, 1998.

[12] P. Zhong et al.: "Accelerating Boolean Satisfiability with Configurable Hardware". In *Proceedings of the 6th Annual IEEE Symposium on FPGAs for Custom Computing Machines (FCCM)*, pp. 186-195, Napa, California, April 1998. IEEE Computer Society. ISBN 0-8186-8900-5.

[13] J. Eldredge, B. Hutchings: "Density Enhancement of a Neural Network Using FPGAs and Run-Time Reconfiguration". In *Proceedings of the Second Annual IEEE Symposium on FPGAs for Custom Computing Machines (FCCM)*, pp. 180-188, Napa, California, April 1994. IEEE Computer Society.

[14] T. Kean, A. Duncan: "A 800 Mpixel/sec Reconfigurable Image Correlator on XC6216". In *Proceedings of the International Workshop on Field-Programmable Logic and Applications (FPL)*, 1997.

[15] K. Simha: "NEBULA: A Partially and Dynamically Reconfigurable Architecture". Master's thesis, University of Cincinnati, 1998.

[16] Altera Corporation: Reconfigurable Interconnect Peripheral Processor (RIPP10). http://www.altera.com.

[17] Wildforce multi-FPGA board by Annapolis Micro Systems, Inc. http://www.annapmicro.com.

[18] GigaOps multi-FPGA. http://www.gigaops.com.

[19] J. Hauser, J. Wawrzynek: "GARP: A MIPS processor with a Reconfigurable Coprocessor". In *International Symposium on Field-Programmable Custom Computing Machines*, April 1997.

[20] T. Miyamori, K. Olukotun: "REMARC: Reconfigurable Multimedia Array Coprocessor". In *Proceedings of the CAN/SIGDA International Symposium on FPGAs*, 1998.

[21] E. Waingold et al.: "Baring it All to Software: Raw Machines". In *IEEE Computer*, pp. 86-93, September 1997.

[22] Xilinx Inc.: "XC6200 FPGAs Product Description", April 1997.

[23] Firefly XC6200-based single-FPGA board by Annapolis Micro Systems, Inc. http://www.annapmicro.com.

[24] Virtual Workbench Virtex-based Rapid Prototyping Board. http://www.vcc.com.

[25] ACEcard Hardware Designer's Manual. http://www.tsi-telsys.com.

[26] Wildstar Virtex-based multi-FPGA board by Annapolis Micro Systems, Inc. http://www.annapmicro.com.

[27] S. Trimberger: "Scheduling Designs into a Time-multiplexed FPGA". In *Proceedings of the ACM/SIGDA International Symposium on FPGAs*, 1998.

[28] S. M. Scalera, J. R. Vazquez: "The Design and Implementation of a Context Switching FPGA". In *Proceedings of the ACM/SIGDA IEEE Symposium on FPGAs for Custom Computing Machines (FCCM)*, pp. 78-85, 1998.

[29] C. Rupp et al.: "The NAPA Adaptive Processing Architecture". In *Proceedings of IEEE Symposium on FPGAs for Custom Computing Machines*, 1998.

[30] H. Singh, N. Bagherzadeh, F. Kurdahi, G. Lu, M. Lee, E. Filho: "MorphoSys: a Reconfigurable Processor Targeted to High Performance Image Applications". In *Reconfigurable Architectures Workshop, RAW in IPPS/SPDP*, pp. 660-669, 1999.

[31] F. Vahid et al.: "Functional Partitioning Improvements Over Structural Partitioning Constraints and Synthesis: Tool Performance". In *ACM transactions on Design Automation of Electronic Systems*, volume 3, No. 2, pp. 181-208, April 1998.

[32] G. De Micheli: *"Synthesis and Optimization of Digital Circuits"*. McGraw-Hill, 1994.

[33] A. C. H. Wu, Y. L. Lin: "High-Level Synthesis-A Tutorial". In *IEICE transactions on information and systems*, vol. 17, No. 3, November 1995.

[34] R. Murgai, R. K. Brayton, A. S. Vincentelli: *"Logic synthesis for field-programmable gate arrays"*. Kluwer Academic Publishers, 1995.

[35] R. K. Brayton et al.: *"Logic minimization algorithms for VLSI synthesis"*. Kluwer Academic Publishers, 1984.

[36] Proceedings of FCCM: *"Proceedings of Annual IEEE Symposium on Field-Programmable Custom Computing Machines (FCMM)"*. IEEE Computer Society, 1992-Current.

[37] Proceedings of FPGA: *"Proceedings of the Annual International ACM Symposium on FPGAs"*. ACM Publications, 1992-current.

[38] IEEE Standard 1076-1993. *IEEE Standard VHDL Language Reference Manual*.

[39] C. Hoare: "Communicating Sequential Processes". In *ACM Communications*, vol. 21, No. 98, pp. 666-677, 1978.

[40] E. Lee, D. Messerschmitt: "Synchronous Data Flow". In *IEEE Proceedings*, vol. 75, No. 9. Pp. 1235-1245, 1987.

[41] F. Vahid, D. Gajski: "SLIF: A specification-level intermediate format for system design". In *Proceedings of the European Design and Test (EDTC)*, pp. 185-189, 1995.

[42] D. D. Gajski, N. D. Dutt, A. C. Wu, S. Y. Lin: *"High-Level Synthesis: Introduction to Chip and System Design"*. Kluwer Academic Publishers, 1992.

[43] M. J. Farland: *"Value Trace"*. Carnegie Mellon University, Internal Report, Pittsburgh, PA, 1978.

[44] D. C. Ku, G. D. Michelli: *"High level synthesis of ASICs under timing and synchronization constraints"*. Kluwer Academic Publishers, 1992.

[45] Tessier et al.: "The virtual wires emulation system: A gate-efficient ASIC prototyping environment". In *Proceedings of the 3rd International ACM Symposium on FPGAs*, Monterey, CA, 1995.

[46] F. Johannes: "Partitioning of VLSI Circuits and Systems". In *Proceedings of the 33rd Design Automation conference (DAC)*, 1996.

[47] S. Antoniazzi et al.: "A methodology for control-dominated systems codesign". In *Proceedings of the International Workshop on Hardware-Software Codesign*, pp. 2-9, 1994.

[48] R. K. Gupta, G. De Michelli: "Hardware-software co-synthesis for digital systems". In *IEEE Design and Test*, vol. 10, No. 3, pp. 29-41, September 1993.

[49] W. J. Fang, A. C. H. Wu: "Integrating HDL Synthesis and Partitioning for Multi-GPGA Designs". In *IEEE Design and Test of Computers*, pp. 65-72, April-June 1998.

[50] N. Kumar, V. Srinivasan, R. Vemuri: "Hierarchical Behavioral Partitioning for Multi Component Synthesis". In *Proceedings of the European Design Automation Conference*, pp. 212-219, 1996.

[51] S. Chaudhuri, S. A. Blythe, R. A. Walker: "A Solution Methodology for Exact Design Exploration in a Three-Dimensional Design Space". In *IEEE Transactions on VLSI Systems, vol. 5, No. 1, March 1997.*

[52] S. A. Blythe, R. A. Walker: "Toward a Practical Methodology for Completely Characterizing the Optimal Design Space". In *9th IEEE International Symposium on System Synthesis (ISSS)*, 1996.

[53] S. Chaudhuri, S. A. Blythe, R. A. Walker: "An Exact Methodology for Scheduling in 3D Design Space". In *8th IEEE International Symposium on System Synthesis (ISSS)*, 1995.

[54] M. Xu, F. J. Kurdahi: "Layout-driven RTL Binding Techniques for High-Level Synthesis Using Accurate Estimators". In *ACM Transactions on Design Automation of Electronic Systems*, 1996.

[55] J. M. Jou, S. R. Kuang: "A Library-Adaptively Integrated High-Level Synthesis System". In *Proceedings of the National Science Council, Rep.*, vol. 19, No. 3, May 1995.

[56] I. Ahmad, M. K. Dhodhi, C. Y. R. Chen: "Integrated scheduling, allocation and module selection for design-space exploration in high-level synthesis". In *IEEE Proceedings on Computers and Digital Techniques*, vol. 142, No. 1, pp. 65-71, January 1995.

[57] I. Ouaiss, S. Govindarajan, V. Srinivasan, M. Kaul, R. Vemuri: "An Integrated Partitioning and Synthesis System for Dynamically Reconfigurable Multi-FPGA Architectures". In *Proceedings of the 5th Reconfigurable Architectures Workshop (RAW), Lecture Notes in Computer Science 1388*, pp. 31-36, April 1998.

[58] S. Govindarajan, I. Ouaiss, V. Srinivasan, M. Kaul, R. Vemuri: "An Effective Design System for Dynamically Reconfigurable Architectures". In *Proceedings of 6th Annual IEEE Symposium on FPGAs for Custom Computing Machines (FCCM)*, pp. 312-313, Napa, California, April 1998. IEEE Computer Society.

[59] M. Kaul, V. Srinivasan, S. Govindarajan, I. Ouaiss, R. Vemuri: "Partitioning and Synthesis for Run-Time Reconfigurable Computers Using the SPARCS System". In *Proceedings of the 1998 Military and Aerospace Applications of Programmable Devices and Technologies Conference (MAPLD'98)*, 1998.

[60] I. Ouaiss, S. Govindarajan, V. Srinivasan, M. Kaul, R. Vemuri: "A Unified Specification Model of Concurrency and Coordination for Synthesis from VHDL". In *Proceedings of the 4th International Conference on Information Systems Analysis and Synthesis (ISAS)*, July 1998.

[61] N. Narasimhan: "*Formal-Assertions Based Verification in a High-Level Synthesis System*". Ph. D. Thesis, University of Cincinnati, ECECS Department, 1998.

[62] J. Spillane, H. Owen: "Temporal Partitioning for Partially-Reconfigurable-Field-Programmable Gate". In *Reconfigurable Architectures Workshop, RAW in IPPS/SPDP*, pp. 37-42. Springer, 1998.

[63] D. Chang, M. Marek-Sadowska: "Partitioning Sequential Circuits on Dynamically Reconfigurable FPGAs". In *ACM/SIGDA International Symposium on Field Programmable Gate Arrays, FPGA*, pp. 161-167, ACM Press, 1998.

[64] P. G. Paulin, J. P. Knight: "Force Directed Scheduling for the Behavior Synthesis of ASICs". In *IEEE Transactions ON CAD*, vol. 8, pp. 661-679, June 1989.

[65] S. Trimberger, D. Carberry, A. Johnson, J. Wong: "A Time-Multiplexed FPGA". In *FPGAs for Custom Computing Machines, FCCM*, pp. 22-28. IEEE Computer Society Press, 1997.

[66] M. Vasilko, D. Ait-Boudaoud: "Architectural Synthesis for Dynamically Reconfigurable Logic". In *International Workshop on Field-Programmable Logic and Applications, FPL*, pp. 290-296. Springer, 1996.

[67] K. M. GajjalaPurna, D. Bhatia: "Temporal Partitioning and Scheduling for Reconfigurable Computing". In *FPGAs for Custom Computing Machines, FCCM*, pp. 329-330. IEEE Computer Society Press, 1998.

[68] K. M. GajjalaPurna, D. Bhatia: "Emulating Large Designs on Small Reconfigurable Hardware". In *IEEE Workshop on Rapid System Prototyping, RSP*, pp. 58-63. IEEE Computer Society Press, 1998.

[69] J. M. P. Cardoso, H. C. Neto: "Macro-Based Hardware Compilation of Java ByteCodes into a Dynamic Reconfigurable Computing System". In *Proceedings of FPGAs for Custom Computing Machines (FCCM)*, Napa Valley, California, 1999.

[70] M. Wolfe: "High Performance Compilers for Parallel Computing". Addison-Wesley Publishers, 1996.

[71] S. Y. Kung: *VLSI Array Processors*. Prentice Hall, 1988.

[72] M. Kaul, R. Vemuri: "Integrated Block processing and Design-Space Exploration in Temporal Partitioning for RTR Architectures". In Jose Rolim, editor, *Parallel and Distributed Processing*, vol. 1586, pp. 606-615. Springer-Verlag, 1999.

[73] M. Kaul, R. Vemuri: "Temporal Partitioning combined with Design Space Exploration for Latency Minimization of Run-Time Reconfigured Designs". In *Design, Automation and Test in Europe, DATE*, pp. 202-209. IEEE Computer Society Press, 1999.

[74] A. Pandey, R. Vemuri: "Combined Temporal Partitioning and Scheduling for Reconfigurable Architectures". In *SPIE Conference on Configurable Computing: Technology and Applications*, September 1999.

[75] A. Pandey: "Temporal Partitioning and Scheduling for Reconfigurable Architectures". Master's thesis, University of Cincinnati, ECECS Department, 1999.

[76] W. Luk, N. Shirazi, P. Cheung: "Automating Product of Run-Time Reconfigurable Designs". In *FPGAs for Custom Computing Machines, FCCM*, pp. 147-156. IEEE Computer Society Press, 1998.

[77] S. Hauck, Z. Li, E. Schwabe: "Configuration Compression for the Xilinx XC6200 FPGA". In *FPGAs for Custom Computing Machines, FCCM*, pp. 138-146. IEEE Computer Society Press, 1998.

[78] E. Lechner, S. A. Guccione: "A Java environment for reconfigurable computing". In *International Workshop on Field-Programmable Logic and Applications, FPL*, pp. 284-293. Springer, 1997.

[79] S. A. Guccione, D. Levi: "XBI: A Java-Based Interface to FPGA Hardware". In *SPIE Conference on Configurable Computing: Technology and Applications*, pp. 97-102, 1998.

[80] S. Ganesan, A. Ghosh, R. Vemuri: "High-level Synthesis of Designs for Partially Reconfigurable FPGAs". In *Proc. of 2nd annual Military and Aerospace Applications of Programmable Devices and Technologies Conference, MAPLD 99*, September 1999.

[81] S. Ganesan: "A Temporal Partitioning and Synthesis Framework to Improve Latency of Design Targeted towards Partially Reconfigurable Architectures". Master's thesis, University of Cincinnati, ECECS Department, 1999.

[82] N. A. Sherwani: *Algorithms for VLSI Physical Design Automation*. Kluwer Academic Publishers, Boston, 1993.

[83] P. K. Chan, M. Schlag, J. Zien: "Spectral-Based Multi-Way FPGA Partitioning". In *Proc. of 3rd Int. Symp. FPGAs*, pp. 133-139, 1995.

[84] S. Hauck, G. Borriello: "Logic Partition Ordering for Multi-GPGA Systems". In *Proc. of 3rd Int. Symp. FPGAs*, pp. 32-38, 1995.

[85] K. Roy-Neogi, C. Sechen: "Multiple FPGA Partitioning with Performance Optimization"" In *Proc. of 3rd Int. Symp. FPGAs*, pp. 146-151, 1995.

[86] W.-J. Fang, A. Wu: "A Hierarchical Functional Structuring and Partitioning Approach for Multi-FPGA Implementations". In *IEEE Trans. on CAD*, vol. 9, No. 5, pp. 500-511, Nov. 1990.

[87] N.-S. Woo, J. Kim: "An Efficient Method of Partitioning Circuits for Multi-FPGA Implementations". In *Proc. 30th ACM/IEEE Design Automation Conference*, pp. 202-207, 1993.

[88] R. Kuznar, F. Brglez, B. Zajc: "Multi-way Net-list Partitioning into Heterogeneous FPGA and Minimization of Total Device Cost and Interconnect". In *Proc. 31st ACM/IEEE Design Automation Conference*, pp. 228-243, 1994.

[89] D. Huang, A. B. Kahng: "Multi-Way System Partitioning into a Single Type or Multiple Types of FPGAs". In *Proc. of 3rd Int. Symp. FPGAs*, pp. 140-145, 1995.

[90] P. Sawkar, D. Thomas: "Multi-way Partitioning for Minimum Delay for Look-Up Table Based FPGAs". In *Proc. 32nd ACM/IEEE Design Automation Conference*, pp. 201-205, 1995.

[91] N. Kumar: *High Level VLSI Synthesis for Multichip Designs*. Ph. D. Thesis, University of Cincinnati, 1994.

[92] N. Kumar, V. Srinivasan, R. Vemuri: "Hierarchical Behavioral Partitioning for Multi Component Synthesis". In *Proc. European Design Automation Conference*, pp. 212-219, 1996.

[93] R. K. Gupta, G. De Micheli: "System-level Synthesis using Reprogrammable Components". In *Proc. European Design Automation Conference*, pp. 2-7, 1992.

[94] K. Kucukcakar: *System-Level Synthesis Techniques with Emphasis on Partitioning and Design Planning*. Ph. D. Thesis, University of Southern California, CA, 1991.

[95] F. Vahid, D. D. Gajski: "Specification Partitioning for System Design". In *Proc. Of 29th Design Automation Conference*, pp. 219-224, 1992.

[96] V. Srinivasan, R. Vemuri: "Task-level Partitioning and RTL Design Space Exploration for Multi-FPGA Architectures". In *Int. Symposium on Field-Programmable Custom Computing Machines*, April 1999.

[97] M. Gokhale, J. Stone: "Automatic Allocation of Arrays to Memories in FPGA Processors with Multiple Memory Banks" In *Int. Symposium on Field-Programmable Custom Computing Machines*, April 1999.

[98] V. Srinivasan: *Partitioning for FPGA-Based Reconfigurable Computers*. Ph. D. Thesis, University of Cincinnati, USA, August 1999.

[99] S. Kirkpatrik, C. D. Gelatt, M. P. Vecchi: "Optimization by Simulated Annealing". In *Science*, vol. 220, No. 4598, pp. 671-680, 1983.

[100] J. Holland: *Adaptation in Natural and Artificial Systems*. Ann Arbor: University of Michigan Press, 1997.

[101] C. Fiduccia, R. Mattheyses: "A linear time heuristic for improving network partitions". In *Proceedings of the 19th Design Automation Conference (DAC)*, pp. 175-181, 1982.

[102] P. Lakshmikanthan: "Partitioning of Behavioral Specifications for Reconfigurable Multi-FPGA Architectures". Master's thesis, University of Cincinnati, ECECS Department, 1999.

[103] S. Hauck, G. Boriello: "Pin Assignment for Multi-FPGA Systems". In *Proc. of FPGAs for Custom Computing Machines*, pp. 11-13, 1994.

[104] W. Mak, D. F. Wong: "On Optimal Board-Level Routing for FPGA based Logic Emulation". In *Proc. 32nd ACM/IEEE Design Automation Conference,* pp. 552-556, 1995.

[105] C. Selvidge, A. Agarwal, M. Dahl, J. Babb: "TIERS: Topology Independent Pipelined Routing and Scheduling for Virtual Wire Compilation". In *Proc. Int. Symp. FPGAs*, pp. 25-31, Feb. 1995.

[106] M. Khalid, J. Rose: "A Hybrid Complete - Graph Partial-Crossbar Routing Architecture for Multi-FPGA Systems". In *Proc. Int. Symp. FPGAs*, pp. 45-54, Feb. 1998.

[107] V. Srinivasan, S. Radhakrishnan, R. Vemuri, J. Walrath: "Interconnect Synthesis for Reconfigurable Multi-FPGA Architectures". In *Proceedings of Parallel and Distributed Processing (RAW'99)*, pp. 597-605. Springer, April 1999.

[108] S. Radhakrishnan: "Interconnect Synthesis for Reconfigurable Multi-FPGA architectures". Master's thesis, University of Cincinnati, ECECS Department, April 1999.

[109] R. Vemuri, J. Walrath: "Abstract models of reconfigurable computer architectures". In *SPIE'98*, Nov. 1998.

[110] J. Walrath, R. Vemuri: "A Performance Modeling and Analysis Environment for Reconfigurable Computers". In *Proceedings of Parallel and Distributed Processing*, pp. 19-24. Springer, March 1998.

[111] D. D. Gajski, F. Vahid et al.: "Specification and Design of Embedded Systems". In *Prentice-Hall Inc.*, Upper Saddle River, NJ, 1994.

[112] K. Kucukcakar, A. Parker: "CHOP: A constraint-driven system-level partitioner". In *Proceedings of the Conference on Design Automation*, pp. 514-519, 1991.

[113] R. K Gupta, G. De Micheli: "Partitioning of functional models of synchronous digital systems". In *Proceedings of the International Conference on Computer-Aided Design*, pp. 216-219, 1990.

[114] A. A. Duncan, D. C. Hendry, P. Gray: "An Overview of the Cobra-ABS High-Level Synthesis System for Multi-FPGA Systems". In *Proceedings of FPGAs for Custom Computing Machines (FCCM)*, pp. 106-115, Napa Valley, California, 1998.

[115] Y. Chen, Y. Hsu, C. King: "MULTIPAR: Behavioral partition for synthesizing multiprocessor architectures". In *IEEE Transactions on VLSI systems*, vol. 2, No. 1, pp. 21-32, March 1994.

[116] S. Govindarajan, V. Srinivasan, P. Lakshmikanthan, R. Vemuri: "A Technique for Dynamic High-Level Exploration During Behavioral-Partitioning for Multi-Device Architectures". In *Proceedings of the 13th International Conference on VLSI Design (VLSI 2000)*, 2000.

[117] R. Walker, R. Camposano: "*A Survey of High-Level Synthesis Systems*". Kluwer Academic Publishers, 1991.

[118] H. Mecha, M. Fernandez and K. Olcoz: "A Method for Area Estimation of Data-Path in High Level Synthesis". In *IEEE Transactions on Computer-Aided Design*, Vol. 15, No. 2, Feb. 1998.

[119] J. Roy, N. Kumar, R. Dutta and R. Vemuri: "DSS: A Distributed High-Level Synthesis System". In *IEEE Design and Test of Computers*, June 1992.

[120] J. Babb, R. Tessier, A. Agarwal: "Virtual Wires: Overcoming Pin Limitations in FPGA-based Logic Emulators". In *Proceedings of FPGAs for Custom Computing Machines*, 1993.

[121] F. Vahid: "Techniques for Minimizing and Balancing I/O During Functional Partitioning". In *IEEE Transactions on Computer-Aided Design of Integrated Circuits and Systems*, Vol. 18, January 1999.

[122] I. Ouaiss, R. Vemuri: "Efficient Resource Arbitration in Reconfigurable Computing Environments". In *Design, Automation and Test in Europe, DATE,* pp. 560-566. IEEE Computer Society Press, 2000

[123] J. Rabaey: *"Digital Integrated Circuits: A Design Perspective"*. Prentice Hall, 1996.

[124] S. Cadambi, S. C. Goldstein: "CPR: A Configuration Profiling Tool". In *Proceedings of FPGAs for Custom Computing Machines (FCCM)*, 1999.

[125] D. S. Rao, F. Kurdahi: "On Clustering for Maximal Regularity Extraction". In *IEEE Transactions on CAD,* August 1993.

[126] S. Sundararaman: *"Application Specific Macro Based Synthesis"*. Master's thesis, University of Cincinnati, ECECS Department. 1999.

Chapter 2

High-Performance Hardware Design and Implementation of Genetic Algorithms

Barry Shackleford[1], Etsuko Okushi[2], Mitsuhiro Yasuda[2], Hisao Koizumi[2], Katsuhiko Seo[2], Takahashi Iwamoto[2], and Hiroto Yasuura[3]

[1]Hewlett-Packard Laboratories, Computer Systems and Technology Laboratory, 1501 Page Mill Road, Palo Alto, CA 94304-1100, USA
[2]Mitsubishi Electric Corporation, Kamakura-shi, 247-8501 Japan
[3]Kyushu University, Graduate School of Engineering Sciences, Kasuga-shi, 816 Japan

In this chapter, we present a survival-based, steady-state GA designed for efficient implementation in hardware and the design of a pipelined genetic algorithm processor that can generate one new, evaluated chromosome per machine cycle. High performance is obtained by implementing the functions of parent selection, crossover, mutation, evaluation, and survival in hardware in such a manner that each function can be executed in a single machine cycle. When these hardware functions are connected in a linear pipeline (much the same as an assembly line), the net result is the generation a new child chromosome on each machine cycle. The key features of the survival-based, steady-state GA are low selection pressure due to random parent selection, steady-state population maintenance, and replacement of randomly discovered, lesser-fit chromosomes by more-fit offspring. A GA machine prototype is also presented, running at 1 MHz and generating one million new chromosomes per second.

1
Introduction

Genetic algorithms (GAs) [1]–[3] were described in 1975 by John Holland [1] as a method for finding solutions to difficult optimization problems [4], [5] by means of simulated evolution. Perhaps the most compelling reason for using a GA is simplicity: All that is required to solve a wide range of optimization problems is (1) the ability to express a potential solution as a bit string and (2) a fitness function to evaluate the goodness of the solution expressed in the bit string.

However, the major drawback of GAs is their slow execution speed when emulated by software on a conventional computer. Parallel processing [6] has been one approach to overcoming the speed problem of GAs. Andre and Koza have used a transputer network for genetic programming [7] and Nordin has developed a genetic programming system that produces compiled machine code [8].

The problem of speeding up the execution of the GA via special purpose hardware has been addressed by Graham [9] and Sitkoff [10] with moderate success (speed-up factors of roughly 10×).

Graham incorporated the Splash 2 machine [11] to solve a 24-city Traveling Salesman Problem. With a population of 256, the hardware running time for the problem was 11.2 s, which was a 10.6× speed-up over a software implementation of their algorithm running on a 125 MHz workstation. Sitkoff used the Armstrong III machine [12] to solve a 500-component circuit partitioning problem. With a population of 96, the hardware running time for the problem was 48.5 s, which was a 3.0× speed-up over a software version of the algorithm running on a 60 MHz workstation. A distributed version of the algorithm incorporating three nodes of the Armstrong III machine achieved an 8.6× speed-up.

Our approach for accelerating the execution speed of a GA was to adapt Holland's original algorithm for efficient implementation in hardware and then to provide an FPGA-based (field programmable gate array) framework to manage the parent selection, crossover, mutation, and survival of new population members [13], [14]. Programming of the GA machine is accomplished by designing a general fitness function circuit for the problem to be solved and then synthesizing a problem-specific fitness function FPGA according to the problem parameters. Operating at a clock rate of 1 MHz, with the fitness function programmed for a 94 row × 521 column set-coverage problem, the prototype achieves a processing rate of one million crossovers per second which is 2,200× faster than a 100 MHz workstation running the same algorithm.

Next, we will describe our modified GA, contrasting it with the original GA proposed by Holland. Then, we will discuss the architecture of a high-performance pipelined implementation of the algorithm. Next, programming of the GA machine will be illustrated with the set-coverage problem and a logic circuit synthesis problem. Finally, we will describe the FPGA-based prototype implementation and experimental results.

2
Modifying the Genetic Algorithm for Efficient Hardware Implementation

In this section, we will explain our modified GA and contrast it with Holland's original GA. Then we will provide some empirical assurance that the functional performance of the original GA has not been sacrificed for the sake of temporal performance and implementation efficiency.

2.1
Algorithm Explanation

We will term our algorithm (Figure 1) a *survival-based, steady-state* GA because it relies on the survival of fitter offspring over less-fit parents to promote evolution and uses a single rather than generational population memory. This is in contrast to Holland's original GA that uses parent selection according to fitness to promote evolution and a separate memory for the new generation.

Initially, a population of n_p randomly generated chromosomes is created, evaluated (i.e., assigned fitness values), and stored in the *Population* array. A single location in the array contains n_d bits of *chromosome$_{data}$* and n_f bits of *chromosome$_{fitness}$*.

Since the basis of the algorithm is survival of fitter offspring over less-fit parents, a record of the least-fit parent encountered during random selection is kept in the two variables: *worst_fitness_encountered* and *worst_adrs*. As parents are randomly selected, their fitness values are compared with the *worst_fitness_encountered*. If a parent is less fit, then it becomes the new candidate for replacement, with its fitness and address being held in *worst_fitness_encountered* and *worst_adrs* respectively.

After two parent chromosomes have been selected, a child chromosome is created by the Crossover function. It is then exposed to the possibility of mutation. After mutation, the child is ready for evaluation by the problem-specific Fitness function. The survival of the child chromosome is determined by comparing its fitness value with that of the least fit parent encountered since the last survival/replacement operation.

If the fitness of the new child chromosome is greater than *worst_fitness_encountered*, then the child data and fitness are stored in the *Population* array at the location pointed to by *worst_adrs*. The value of *worst_fitness_encountered* is then set to maximum so that the next parent selected will automatically become the first of the next series of replacement candidates.

—Initial Population Creation—

```
for i = 0 to np − 1 do
    chromosomedata = Random(2^nd);
    chromosomefitness = Fitness(chromosomedata);
    Population(i) = chromosome;
end for
```

—Algorithm Body—

```
worst_fitness_encountered = 2^nf − 1;
while not Evolutionary_Stasis(Population) do

    • prior first-parent becomes second-parent
    parent2 = parent1;

    • new first-parent selection
    parent1_adrs = Random(np);
    parent1 = Population(parent1_adrs);

    • check fitness and possibly update least-fit parent pointer
    if parent1fitness < worst_fitness_encountered then
        worst_fitness_encountered = parent1fitness;
        worst_adrs = parent1_adrs;
    end if

    childdata = Crossover(cut_prob, parent1data, parent2data);
    childdata = Mutation(mutation_prob, childdata);
    childfitness = Fitness(childdata);

    • survival determination
    if childfitness > worst_fitness_encountered then
        worst_fitness_encountered = 2^nf − 1;
        Population(worst_adrs) = child;
    end if
end while
```

Fig. 1. Survival-based genetic algorithm designed for efficient hardware implementation.

As the process of selection, generation, and survival/replacement continues, the overall fitness of the population will increase and the survival rate of new offspring will diminish. At some point, the entire population will achieve the same fitness (but not necessarily the same solution) and the offspring survival rate will drop to zero. At this point, evolution has probably ceased and the algorithm should be terminated.

2.2
Contrast with Original GA

The survival-based, steady-state genetic algorithm has been devised specifically for efficient implementation in hardware. To this end, the methods of population storage, parent selection, crossover, and chromosome survival are significantly different from Holland's original GA.

Population storage

In the original GA, the population consists of a current population, from which the parents are chosen, and a new population, which serves as the repository of the next generation. This is disadvantageous to hardware implementation in that the size of the memory used to implement the population memory must be doubled. The survival-based, steady-state GA uses a single population to hold both parent chromosomes and their offspring in a manner similar to Syswerda's steady-state GA [15], [16].

Parent selection

Parent selection with a probability proportional to fitness is used in the original GA which allows chromosomes with higher fitnesses to have a greater influence on subsequent generations. However this method of selection is disadvantageous to hardware implementation in that a fitness distribution must be maintained and the means for performing a probabilistic selection requires extra hardware and computational cycles.

The intent of probabilistic selection is to allow more-fit chromosomes to have a greater influence of subsequent generations owing to increased participation in the crossover process. Our implementation accomplishes the same intent by using simple *random* selection, without regard to fitness, in which the longer lifetime of the more fit chromosome will account for an increased participation in the crossover process.

Crossover probability

In the original GA, crossover is performed probabilistically. When crossover is not performed, the parent chromosomes are simply copied to the new population memory after being exposed to the mutation process. In contrast, the survival-based GA performs crossover on all chromosomes selected from the population memory. Since all chromosomes tend to remain in the population memory a period of time proportional to their fitness, there is no need to perform the copy operation, which in effect, is an overhead operation that reduces the processing throughput of the GA.

Survival

In the original GA, all offspring survive to be transferred to the new population. In the survival-based GA, an offspring will survive only if it is more fit than the current least-fit parent, which it will then replace.

2.3
Validity of Survival-Based Genetic Algorithm

The survival-based GA was created expressly for efficient implementation in hardware in terms of both component cost (i.e., chip area) and system speed (crossovers/s). The question then arises: *have compromises been made that damage the functional integrity of the GA?*

To provide some preliminary empirical assurance that our GA was still valid, we evaluated its performance using the Royal Road R_1 function (Figure 2) designed by Mitchell, Forrest, and Holland [17]–[19].

The intend of the Royal Road function (actually a class function) was to test the Building Block Hypothesis [2] which states that crossover combines highly-fit portions of chromosomes (called *schemas*) into increasingly fit chromosomes. The function was so named because it was thought that the presence of the first-level schemas would $s1-s8$ act as a "royal road," leading the GA quickly to the optimum solution of all 1s. However, this did not turn out to be the case and the function proved to be somewhat difficult for the GA to solve; taking, on average, over 61,000 crossovers to generate the optimum solution.

The first-level schemas for the R_1 function s_1-s_8 are defined to be eight contiguous 1s aligned on 8-bit boundaries as shown in Figure 2. These are shown as being detected by 8-input AND gates. Each valid, first-level schema contributes a fitness of 8 to the overall fitness score.

The second-level schemas s_9-s_{12} are aligned on 16-bit boundaries and are composed of first-level schemas. Each valid second-level schema contributes a fitness of 16 to the overall fitness score. In a similar manner, the two third-level schemas s_{13} and s_{14} each contribute a fitness of 32 and the single, fourth-level schema s_{15} contribute a fitness of 64.

The optimum solution of 64 contiguous 1s has a fitness of 256. The quantization of fitness values can be seen in Figure 3, where the fitness of each surviving chromosome is plotted according to the crossover count.

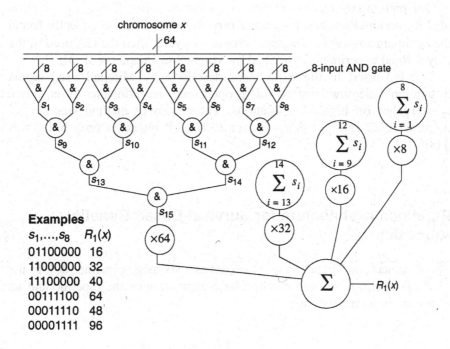

Fig. 2. Fitness vs. crossover count for the Royal Road R_1 function.

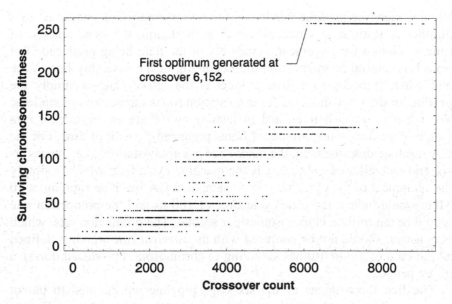

Fig. 3. Fitness vs. crossover count for the Royal Road R_1 function.

Our preliminary results (Figure 3) are encouraging. Using a population of 256, no mutation and a cutpoint probability of 0.1, we typically found the optimum answer in 10× *fewer* crossover cycles then the GA used in the Royal Road experiment, described by Mitchell in Chapter 4 of [3].

The GA used in the experiment described by Mitchell used sigma truncation selection instead of proportional selection to slow down convergence on highly fit solutions. The crossover method was single-point with 0.7 rate per pair of parents. The bit mutation probability was 0.005.

3
Pipelined Architecture for Survival-Based Genetic Algorithm

The GA machine (Figure 4) is organized as a six-stage pipeline [20]. In the next two sections we will discuss the organization of the pipeline and its hardware implementation.

3.1
Pipeline Description

We can view the pipeline much as a factory assembly line composed of a number of stations in series, where at each station, the same amount of time is allotted for incremental assembly of the item being produced. The time for material to travel from the beginning of the assembly line to the end where it becomes a final product is the *latency* and is simply the product of the time allocated for each station times the number of stations. We are not so much interested in latency as we are in *production rate* which is defined as the number of items produced per unit of time. For the GA machine describe here, the number of assembly stations (i.e., stages) is six and time allotted each stage is the machine cycle time which is simply the reciprocal of the clock rate. For example, a GA machine running at 10 MHz would have a machine cycle time of 100 ns and the production rate would be ten million chromosomes per second. The production rate, which is constant, should not be confused with the *survival rate* which is defined as the ratio of chromosomes surviving to chromosomes produced during a given period.

The first three stages of the six-stage pipeline are devoted to parent selection. The fourth stage performs crossover and mutation. Fitness evaluation is performed in the fifth stage and survival is determined in the sixth stage. The next six subsections will respectively detail the operation of each stage.

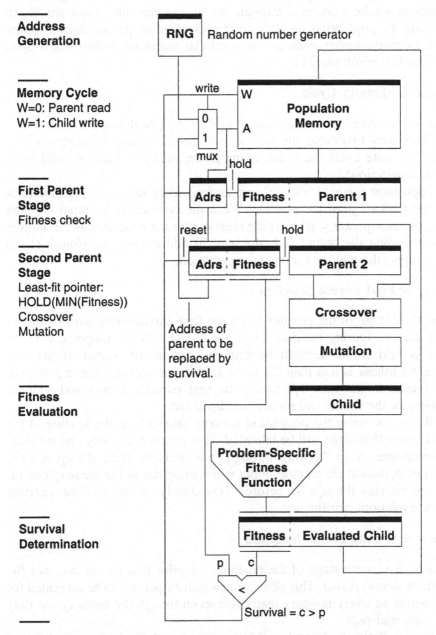

Address Generation

RNG Random number generator

Memory Cycle
W=0: Parent read
W=1: Child write

write W

0 A
1
mux

Population Memory

hold

First Parent Stage
Fitness check

Adrs Fitness   Parent 1

reset   hold

Second Parent Stage
Least-fit pointer:
HOLD(MIN(Fitness))
Crossover
Mutation

Adrs Fitness   Parent 2

Crossover

Address of
parent to be
replaced by
survival.

Mutation

Fitness Evaluation

Child

Problem-Specific Fitness Function

Survival Determination

Fitness Evaluated Child

p   c

<

Survival = c > p

Fig. 4. Block diagram of pipelined hardware implementation of a genetic algorithm. Blocks with heavy horizontal lines are registers or memory.

Stage 1: Address Generation

The first stage of the pipeline is devoted to random number generation. Random numbers are used through out the GA machine, most notably to address the population memory in the selection of parent chromosomes. The random number generator is a cellular-automata design based upon the work of Wolfram [21].

Stage 2: Memory Cycle

The second stage of the pipeline is used as the population memory access cycle. During this cycle, the memory will either be read, or written, with a memory write cycle (survival) taking precedence or a memory read cycle (parent selection).

Population memory read/write is determined by the survival comparator in the sixth stage of the pipeline. When the comparator's output is 0, the address multiplexer will select the random number generator as the address source; when the output is 1, the least-fit address register (fourth stage) will supply the address for the write operation.

Stage 3: First Parent Selection

The third stage of the pipeline holds the first parent along with its fitness and address. During the third stage, the fitness will be compared with the fitness held in the least-fit holding register (fourth stage). If the first parent's fitness is less than the value held in the register, the register will be loaded in the next cycle with the first parent's fitness and address. Otherwise the fitness and address are discarded.

When a write to the population memory takes place, the loading of the registers at this stage will be inhibited. This prevents a newly created child chromosome from "writing through" the memory (i.e., during a write operation, data at the memory input will also appear at the memory output) and re-entering the pipeline before it is randomly chosen, and thus exerting undo evolutionary influence.

Stage 4: Second Parent Selection

During the fourth stage of the pipeline, the prior first parent becomes the current second parent. This allows a new pair of parents to be presented for crossover on every memory read cycle, even though the memory has only a single read-port.

Due to their short logic paths (Figures 5 and 6), both crossover and mutation can be accomplished during this stage. The output of the crossover circuit is connected directly the mutation circuit whose output is connected to the child register.

As in the prior stage, the survival signal is used to inhibit the loading of the parent register. It is also used to reset the least-fit holding circuit by causing the maximum possible value to be loaded into the fitness portion of the register. This means that the next parent to be read from the population memory will automatically become a candidate for replacement, even if its fitness is high. If its fitness is high, then a survival operation probably can not take place, in which case, the next parent to be read from the population memory will probably have a lower fitness and in turn become the new replacement candidate.

Stage 5: Fitness Evaluation

During the fifth stage, the child chromosome is evaluated by the problem-specific fitness function. If the fitness function contains extremely long logic paths, it can also be pipelined to bring its cycle time in line with the rest of the machine as long as an equal number of delay stages are inserted between the child register and the evaluated child register.

Stage 6: Survival Determination

At the sixth and final stage of the pipeline, a new child chromosome and its fitness are held in the evaluated child register. During this stage, the fitness is compared with the fitness held in the least-fit register. If the child chromosome is more fit, it is written into the population memory at the address held by the least-fit register, replacing the parent at that address. A less fit child chromosome is discarded at this point.

3.2
Hardware Implementation

As component counts for chips grow (over 100M gates per chip by 2010), the problem is not so much having enough components for a circuit, but being able to wire them together efficiently. One solution to this problem is to devise a macro component out of elemental chip components. This macro component is called a *bit-slice*. Identical bit-slices can be assembled side-by-side, much like floor tiles, according to the size of the problem. The global wiring problem is effectively solved because the wiring between bit-slices can be arranged such that when they are laid side-by-side, the outputs of one slice automatically connect to the inputs of the other. However, the problem for GA machine application is the distribution of individual bit control signals. The solution to the distributed control problem along with implementation details of the crossover and mutation functions will be discussed in the following two subsections. After that, we will look at the datapath bit-slice in detail.

Crossover

As shown in Figure 5, each chromosome bit position requires a two-input multiplexer to select between the two parents. As mentioned above, the problem is how to control the multiplexer aggregate.

Control based at a single point would require lines to all multiplexer address inputs. This would pose a burden on chip routing capacity and chip I/O pins if the datapath were sliced across chips.

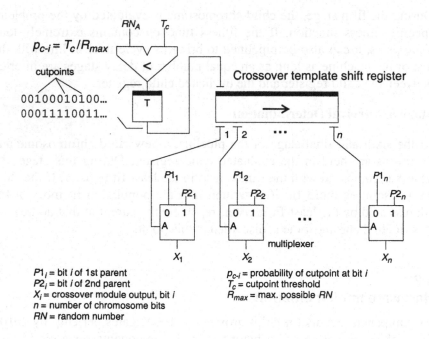

$p_{c-i} = T_c / R_{max}$

$P1_i$ = bit i of 1st parent
$P2_i$ = bit i of 2nd parent
X_i = crossover module output, bit i
n = number of chromosome bits
RN = random number

p_{c-i} = probability of cutpoint at bit i
T_c = cutpoint threshold
R_{max} = max. possible RN

Fig. 5. Block diagram of hardware implementation of the crossover function

Our solution was to send a crossover template to all multiplexers via a shift register (one bit per bit-slice). This requires one flip-flop per slice, but has the advantage of only needing two adjacent-slice connections. It also allows the number of cutpoints to be varied dynamically by controlling the input pattern to the template shift register.

We create the crossover pattern probabilistically by a comparator connected to a threshold register and the random number generator. When the random number is less than the threshold, the comparator's output is true which causes a toggle flip-flop to change state and thus change the selection pattern being applied to the template shift register. Increasing the threshold increases the number of cutpoints. Syswerda's uniform crossover algorithm [15] can be implemented by removing the toggle flip-flop and using the comparator's output as the template input.

Mutation

The mutation function (Figure 6) uses a technique very similar to crossover in that the mutation information is conveyed to the data bits serially via shift registers In order to lessen the possibility of correlation between mutation and crossover, we have chosen to have two random number streams traveling in opposite directions. A mutation occurrence for bit i is defined as two ones appearing simultaneously at position i in each of the shift registers. The event is detected by a two-input AND function which causes and XOR function to invert bit i coming from the crossover multiplexer.

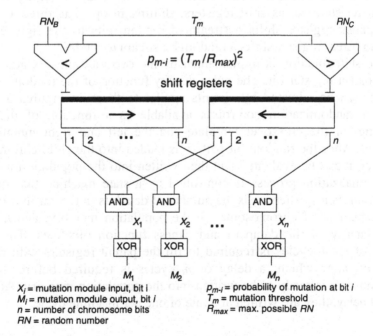

X_i = mutation module input, bit i
M_i = mutation module output, bit i
n = number of chromosome bits
RN = random number

p_{m-i} = probability of mutation at bit i
T_m = mutation threshold
R_{max} = max. possible RN

Fig. 6. Block diagram of hardware implementation of the mutation function.

The two random number streams are implemented similarly to the crossover template stream, except that a toggle flip-flop is not connected to the comparator's output, so a probability of a one in the stream is the ratio of the threshold value to the maximum value of the random number. The probability of a mutation at any single bit is then the product of the one's probability in each of the two streams.

Datapath Bit-Slice

Figure 7 shows the logic flow and quasi-physical representation of the datapath bit-slice. The point that we wish to illustrate is that as the bit-slices are tiled together, the inputs and outputs of respective slices can be made to align thus eliminating the global wiring problem. With the exception of the mode select bits S1 and S2, all connections between slices originate from flip-flops and should be very fast. Since the mode select bits must drive all slices simultaneously, they need to be either driven by special high-power drivers or a fanout tree of buffers.

As shown in the table in Figure 7, the GA machine has three operational modes: initalization, run, and hold. During initalization, the population memory must be filled with random chromosomes and their respective fitnesses. The random chromosomes are generated by letting the two parent registers act as shift registers, shifting in opposite directions. The first parent register shifts a stream of random bits to the right and the second parent register shifts a random bit stream to the left.

The shift function is implemented by the two multiplexers attached to each parent register bit. The pulse density function of the random number stream can be adjusted by circuits similar to those in Figures 5 and 6. Further randomization control is available as a function of the pulse densities of the crossover template and the left and right mutation bit streams. After the random bit pattern is loaded into the child chromosome register, it can be evaluated and then written into the population memory. The initialization process is controlled by a state machine that runs for $n_d+n_p+n_l$ cycles, where n_d is the number of data bits in the chromosome, n_p is the number of chromosomes in the population memory, and n_l is the total latency of the datapath and fitness function pipelines. The initial delay of n_d+n_l cycles is required to fill the parent registers with random patterns, after which, a delay of n_l cycles is required before the first chromosome is ready to be written into the population memory. After the initial delay, they are written at a rate of one per machine cycle.

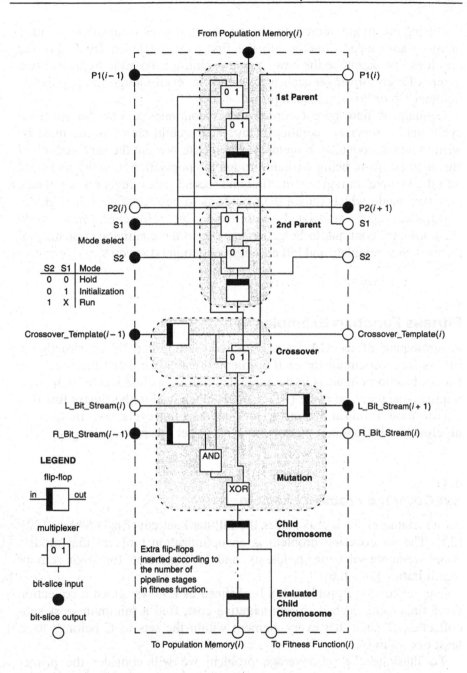

Fig. 7. Bit-slice *i* of the GA machine datapath pipeline.

During run mode, randomly chosen chromosomes from the population memory are loaded directly into the first parent register. By letting the previous first parent be the new second parent, it is possible to present two parents for crossover on each machine cycle, even though the population memory has only a single read port.

Loading of new parent chromosomes continues at one per machine cycle until a survival operation occurs and a child chromosome must be written into the population memory. In order to prevent the surviving child chromosome from being written through the population memory and back into the first parent register, the first and second parent registers are placed into hold mode which causes their contents to be recirculated through the multiplexer pair associated with each bit. However, new child chromosomes continue to be generated due to the continuous updating of the crossover template and left and right mutation bit streams.

4
Fitness Function Examples

Programming of the GA framework is accomplished by constructing a fitness function circuit for each problem. It should be noted that since the fitness function circuit is to be integrated into a pipeline where each stage requires one machine cycle (i.e., a single clock cycle), the fitness function circuit must produce its result in one machine cycle, *or*, in turn be pipelined itself, so that it produces one result per machine cycle.

4.1
Set-Coverage Problem Example

As an example, we will consider the NP-hard set covering problem [22], [23]. The set covering problem is an optimization problem that models many resource-selection problems and is important for logic circuit minimization [24]–[26].

The set covering problem can be defined as follows: given a collection C of finite sets, each with non-negative cost, find a minimum-cost sub-collection C' such that every element within the sets in C belongs to at least one set in C'.

To illustrate the set-coverage problem we will consider the prime-implicant reduction sub-problem of the logic minimization problem [27] shown in Figure 8: The truth table describes the logic function to be implemented. The 1s of this function are plotted on a Karnaugh map [28] which allows us readily see the prime implicants.

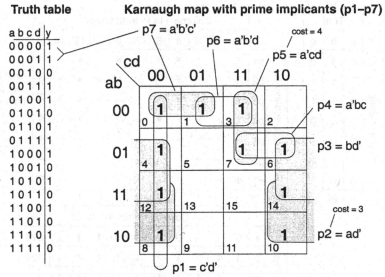

Objective: Find minimum-cost set of prime implicants that covers all 1s in the truth table (column y).

Fig. 8. Example of set-coverage problem: minimal-cost prime implicant set problem (NP-complete subproblem of the logic minimization problem).

Immediately, we can see that all but one of the 1s are covered by at least two prime implicants. The problem is to select a minimum-cost set of prime implicants that covers all 1s on the map. We will use the number of gate inputs required to implement the prime implicant as its cost.

The prime implicants can now be plotted onto a set-coverage table (Figure 9) with the rows representing each set (prime implicant) and the columns representing the elements within the sets (1s of the logic function covered by the prime implicant). If an element is contained within a set, the column representing that item is said to be covered by the set. The objective then, is to find a minimum-cost set of rows whose elements cover all columns.

Chromosome Data Format

Mapping of the trial solution on to the chromosome is straight forward: each row in the table is represented by a bit in the chromosome. If the bit is a 1, then the row is considered to be a part of the trial solution. The cost of the solution is the sum of the costs of the selected rows. However, the fitness of the solution must consider both the legality (all columns might not be covered) and cost of the trial solution.

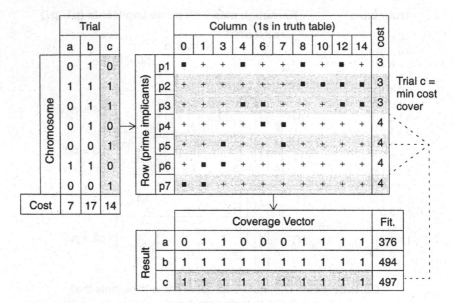

Objective: Find minimum-cost set of rows that covers all columns.
Example: Row 6 covers columns 1 and 3.

Fig. 9. Set-coverage problem

Fitness Function Circuit

In order to provide an evolutionary gradient that will move the population towards legal solutions (all columns covered), the number of covered columns must be integrated into the fitness function. The fitness function circuit in Figure 10 achieves this by counting the number of covered columns (by means of a carry-save adder [20], [22] connected to the outputs of the OR gates that detect column cover) and then subtracting this value from the total number of columns. The 1's complement of the difference is then used as the most-significant portion of the fitness value. This will cause the most-significant portion of the fitness value to be all 1s when all columns are covered. Thus maximizing the fitness values of legal solutions. The least significant portion of the fitness value is composed of the 1's complement of the total cost of the selected rows. Thus, as the cost decreases, the fitness will increase.

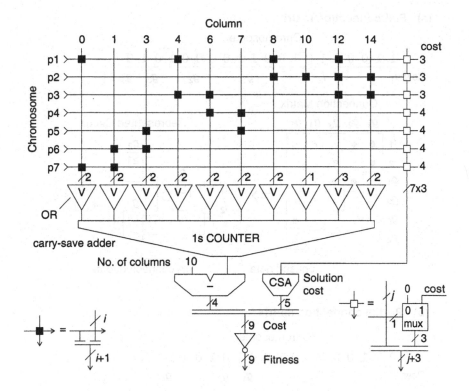

Fig. 10. Fitness function circuit for set-coverage problem.

4.2
Logic Circuit Synthesis Example

In this section, the problem of synthesizing a minimum-cost logic network is formulated for a genetic algorithm. When benchmarked against the a commercial logic synthesis tool, an odd parity circuit required 24 basic cells (BCs) versus 28 BCs for the design produced by the commercial system. A magnitude comparator required 20 BCs versus 21 BCs for the commercial system's design. The design of a hardware-based cost function that would accelerate the GA by several thousand times is described.

Chromosome Data Format

A full connection matrix similar to that in Figure 11a can describe any network not incorporating feedback and comprised of similar circuit elements (in this case, NOR gates).

(a)   Full connection matrix

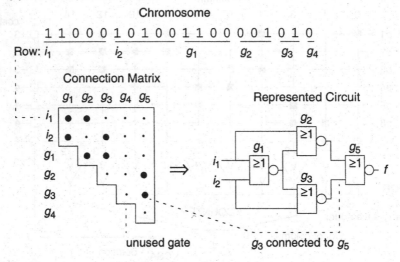

(b)   Partial connection matrix

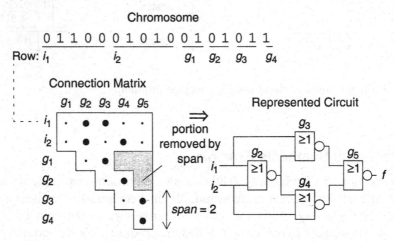

Fig. 11. Chromosome data format: (a) The chromosome represents a full connection matrix of NOR gates and primary inputs to the logic function. A 1 in the chromosome represents a connection (shown by a "•" in the connection matrix). The output of the circuit is defined to be that of the rightmost gate in the connection matrix. (b) Partial connection matrix only allows gates within the range of *span* to be connected.

The rows of the connection matrix represent either function inputs (the rectangular upper portion of the matrix) or gate outputs (the triangular lower portion of the matrix). The columns represent inputs to the gates. A one in the connection matrix represents a connection *from* the signal represented by the row *to* the gate represented by the column.

The connection matrix is arranged so that any function input can be connected to any gate and any gate g_j can be connected to any other gate g_k where $k > j$. The full connection matrix is capable of describing all circuits of up to n_g gates and n_i function inputs. The size of the upper, rectangular portion of the matrix is $n_i n_g$ cells. The size of the lower, triangular portion of the matrix is $n_g(n_g - 1)/2$ cells. Letting each cell in the connection matrix be represented by a single bit in the chromosome, the length n_c of the chromosome is given by:

$$n_c = n_i n_g + \frac{n_g(n_g - 1)}{2}$$

The number of possible network configurations is 2^{n_c}.

The size of the full connection matrix grows as n_g^2. If the span s of connectability is limited such that a gate g_j can only be connected to another gate g_k subject to the constraint $j - s \leq k < j$, then the size of the connection matrix will increase linearly as the number of gates increases. We term this a partial connection matrix (Figure 11b). The size reduction of the connection matrix (shaded area in Figure 11b) is given by $(n_g - s)(n_g - s - 1)/2$, so the chromosome length of the partial connection matrix becomes:

$$n_c = n_i \cdot n_g + \frac{n_g \cdot (n_g - 1)}{2} - \frac{(n_g - s) \cdot (n_g - s - 1)}{2}.$$

Fitness Function

For the logic minimization problem, higher fitness is associated with lower cost, so we will address the cost function directly. We will take the cost of a logic network to be the sum of the costs of the individual gates comprising the network. For the CMOS technology that we used as our target technology, gate costs are measured in basic cells (BCs). For NAND and NOR gates the cost C_B of a gate g in BCs is given by:

$$C_B(g(fanin)) = \begin{cases} fanin + 1 & if \_ fanin \geq 1 \\ 0 & \text{otherwise.} \end{cases}$$

However, we still need to account for cost of logic networks that don't correctly implement the supplied logic function. For these networks, we add a penalty cost increment for every instance in which the synthetic network F does not provide the output specified by the source function T when tested against all possible input combinations. By choosing the penalty increment to be the maximum possible cost (i.e., $n_c + n_g$) for a connection matrix we can be assured that a network with n_e errors will have a lower cost than a network with $n_e + 1$ errors. The penalty cost is given by:

$$C_P = \left(n_c + n_g\right) \sum_{i=0}^{2^{n_i}-1} \begin{cases} 1 & \text{if } T(i) \neq F(i) \\ 0 & \text{otherwise.} \end{cases}$$

Thus, the cost C for a given chromosome is composed of a penalty cost plus the intrinsic cost of the network:

$$C = C_P + \sum_{i=1}^{n_g} C_B(g_i).$$

Hardware Implementation of Cost Function

By implementing 2^{n_i} connection matrix circuits (one for each row in the truth table), a synthetic circuit's compliance the target logic function can be evaluated in one machine cycle (Figure 12).

The circuit is, in effect, a custom FPGA (field programmable gate array) that directly implements the circuit described by the chromosome's bit pattern. The circuit, however, can only evaluate a single row of logic function's truth table. In order to evaluate a chromosome in a single cycle, the basic connection matrix circuit has to be replicated for each row in the truth table.

Figure 13 shows a pipelined implementation of the concept. Each stage of the pipeline evaluates one row of the truth table. If the output off the synthetic circuit does not match the target function at any stage, the penalty cost is incremented and passed to the next stage.

The final stage of the pipeline combines the penalty cost with the intrinsic cost of the synthetic circuit. The penalty cost comprises the most significant portion of the solution cost with the actual cost in BCs comprising the least significant portion.

Since the cost in BCs for a gate is effectively the number of inputs plus one for the output, the actual cost of the circuit represented by the chromosome can be determined by summing the number of inputs with the number of outputs. A carry-save adder connected to the chromosome will calculate the number of inputs since each 1 in the chromosome represents a gate input. Gate outputs can be detected by ORing bits in the chromosome that are associated with a single column in the connection matrix. The outputs of these n_g OR gates are summed in the same carry-save adder to produce the intrinsic circuit cost.

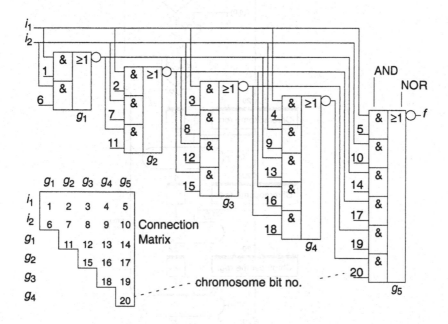

Fig. 12. Hardware circuit to evaluate any circuit expressed by connection matrix: The circuit is simulated by NOR gates g_{1-5} and the circuit interconnections are effected by the AND gates abutted to each NOR gate. Each AND gate is in turn controlled by a bit in the chromosome.

The cost of hardware fitness function C_F increases exponentially with the number of function inputs as given by:

$$C_F = 2^{n_i} \cdot C_C.$$

The cost of a single-cycle-evaluation fitness function circuit as a function of the number of logic function inputs and the maximum number of gates to be considered is plotted in Figure 14.

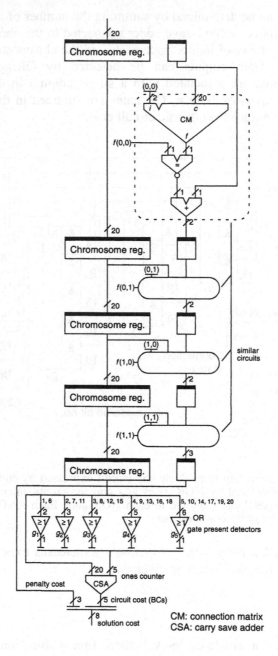

Fig. 13. Pipelined hardware implementation of the logic circuit fitness function that will produce one chromosome evaluation per machine cycle.

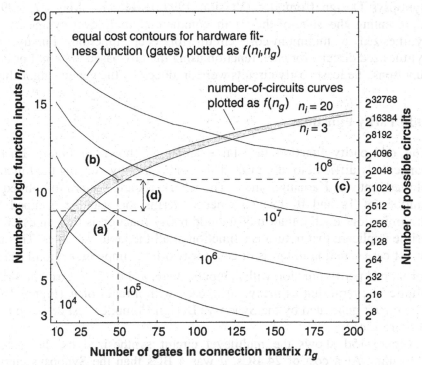

Fig. 14. Equal-cost contours for the single-cycle fitness function circuit are plotted as a function of n_i and n_g.

Circuit Synthesis Experiments

We performed synthesis experiments on two logic functions: (1) a three-bit odd parity function, and (2) a two-bit magnitude comparator. The implementation technology in all cases was a library composed only of NOR gates with the gate cost in basic cells (BCs) being computed as the gate's fanin plus one.

For each function we took the cheaper of either the sum-of-products or the product-of-sums to use as a baseline implementation. Then using the

Synopsys Design Compiler (Version 1997.01-44683 - May 27, 1997), representing the state-of-the-art in commercial multilevel synthesis, we synthesized a minimum-cost circuit for each function. Finally, we synthesized circuits for each function using the GA-based system. For both functions, the least costly circuits were produced by the genetic algorithm.

Odd Parity Function

The odd parity function (a 3-bit example is shown in Figure 15a) is particularly difficult to minimize. This can be seen by viewing the function plotted onto a Karnaugh map. The checkerboard pattern of an equal number of 1s and 0s has no adjacent terms that can be grouped for minimization. Each minterm of the odd parity function is thus an essential prime implicant that in turn is a function of all the input variables. This is a worst-case function in terms of cost for two-level implementation because for an odd parity function with n_i inputs, there will be 2^{n_i-1} essential prime implicants, requiring as many gates, each with a fanin of n_i (Figure 15b). The circuit generated by the Synopsys Design Compiler cost 28 basic cells (Figure 15c).

Figure 15d shows the multilevel circuit synthesized by the genetic algorithm. At a cost of 24 BCs, it was 4 BCs than the Synopsys circuit. Overall, the circuit has a delay of five gate-levels, a maximum gate fanin of three, and a maximum gate fanout of two.

We have included the circuit in Figure 15e as a point of interest. It is a three-bit even parity circuit, which is the inverse of the logic function implemented in Figure 15b. The circuit requires one less gate and one less BC than the odd parity circuit.

Figure 16 shows a plot of circuit cost vs. crossover count of surviving chromosomes for the odd parity function. The stratification of the plot is due to the penalty cost function for circuits that fail to satisfy all rows of the function's truth table. The bottom stratum represents the costs of circuits that properly implement the odd parity function. The next stratum up (costs around 100 BCs) represents circuits that satisfied all but one row of the odd parity truth table (Figure 15a). Successive strata are due to additional errors in satisfying the function.

(a) Odd parity function

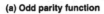

Function symbol

Karnaugh map

Truth table

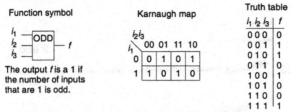

The output f is a 1 if
the number of inputs
that are 1 is odd.

i_1 i_2 i_3	f
0 0 0	0
0 0 1	1
0 1 0	1
0 1 1	0
1 0 0	1
1 0 1	0
1 1 0	0
1 1 1	1

(b) Two-level product-of-sums circuit: cost = 27 BCs

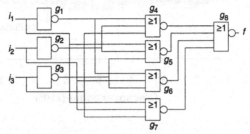

(c) Synopsys-generated circuit: cost = 28 BCs

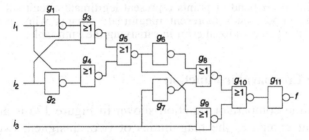

(d) GA-generated circuit: cost = 24 BCs

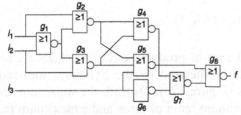

(e) GA-generated circuit (inverse function): cost = 23 BCs

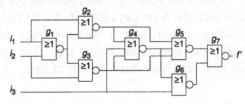

Fig. 15. Three-input odd parity function.

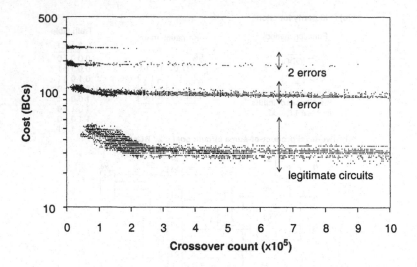

Fig. 16. Cost vs. crossover count of surviving chromosomes for parity circuit synthesis. The lower band of points represent legitimate circuit solutions for the function. The upper bands represent illegitimate circuits with each successive stratum indicating an additional error in satisfying the truth table.

Magnitude Comparator Function

The magnitude comparator function shown in Figure 17a is an arithmetic function that compares the magnitudes of two, unsigned, two-bit binary integers $<i_1, i_2>$ and $<i_3, i_4>$. The function output is 1 when:

$$(i_1 \cdot 2 + i_2 \cdot 1) > (i_3 \cdot 2 + i_4 \cdot 1).$$

The two-level sum-of-products circuit cost 23 BCs (Figure 17b). The multilevel circuit synthesized by the Synopsys tool required eight gates, but only 21 BCs (Figure 17c). Overall, the maximum delay was five gate levels with a maximum fanin of three and a maximum fanout of four.

Figure 17d shows the least costly circuit found by the genetic algorithm. It has one less gate than the Synopsys circuit. Its 20 BC cost was one BC less than the Synopsys circuit and it was the least costly of the three approaches. Overall, the maximum delay was five gate levels with a maximum fanin of three and maximum fanout of two.

(a) Magnitude comparator

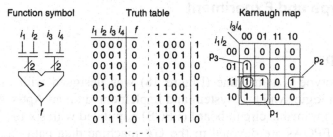

(b) Two-level sum-of-products: cost = 23 BCs

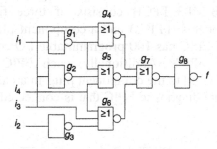

(c) Synopsys-generated circuit: cost = 21 BCs

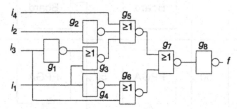

(d) GA-generated circuit: cost = 20 BCs

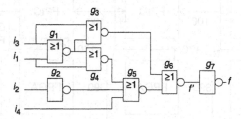

Fig. 17. Two-bit, greater-than comparator function.

5
Prototype and Experiment

5.1
Prototype

The prototype GA machine (Figure 18) was designed with the *Tsutsuji* [29], [30] logic synthesis system and implemented on an Aptix AXB-MP3 field programmable circuit board (FPCB) populated with six FPGAs.

Three FPGAs are devoted to the GA machine data path and three are devoted to the fitness function for the set coverage problem.

The Aptix AXB-MP3 FPCB consists of three field programmable interconnect components (FPICs) and a component plug-in area wired to the FPIC I/O. Each FPIC has 100 programmable I/O connections wired to each of the other FPICs. Additionally, each FPIC has 640 external programmable I/O wired to the component plug-in area. Connected to each FPIC is an additional diagnostic FPIC that is connected to a logic analyzer interface.

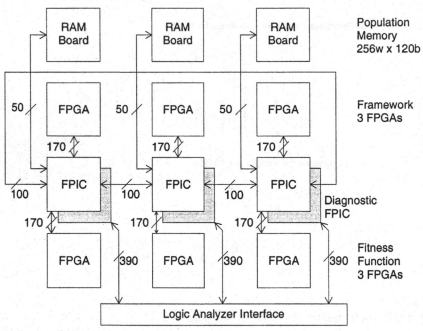

FPGA = Field Programmable Gate Array
FPIC = Field Programmable Interconnect Component

Fig. 18. System prototype block diagram.

Connected to each FPIC via 170 programmable I/O each are two Altera EPF81188A FPGAs. This particular FPGA is described as having 1,008 logic elements or 12,000 "usable gates." Also connected to each FPIC via a 50-bit bus is a RAM memory board. The three memory boards form the population memory. The system is monitored via the logic analyzer interface.

The fitness function circuit for the set coverage problem is designed directly by logic synthesis as a function of a set-specification file. The set-specification file is first transformed into a logic equation file according to a structure similar to that of Figure 10. The logic equation file is then partitioned according to expected FPGA capacity and then each partition is compiled into a gate-level design that can be mapped onto an FPGA.

5.2
Experiment

The set coverage problem considered had 94 rows and 521 columns. This is to say that the objective was to find a minimum-sized set of rows whose elements covered all of the 521 columns. For this problem, the cost of each row was unity. The minimum set size was known before hand to be 15.

The FPGA-based prototype running at 1MHz produces one million crossovers per second. Our software emulation of the survival-based GA, written in C and running on a 100 MHz workstation, produces about 450 crossovers per second for the same set coverage problem. This is an acceleration of over 2,200× for this particular problem.

Figure 19 shows cost data of surviving chromosomes plotted according to the crossover count at which they were generated. At first, many of the solutions are illegal since all columns are not covered in the set-coverage table. These solutions are tagged with very high costs (low fitnesses) because the number of uncovered columns is recorded in the upper 10 bits of the cost function.

Once all columns have been covered, the upper 10 bits of the fitness function will all be 0. The solution cost is then determined by the number of 1s in the chromosome (since all solution rows have a cost of 1). The worst cost for a legal solution is therefore 94 (all chromosome bits set to 1).

The lower plot in Figure 19 shows, at expanded scale, the progression of legal solutions to where the first optimum solution was generated at crossover 18,098.

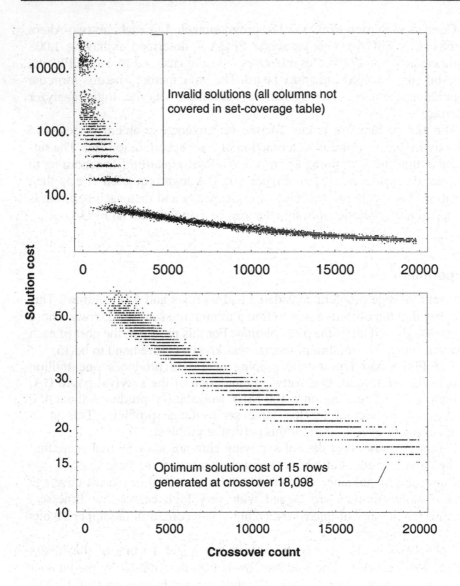

Fig. 19. Fitness of surviving chromosomes vs. crossover count for the set-coverage problem. Bottom plot shows expanded scale.

6
Conclusions

In this chapter, we have addressed the problem of slow execution speed of the software-emulated genetic algorithm by modifying Holland's original

GA for efficient implementation in hardware and then designing a pipelined genetic algorithm processor that can generate one new, evaluated chromosome per machine cycle.

High performance is obtained by implementing the functions of parent selection, crossover, mutation, evaluation, and survival in hardware such a manner that each function can be executed in a single machine cycle. When these hardware functions are connected in a linear pipeline (much the same as an assembly line), the net result is the generation a new child chromosome on each machine cycle.

Preliminary empirical validation of the survival-based genetic algorithm has been obtained by finding the optimum answer to the Royal Road R_1 function in 10× fewer crossover cycles than the original GA.

The key features of the survival-based, steady-state GA are low selection pressure due to random parent selection, steady-state population maintenance, and replacement of randomly discovered, lesser-fit chromosomes by more-fit offspring.

The data path of the GA machine prototype was implemented with three 12,000-gate FPGAs in addition to the population memory. The fitness function circuit to solve a 94 row by 521 column set coverage problem required three additional similar size FPGAs. Running at 1 MHz, the GA machine generated one million new chromosomes per second which was over 2,200× faster than a 100 MHz workstation executing the same algorithm written in C.

References

[1] J. H. Holland, *Adaptation in Natural and Artificial Systems*, University of Michigan Press, 1975. (Second edition: MIT Press, 1992.)
[2] D. E. Goldberg, Genetic Algorithms in Search, Optimization, and Machine Learning, Addison-Wesley, 1989.
[3] M. Mitchell, An Introduction to Genetic Algorithms, MIT Press, 1996.
[4] K. A. De Jong and W. M. Spears, "Using genetic algorithms to solve NP-complete problems," *Proceedings of the Third International Conference on Genetic Algorithms*, Morgan Kaufmann, pp. 124–132, 1989.
[5] J. J. Grefenstette, R. Gopal, B. Rosmaita, D. Van Gucht, "Genetic algorithms for the traveling salesman problem," *Proceedings of the First International Conference on Genetic Algorithms*, Morgan Kaufmann, pp. 160–168, 1985.
[6] H. Mühlenbein, "Parallel genetic algorithms, population genetics, and combinatorial optimization," *Proceedings of the Third International Conference on Genetic Algorithms*, Morgan Kaufmann, pp. 416–421, 1989.
[7] D. Andre and J. R. Koza, "Parallel genetic programming: A scalable implementation using the transputer network architecture," in P. J.

Angeline and K. E. Kinnear Jr., eds., *Advances in Genetic Programming 2*, MIT Press, ch. 16, 1996.

[8] P. Nordin, "A compiling genetic programming system that directly manipulates the machine code," in K. E. Kinnear Jr., ed., *Advances in Genetic Programming*, MIT Press, pp. 311–331, 1994.

[9] P. Graham and B. Nelson, "A hardware genetic algorithm for the traveling salesman problem on Splash 2," in *Field-Programmable Logic and Applications*, ed. W. Moore and W. Luk, pp. 352–361, Springer, Oxford, 1995.

[10] N. Sitkoff, M. Wazlowski, A. Smith, and H. Silverman, "Implementing a genetic algorithm on a parallel custom computing machine," *Proceedings of the IEEE Workshop on FPGAs for Custom Computing Machines*, pp. 180–187, 1995.

[11] J. M. Arnold, D. A. Buell, and E. G. Davis, "Splash 2," Proceedings of the 4th Annual ACM Symposium on Parallel Algorithms and Architectures, pp. 316–324, June 1992.

[12] M. Wazlowski, A. Smith, R. Citro, and H. Silverman, "Armstrong III: A loosely coupled parallel processor with reconfigurable computing capabilities," Technical Report, Division of Engineering, Brown University, 1994.

[13] B. Shackleford, E. Okushi, M. Yasuda, H. Koizumi, K. Seo, and T. Iwamoto, "Hardware framework for accelerating the execution speed of a genetic algorithm," *IEICE Transactions on Electronics*, vol. E80-C, no. 7, pp. 962–969, July 1997.

[14] B. Shackleford, E. Okushi, M. Yasuda, H. Koizumi, K. Seo, T. Iwamoto, and H. Yasuura, "A high-performance implementation of a survival-based genetic algorithm," *The Fourth International Conference on Neural Information Processing—ICONIP'97*, Dunedin, New Zealand, pp. 686–691, Nov. 1997.

[15] G. Syswerda, "Uniform crossover in genetic algorithms," *Proceedings of the Third International Conference on Genetic Algorithms*, Morgan Kaufmann, pp. 2–9, 1989.

[16] G. Syswerda, "A study of reproduction in generational and steady-state genetic algorithms," *Foundations of Genetic Algorithms*, G. Rawlins, ed., Morgan Kaufmann, pp. 94–101, 1991.

[17] M. Mitchell, S. Forrest, and J. H. Holland, "The royal road for genetic algorithms: Fitness landscapes and GA performance," in F. J. Varela and P. Bourgine, eds., *Towards a Practice of Autonomous Systems: Proceedings of the First European Conference on Artificial Life*, MIT Press, 1992.

[18] S. Forrest and M. Mitchell, "Relative building block fitness and building block hypothesis," in L. D. Whitley, ed., *Foundations of Genetic Algorithms 2*, Morgan Kaufmann, 1993.

[19] M. Mitchell, J. H. Holland, and S. Forrest, "When will a genetic algorithm outperform hill climbing?" in J. D. Cowan, G. Tesauro, and J. Alspector, eds., *Advances in Neural Information Processing Systems 6*, Morgan Kaufmann, 1994.

[20] D. A. Patterson and J. L. Hennessy, *Computer Architecture: A Quantitative Approach*, Morgan Kaufmann, 1990.

[21] S. Wolfram, "Random sequence generation by cellular automata," *Advances Appl. Math.*, vol. 7, pp. 123–169, 1986. (Also in S. Wolfram, *Theory and Applications of Cellular Automata*, World Scientific, 1986.)

[22] T. H. Cormen, C. E. Leiserson, and R. L. Rivest, *Introduction to Algorithms*, MIT Press, 1990.

[23] T. Iwamoto, "Genetic algorithms for set covering problems" (in Japanese), *The Sixth Intelligent System Symposium, The Japan Society of Mechanical Engineers*, Osaka, pp. 73–74, Oct. 1996.

[24] O. Coudert, "On solving covering problems," *Proceedings of the 33rd Design Automation Conference*, pp. 197–202, June 1996.

[25] E. L. McCluskey Jr., "Minimization of boolean functions," *Bell System Technical Journal*, vol. 35, pp. 1417–1444, April 1959.

[26] W. V. Quine, "On cores and prime implicants of truth functions," *American Math. Monthly*, vol. 66, pp. 755–760, 1959.

[27] D. D. Gajski, *Principles of Digital Design*, Prentice Hall, 1997.

[28] M. Karnaugh, "A map method for synthesis of combinatorial logic circuits," *Transactions of the AIEE, Communications and Electronics*, vol. 72, part I, pp. 593–599, Nov. 1953.

[29] W. B. Culbertson, T. Osame, Y. Otsuru, J. B. Shackleford, and M. Tanaka, "The HP Tsutsuji logic synthesis system," *Hewlett-Packard Journal*, pp. 38–51, Aug. 1993.

[30] H. Koizumi, K. Seo, F. Suzuki, Y. Ohtsuru, and H. Yasuura, "A proposal for a co-design method in control systems using combination of models," *IEICE Transactions on Information and Systems*, vol. E78-D, no. 3, pp. 237–247, March 1995.

Part 2

Fuzzy Logic Hardware Implementations

Chapter 3

Hardware Implementation of Intelligent Systems

Marco Russo[1] and Luigi Caponetto[2]

[1]Dept. of Physics, Faculty of Engineering, University of Messina, Contrada Papardo, Salita Sperone 31, Sant'Agata 98166 (ME) – ITALY and INFN Section of Catania – Corso Italia 57, 95129 (CT) – ITALY
[2]INF Section of Catania – Corso Italia 57, 95129 (CT) – ITALY

Neural computing, fuzzy logic and evolutionary computing are widely used in a broad range of application fields. While many fields take full advantage from conventional von Neumann processors, there are still classes, such as for example intelligent systems in high-energy physics, requiring the speed of fully hardware implementations.

In the first part of this chapter, we discuss the hardware specifications of intelligent systems. These are outlined as basic specifications (including external input/output architecture, topology for neural networks or defuzzification function for fuzzy systems), hardware specifications (including the technology and the precision required), and performance specifications. These specifications are mapped over existing architectures such as general purpose (micro controllers and digital signal processors, extended instruction set architectures and coprocessors), and dedicated ones. Further, we review a sample of various VLSI implementations including digital and analog. We also investigate a selection of basic building blocks suitable for neural networks, fuzzy logic and genetic algorithms.

1
Introduction

In this chapter, we present an overview of hardware techniques used to implement Soft Computing (SC) systems. The theory behind these systems is not outlined in this survey. For theoretical details, the reader is referred to the wide literature regarding introductory and tutorial material [33], [35].

Fuzzy Logic (FL) and Neural Networks (NNs) are two widespread accepted design methods. The parallelism of FL and NNs is directly mapped in hardware and significant speeds are achievable [31]. Genetic Algorithms (GAs) are also used as an optimization method, based on the evolution of species, and has been applied to many optimization problems. However, the inherent parallel structure of this technique greatly benefits from hardware implementation [29], [43], [50]. These techniques are very different from each other. Often two or three of these techniques are used together to obtain better performance [32], [34].

Several specific terms are used related to soft computing hardware solutions. Unfortunately, many of them are not universally accepted yet. Thus, we will introduce with brief explanations the main terms used throughout this chapter.

A fuzzy *processor* (often *coprocessor*, when it implements host interface logic combined in a single chip) is an integrated circuit (IC) performing complete fuzzy computations, including premise, rule and conclusion evaluation, defuzzification, moreover implementing rule base memory interface. Generally, these processors are digital-based designs. We refer to a fuzzy *micro-controller, Fuzzy Logic Controller (FLC)* or *controller* as a system whose general purpose features are limited to enhanced specific control capabilities (i.e. extremely fast latency times, easy and efficient input and output). Analog-based implementations of these systems benefit of no Analog to Digital Converters (ADCs) and Digital to Analog ones (DACs). Further analysis of such arguments can be found in Section 2.1.

Research in hardware design of NNs was initiated before FL and GA. So, a wider spectrum of implementation choice has been investigated. Many solutions are commercially available, too [21]. We refer to a *neuro-microprocessor* as a full programmable architecture efficiently executing a wide range of connectionist computations. Similarly, a *neuro-computer* is a stand-alone system with a quite elaborate software environment, libraries of NN algorithms and an optimizing compiler for developing purpose [26].

There are some examples of GAs designed for hardware realizations [29], [42], [52], attempting to accelerate the execution of the algorithm using pipelining and parallelization. Though general-purpose systems (such as for example Transputers, Hypercube, MasPar and Connection Machine) have been preferred for its superior mapping flexibility of the problem [19], dedicated parallel hardware may be more cost-effective since not all features of such large systems may be needed. The major problem the designer have to face with is the fitness evaluation task [42], [50], because of the limited set of computational blocks available in hardware. Considering that a general-purpose GA requires that the fitness function can be easily changed using very different operators and primitive functions, hardware implementations greatly benefits from the re-programmability provided by FPGA technologies [43].

2
Specifications

In this section, we first introduce those hardware characteristics which, from the user perspective, are often used to choose among many different implementations possibilities. Such attributes are, for example, the number of inputs and outputs, resolution, speed, power, memory, and architectural choices. We discuss, at the end of the section, ways to classify intelligent hardware, too.

2.1
Basics

Comparison between hardware implementations of SC algorithms is difficult due to the large number of parameters involved. Furthermore, such algorithms are strongly applications dependent. Therefore, several hardware variations and extensions exist. Also, many of these algorithms are rapidly changing due to the rapid research developments.

The first parameter to consider when new hardware is evaluated should be the maximum number of inputs/outputs (I/O). While this is usually straightforward for microcontroller chips, some subtleties exist when considering more structured systems as for example fuzzy and neuro coprocessors. Implementing such systems as accelerator boards in fact leads to system-level specifications bounded to the particular host computer to use. For example, some hardware-based GAs implement only crossover, mutation and selection assuming fitness is evaluated externally [29], [43]: this could either happen in a software program running in the host CPU, as well in a hardware module placed within the same board. Both solutions allow for a higher level of abstraction, using a coarse grained parallelism to reduce the memory bottleneck [29].

Above all, in controller-like implementations, the *type* of I/O ports is one of the parameters to evaluate. Main issues are if analog or digital and if parallel or serial ports must be used. Usually, systems more complex than controllers have got their own digital host interface, either integrated in the chip or implemented within the board [21], [26], [43].

When a user is not interested in a very small, embedded system or in a single fixed type of algorithm, a programmable system is required. *Programmability* is one of the main classification issues and means if the overall behavior could be changed applying external control inputs, or if the internal data-flow is hardwired and no modification is possible.

Fuzzy systems are perhaps the best examples showing such issue, ranging from highly user-re-configurable architectures [18] to application-specific [10], through several masked-programmable or field-programmable [1], [45], [48] realizations. Re-configurable analog as well mixed systems are presented in [38]. Conversely, in the NN field, most of such designs are SIMD systems with only minor variations. Several examples could be found in commercial NN realizations [21], while the architecture of a neuro-microprocessor is presented in [56].

The precision of the inputs and outputs as well as their internal representations is also important. Those holds true in particular for digital fuzzy controllers [27], where the transformation from analog to digital and vice versa determines the accuracy of the control action.

Several authors outline the same functional block architecture ([1], [18], [27], [48], [10]), where each fuzzy system design at least consists of three modules: fuzzification, inference and defuzzification (Fig. 1). Rule base memory could also be found inside the system as a fourth unit [27], or its global organization could just be described leaving its implementation within a commercially available external memory [18].

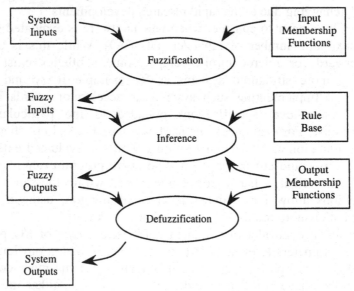

Fig. 1. Three stages Fuzzy Logic Controller functional architecture

Summarizing, we now outline the main classification issues adopted for fuzzy hardware classification together with the typical parameters to determine during (or before) the design process of a fuzzy controller [48]:

- Fuzzifier implementation
  - number of I / O signals;
  - number of Membership Functions (MFs) for each input and for each output;
  - overlap between MFs.
- Defuzzifier implementation
  - implemented algorithm(s);
  - external and internal representation width (in bits).
- Parallel and pipeline architecture
  - overall inference strategy;
  - antecedent combination method;
  - MFs storage technique;
  - fuzzification and defuzzification methods.

2.2
Hardware

Hardware implementations of intelligent systems often aim to provide a final product with low-area, low-power and low-cost properties. That involves several practical difficulties often tied to a lack of a unique structural definition, clearly visible when comparing different architectural issues and overall performance of such systems. The task of mapping basic specifications, as the ones previously described, typically is subjected to restrictions in terms of area, power and time, which may complicated the realization of a chosen algorithm.

In the case of FL systems, 4-bit words often provide the best membership degree resolution regarding design complexity considerations [12], [27], [48]. A wide spectrum of arithmetic computational blocks could be found ranging from the 64 bits floating-point capabilities offered by using a general purpose processor ([46]), ending with analog voltage-mode implementations [10], [38], [49] or current-mode [53]. An even wider implementation range is offered when considering NN-based digital hardware systems (see [21] for a review of commercially available realizations).

An Artificial Neural Network (ANN) is composed of a large number of highly interconnected elements (PE or briefly *neurons* in the ANNs context) working together to solve specific problems. Therefore, a straightforward design technique is using multiprocessor systems made of commercial CPUs (see Section 3.1). Advantages provided by the short design time and the adaptability of use are often balanced with limited size and parallelism.

Custom processor designs are used for higher performances. The simplifications are made possible by several algorithms enabling the integration of many processors on a single die. The design of the processing units thus consists in implementing only a minimal set of computational primitives a required by the target algorithm. The reduced precision required in most models often leads the designer to avoid area-expensive floating point arithmetic units while using simplified integer codings as well as analogue structures (see [21] for digital examples, and [38] for analog examples).

Some VLSI-related implementation issues the designer has to analyze are now briefly discussed: these are widely discussed arguments within the VLSI discipline so we will briefly touch only a few points.

• *Fabrication technology*: The standard technologies that are used for microprocessor fabrication seem suitable to fabricate state-of-the-art fuzzy controllers [27]. Comparing the architectures of today's fuzzy processors and a standard microprocessor we see that many components (ALU, MMU, control unit) are used in both of them [46].

While new emerging technologies such floating-gate MOS [20], could be used in future systems design, the large part of the implementation reviewed here adopt digital design flows methodology used in standard MOS processes ([21], [27], [29], [37], [50], [56]). Modern sub-micron CMOS are now widely available even for research purposes and are not more complicated than a sub-micron BiCMOS process. CMOS integrated circuits, however, have established a dominant position and are manufactured in much greater volume than any other technology [44].

FPGA technologies are the mandatory implementation choice for Genetic Algorithms and in general for evolutionary systems ([19], [43]) though some examples exist in the fuzzy-based area [9], [45].

• *Chip area*: The capacity of the on-chip memory as well as the number of its I/O strongly affect the final chip area and the resulting package.

• *Storage ability*: In a fuzzy-based design, it usually refers to the capacity to store membership functions assigned to different linguistic variable values. The term *rule base* could be considered just as a synonym.

Depending on the specific implementation, the memory demand for the rule base of a typical fuzzy controller varies form a few to several Kbytes [27].

In an Artificial Neural Network chip, the built-in memory demand is for registers to store the weights. Storing analog signals could also result in less occupied area for purely analog systems (see Section 3.2) Depending whether the chip implements on-chip-learning or not, this basic requirement could grow up to twice (see [21] for references) when a back-propagation algorithm is used.

Genetic algorithms usually need large memory banks above all to store the population; depending on the range of values a gene needs, either a shared (with host) external memory [42], or a fully in chip [50] solution is used.

2.3
Performance

Speed is another important hardware specification. In the FL controller literature, at least four performance measures exist [27]:

1. the maximum internal clock frequency;
2. the number of fuzzy logic inferences per second (FLIPS);
3. the number of the elementary fuzzy operations per second (e.g. MIN or MAX);
4. the input-output delay time (*latency*).

While only a few instruction-set-based digital architectures could be rated basing on the first speed index, this is often used when comparing hardware versus software implementations of the same systems.

Because of the not uniquely defined inference scheme (see next section), the FLIPS (or FIPS) measure is usually ambiguously defined. Furthermore, because of the lack of agreement amongst the research community, this would be easily misunderstood as the operation referring to a single rule as well as to a part of the rule [27]. This parameter is generally not related to the actual availability of the output. The presence of a slow defuzzification block for example could lead to an output control action available, say, milliseconds since the input stimulus entered the controller, while the device is claiming a performance of several MFLIPS. A slightly different speed index is the Fuzzy Rules Per Second (FRPS), only useful for such architectures able to evaluate fuzzy rules. Again, it is hard to compare different architectures provided that restrictions often exist on the maximum allowable number of rules [39]. The number of elementary fuzzy operations is even more confusing if used as a speed measure.

Referring to the literature on Artificial Neural Networks, the most common figure of merit used is the Connection-Per-Second (SPC). Here, a connection is normally defined as the result of a multiply and accumulate operation, that is, the typical synapse computation. While a well-accepted agreement exists about this point, the CPS rates can be misleading not taking into account the precision of the inputs and of the weights. The Connection Primitives per Sec (CPPS) has been proposed to address this matter:

$$CPPS = b_{in}b_w CPS \tag{1}$$

where b_{in} and b_w are respectively the number of bits of the inputs and of the weights. To weight the CPS taking into account the number of synapses provided per neuron (N), the CPS Per Weight (CPSPW) was proposed:

$$CPSPW = \frac{CPS}{N} \tag{2}$$

Another parameter, useful for on-chip learning systems, is the Connection-Update-per-Second (CUPS), indicating the rate of weight modifications. However, this parameter does not consider the weights and inputs precision, as well as the accumulator size. This is not good especially for standard back-propagation algorithm, to which CUPS is normally referred, where high precision is needed for many classification tasks [26]. For RBF networks (see Section 2.5), pattern presentation rates are the most relevant performance parameters [25].

Unfortunately, both for fuzzy- and for neural-based systems, there are no accepted benchmark data sets on which hardware implementations could be tested.

2.4
Classification of Fuzzy Architectures

In fuzzy control we usually distinguish two types of rules: Mamdani rules and Sugeno rules. The first ones are by far the most general form of writing rules adopted in fuzzy control theory and was used in the first reported applications of fuzzy control by Mamdani, in 1974 (see [23]). The general form of the k-th rule is:

if $(x_1$ *is* $A_1^k)$ *and* ... *and* $(x_N$ *is* $A_N^k)$ *then* $y = b_k$

where b_k is a constant parameter. A very simple weighted defuzzification is used to obtain the final controller output:

$$y' = \frac{\sum_{k=1}^{n} \theta_k b_k}{\sum_{k=1}^{n} \theta_k} \qquad (3)$$

where θ_k is the premise degree of truth of the k-th rule.

We present more details related to the above discussion in Table 1. Two entries of this table are now briefly discussed, representing each in its own domain *typical* hardware implementation for fuzzy systems.

The SAE 81 C991 digital general-purpose fuzzy controller used as a hardware accelerator is presented in [18]. It is suitable to be integrated as a macro-cell on Siemens 16 bits micro-controllers C16x. Because of the aim of a general-purpose chip, different operation modes, algorithms and operators are offered. The fuzzification block processes 12 bits crisp input values into 12 bits activation degree α values (a maximum of 15 membership functions – 4 bits coding), using the *elementary interval* (EI) method that is independent on the shape of the membership function (see Fig. 1). Furthermore, the inference block supports several different inference operators while the controller exhibits four different defuzzification methods.

Table 1: Fuzzy Classification

Arch. Type and Technology	Short description	Ref. and Year
Three stages digital FLC	Mamdani inference scheme. Memory defined membership function's shapes.	[12] 1990
Three stages FPGA FLC	Mamdani inference scheme with calculation of activated rules. Memory defined membership function's shapes.	[45] 1992
General Purpose Digital CMOS	It supports different fuzzy algorithms and operators. No restrictions on membership function's shapes.	[18] 1996
Three stages analog/digital (BiCMOS) FLC	Mamdani inference scheme. S-shape, Z-shape, triangle, or trapezoid membership functions.	[40] 1996
Three stage analog FLC	Sugeno order zero inference scheme. S-shape, Z-shape, triangle, or trapezoid membership functions.	[10] 1997

Analog chips implemented in voltage mode, like the one in [38], present two main big advantages: small areas and simple connection to several consequent blocks in parallel without additional circuitry. Usually, the fuzzification block offers the possibility to change the membership function shapes (from bell-shapes to triangular) using the same hardware circuit [15], [38]. Re-configurable analog inference engine with analog Mamdani *max-min* technique again is often the implementation choice for such designs. In the reported solution, the rule-base reconfiguration is accomplished via analog demultiplexers, controlled by the content of digital registers [16] or external pins [15].

2.5
Classification of Artificial Neural Networks

We briefly discuss now the mathematics of two types of ANNs, which have been often implemented in hardware systems. These are the multi-layer *sigmoid* and *Radial Basis Function* (RBF) networks [21].

Sigmoid networks at least contain some processing unit computing their outputs as a non-linear sigmoid function $\sigma(\cdot)$ of its input. The purpose of training such networks is to reduce the generalization error and this usually leads to the computation of the negative gradient of the network error with respect to the weights; the best-known algorithm doing that is the back-propagation technique. This algorithm requires considerable amounts of storage for intermediate results and extra circuitry for the backward processing steps [8], [21], [25]. Therefore, every time that chip-in-the-loop systems could be implemented, the solution consists of emulating the network within the host computer for carrying on the learning phase and the downloading resulting weights to the chip.

In the second type of multi-layer ANN, the hidden units have some sorts of distance-limited activation function: the comparison of input vectors to stored training vectors can be done quickly, provided that no multiplication operations are needed in non-Euclidean distances. Here, the learning is local, i.e. no complex information from multiple neurons needs to be exchanged and hence simpler implementations are possible.

Again, like in the previous section, two interesting hardware implementations are briefly discussed. In [56] is described a *neuro-microprocessor* (SPERT). The design of such machine is similar to that of a general-purpose parallel computer, including several 32 bits digital blocks often used in microprocessor or DSPs designs. SPERT is a combination of a RISC 32 bit-wide data-path scalar unit with a SIMD array containing eight 32 bits fixed-point PEs (see Fig. 3). The main idea behind that is to use the RISC scalar unit for handling cases where operations cannot be parallelized across the SIMD data-paths.

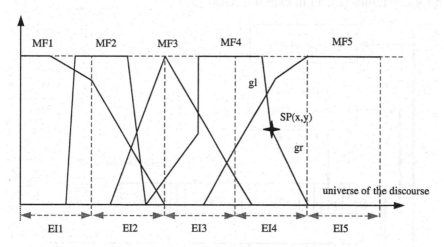

Fig. 2. Example EI classification method: the universe of the discourse is divided in EI within which at least one Supporting Point and one or two gradients gl and gr are allowed to describe up to four membership functions.

This design represents an evolution step from general purpose processors to custom chips; it is leading from a first DSP array (Ring Array Processor) for speech-recognition applications, to the special purpose VLIW SPERT chip and would finally result in a large connectionist server (CNS-1, see [21], [56].

The TOTEM Architecture was implemented to work with the Random Tabu Search (RTS) algorithm, based on combinatorial methods that avoid the need for derivative calculations. One of the major advantages of this method is the low precision weight, as opposed to back propagation-based algorithms that use derivatives and work best with high precision values. This implies simple chips with low precision weights: embedded applications could then be easily implemented with the weights hardwired into the chip. Although the chip is particularly suitable for use in connection with this training method, basically it only runs the forward processing of layered feed-forward networks [58]: the chip implements a SIMD stream using 32 simple processors, each with a buffer of 128 bytes. Inputs and outputs have 16 bits precision and each processor has a 16×8 parallel multiplier using a Baugh-Wooley algorithm (and a 32 bit accumulator) [8]. Multiple chips can be combined to build larger networks. The TOTEM chip could even run the feed-forward processing for other algorithms, such as back propagation, while the full evaluation cycle of a Mamdani type fuzzy controller is claimed to be executed together with a host in [57]. Transfer sigmoidal functions are read from lookup are read from lookup tables (LUT) in external RAM [57].

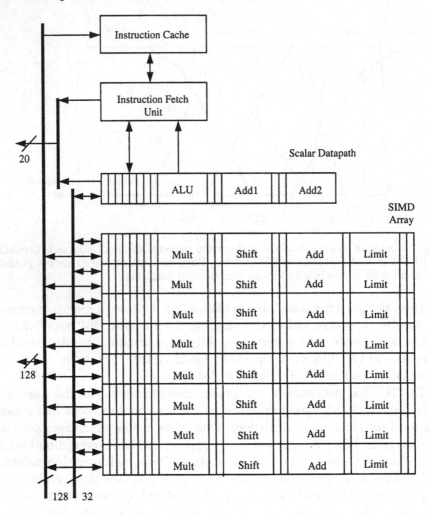

Fig. 3. SPERT neuro-computer architecture

3
Hardware Building Blocks for Computational Intelligence

In this section, we give a brief survey of the basic hardware blocks used when implementing intelligent systems as ICs. Basically we will distinguish between *digital* and *analog*-based design methodology. Within each subsection, we present basic building blocks for fuzzy systems, neural networks and genetic algorithms, though a rigid classification is not possible: some of these block would also fit well in more than one class as well as in conventional ASICs.

3.1
Digital Design

The time needed for the realization of a few projects could be frustrating for its effectiveness in case of a long prototyping phase. This particularly holds true in the research field, where design costs could represent the main issue to deal with, when starting a new project. Nowadays, the high degree of standardization reached by the design flow and the mature fabrication techniques are leading digital hardware implementations to even faster and less expensive developing times. Furthermore, the industry-standard digital development approach, deploying HDLs based design methodologies, fits well the requirements of such type of products. In fact, HDL methodologies have helped in exploring various alternatives for fuzzy logic hardware chip design ([48] and [11], [27]) and constitute the underlying base for all the implementations of genetic algorithms ([29], [43]).

FPGA technology offers high speed to portable systems in low-volume productions [10], as well as effective techniques for rapid prototyping systems [48]. For example, the growing assessment of this technology greatly simplifies fuzzy hardware prototyping though only if FPGA modules will directly support fuzzy primitives the design of such systems should be significantly boosted up [37]. Genetic algorithms based FPGA chips possess the speed characteristics of the hardware, while retaining the flexibility of software implementation [43], [50].

Using Standard Digital Hardware

The most general way to implement intelligent systems is to write software for a specific computer platform to be executed in standard digital processors [21], [37], [39]. Perhaps, the main advantage of such approach is its flexibility to implement even multi-purpose processes, taking full advantage from the huge amount of existing software libraries. Furthermore, such solution benefits of the availability of usable operating systems, given that close interaction with real user applications have to be provided [56]. Another main issue for implementing intelligent systems on general purpose processors is the simulation and optimization of the algorithms before they get hard-wired on chip; such developing technique is a real payoff especially in automatic adaptation tasks of fuzzy rule-based systems with neural and genetic algorithms [46].

Several attempts have been made to compare performance of dedicated hardware with software implementations optimized or not [6], [42], [46]. Perhaps the main concern behind this approach is that it inherently involves very low parallel computation, while all the hardware implementation of intelligent systems aims to exploit its intrinsic parallelism.

However, Amdahl's law shows that only when a substantial part of a task can be parallelized, we can achieve significant acceleration using specialized hardware. The total speedup is thus given by the formula:

$$Overall\ speedup = \frac{1}{(1-f)+(f/s)} \tag{4}$$

where f is the fraction of the process that could be enhanced and s is the speedup of this portion.

While some examples exist of fuzzy-based systems implemented in standard DSPs [22] as well as in 8-bit micro-controller [41], producing inexpensive implementations of fuzzy controllers with medium complexity [46], a more interesting general-purpose based approach has even lead to extended instruction set RISC-like architectures [6], [55].

The FLORA (Fuzzy Logic On RISC Architecture) project proposes a 32-bit RISC whose architectural choice are only starting from instruction analysis and profiling of selected target C code. While such systems could only be considered a general-purpose RISC processor with fuzzy logic special support, it may achieve significantly better performance than other equivalent machines, exploiting advantages coming from an effective exploration of system components and from on-chip data communication capability [46], [47], [54].

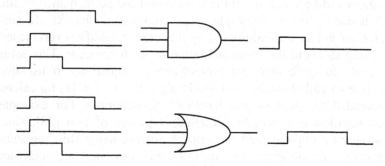

Fig. 4. MIN and MAX implementation with the bit duration technique.

An effective implementation of an intelligent system with standard general purpose hardware requires an analysis of the available operations of today microprocessors and a subsequent adaptation step for algorithm. For example, a possible representation for fuzzy membership value is the so-called pulse duration modulation (PDM) [46], also known as pulse width modulation (PWM) [49], [51]. This technique is particularly suitable for standard digital hardware implementations, when neither MIN nor MAX operations are available. So, using a bit duration technique (see Fig. 4) in conjunction with built-bitwise AND (for MIN) and bitwise OR (for MAX), it is possible to implement fuzzy primitives on standard microprocessors.

The same technique could also be used when implementing current mode ANNs [13]: provided that key operations in ANN are the summation of the weights-outputs products $(\sum_{ij} w_i o_j)$ and the nonlinear outputs transformation, the current-mode technique greatly simplifies the first while PWM could be used instead of the Gilbert cell (see Section 3.2) combined latter with the multiplication.

The use of commercial CPUs based multiprocessor system constitutes an implementation choice only for ANN hardware (especially in the late'80 [21]) with only a known exception in the genetic algorithms field [19], which is a tree structure of processor for executing a GA.

Multipliers

As already mentioned (see Section 2.2), one of the main digital implementation choices is the number of bits used to store words internal to the chip. Considering only custom implementations, it ranges from 32 floating point bits used in the HNC100 ANN system (see [21] and [26] for references) to the 4 bits widths of some fuzzy system implementations. Of course, this would greatly affect the design and the performance of such a system needed for a multiplier as functional block: feasibility considerations are so well addressed by this case to justify several research efforts trying to avoid the implementation of such operator. This solution always leads to quite different weight-change equations to use during learning (the so-called hardware-friendly algorithms – see [2] for reference – are intended to yield simple hardware realizations). For example, a proposed solution uses weights equal to a power of two [28], since it would simply be implemented in digital hardware using shift registers. A back propagation algorithm for training this modified artificial neural network is proposed in [30].

A different approach addressing this matter would be to use a combination of digital (for control and memory issues) and analog (for implementing the actual computation) techniques: see Section 3.2. In some cases though the digital multiplier is the only possible implementation choice.

A custom digital fuzzy system adopting a product operator as the antecedents T-norm and conjunction is presented in [14]. This would be further complicated by the presence of a second multiplier, performing the multiplication between the premise degree of truth θ and the output function 7-bit crisp value Z_i (Sugeno order-zero control). The feasibility final implementation here is allowed by the choice of adopting 4 bits both for the antecedent and the premise degree of matching. Both multipliers are standard cell implementations of the same Wallace tree array multiplier.

A different choice is the one adopted for the SPERT neuro-processor [56], where a 32-bit wide data path is required for each of the 8 SIMD processing units. Here, the fixed-point 32 bit capabilities are provided by a 24b × 8b full custom multiplier. The 50MHz clocked SIMD array is thus able to deliver 400×10^6 fixed-point multiply accumulates per second.

Baugh-Wooley array multipliers (see Fig. 5) are used to multiply positive and negative numbers in two's compliment in the TOTEM chip [3]. The cost is $(n\times n)$ AND gates plus $n\cdot(n+1)+2$ full adders, and the performance is $t_{AND}+(2n-1)\cdot t_{Carry}+t_{Sim}$, where n is the number of bits per word.

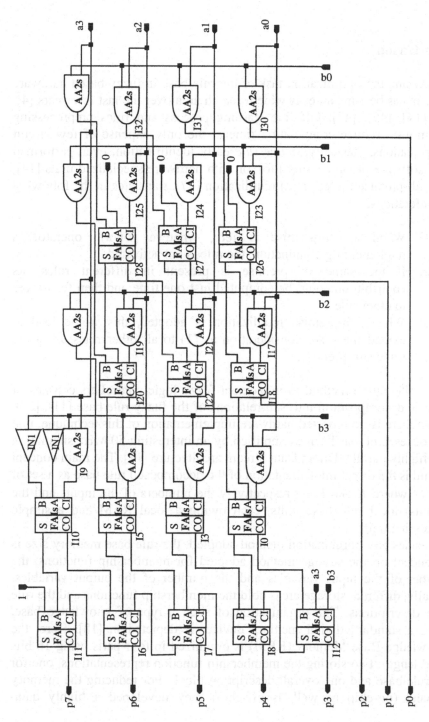

Fig. 5. Example Baugh-Wooley 4 bit array multiplier

Rule Bases

Addressing the optimization task of the rule base in fuzzy based hardware designs has become an ever wide research area over the last few years [4], [5], [14], [46], [47]. Off line learning process and rules preprocessing enormously reduce computation time at the only expense of few circuit complications. Basically, *active rule* early identification, even performed with software preprocessing [46], or with hardware specialized units [14], and sub-premise (antecedent) reutilization [47], translates in the following considerations:

1. When a sub-premise is zero, whatever t-norm operator is implementing conjunction, the rule is not activated.
2. If the same sub-premise is present in different rules, its contribution could be computed just one time and then forwarded to other rules.
3. When sub-premise reutilization is adopted, this would lead to extend the same consideration as (1) to all other rules using the same sub-premise.

An alternative method to implement fuzzy logic controllers consists of the rule decomposition into sub-relations of the fuzzy rule base [11], [27]. While there is no reported hardware implementation of this technique, that line of research has been exemplified by an interesting 50 MHz simulation of a highly parallel Direct Data Stream architecture [11]. The main concept behind is the direct implementation of the decomposed rule base as a set of $K \times L$ (where K and L are respectively the numbers of the inputs and the outputs) local rule base units, each owing a local RAM and a simple processing unit.

Besides any optimization method adopted, the rule base memory size is dependent on the storage method adopted for membership functions, the number of the input variables and the number of the output variables. Usually, different storage areas hold the membership functions and the rule base descriptions. The organization of such a type of knowledge base, using a standard digital memory device, is depicted in [18]. Here, the Knowledge-Base Memory (KBM) is organized in four parts using 16 bits word length: two storing the membership function representations, one for the rule base and one overall description block. For reducing the memory demand (on-chip as well as off-chip) they developed a highly data-compressed format for the input / output membership functions, as well as for the rule base.

For compressed storage of neighbored membership functions, the method firstly proposed by Eichfeld (see [46]) is often used, where at each membership function is assigned a binary number and two different memory banks are used. That system allows a maximum overlap of two between membership functions, thus looking interestingly for large applications (see Fig. 6). Of course the method is generalizable for higher overlaps degree.

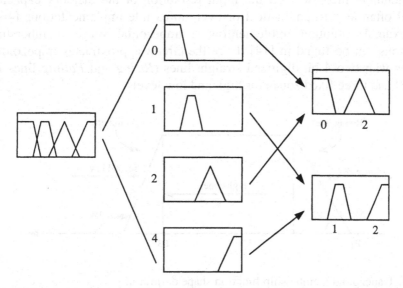

Fig. 6. Compressed storage of neighbor membership functions

A good implementation of methods here depicted is found in [45]. The memory required for storing a rule, assuming a binary code representation for the linguistic labels is:

$$S_R = (m+n) \times \log_2(k) \tag{5}$$

where k is the number of the membership functions (it is assumed to be the same for all the variables) and m and n are the numbers if the I/O variables. The membership functions (in the premise parts) are stored in an external RAM, whose read address is computed from the crisp input value: this is a well adopted technique since early time of fuzzy controllers [12].

Function Generators

Digital function generators are found in fuzzy systems where the required precision is very high. While continuous, monotonically increasing, non-linear sigmoid functions are normally required in multi-layer perceptron implementations, no dedicated digital solutions are reported. Typical solution in that field often adopts primitive block arithmetic computation, or internal or external lookup table based implementations [21], [57]. The latter solution is quite frequent in fuzzy-based design too, though the exponentially increase with the input resolution of the memory capacity would often lead to unpractical or even unfeasible implementations [46]. An example solution implementing a trapezoidal shape membership functions can be found in [14]. Here the circuit approximates trapezoidal shapes with two 4 bit digitized straight lines (*Rising* and *Falling* lines in Fig. 7) and three fixed zones for high and low levels.

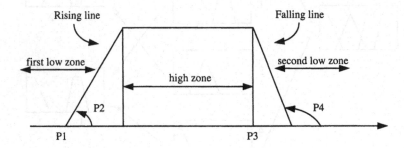

Fig. 7. Trapezoidal membership function shape definition

The four parameters used for representing in memory such shape are the ones depicted in Fig. 7. Thus three zones are easily implemented with three digital comparators (7 bits wide). The hardware implementation of the two straight lines generator only needs a multiplication between the 7 bit slope parameter and the input variable, avoiding implementing a divider (a truncation operation is used instead).

3.2
Analog Design

Analog hardware can exploit physical properties to do primitives operations obtaining high speed and densities compared with digital implementations [38]. Continuous signals and the nonlinear characteristics of the active devices are the most obvious advantages of analog technology.

Real-world interfacing is another key-point requiring analog technology especially when data is applied in massive parallelism: That holds for large Artificial Neural Networks where the use of hundreds or even thousands of high speed A/D converters would not allow feasibility considerations like one required in low-power systems [24].

Furthermore is it possible to view fuzzy systems as well as Artificial Neural Networks like nonlinear systems with less restrictive electrical requirements than general-purpose analog circuits. This would lead to simplified circuits design regarding overall linearity, thermal drift and matching.

Neuron Circuits

One of the major problems reported when designing digital IC's Artificial Neural Networks is the presence of a multiplier implementing the synapse function: for digital design this would be often slowest element in the processing chain. Though for analog designs the multiplier is easily implemented in many different ways. Problems arise when considering linearity over a useful range [26]. Typical analog multipliers are the Gilbert multiplier and the MOS resistive circuit.

The first implementation choice a designer has to face is the need for a 4-quadrant multiplier or not. Weights need in general to be bipolar, thus needing at least 2-quadrant multiplication, though by adding a constant prior of multiplication and afterwards do a subtraction

$$s = w \times z = (w + w_0) \times z - w_0 \times z \tag{6}$$

the problem is reduced to a single-quadrant one. This could however introduce additional offset errors.

Furthermore, some widely adopted neuron sigmoid functions (e.g. *tanh*(.)) yields as output a bipolar value. However, even this problem could easily be solved, 4-quadrant multiplication leads to straightforward implementations of the learning hardware [24].

Perhaps the most popular form of a 4-quadrant multiplier is the one showed in Fig. 8. Here the current output is differential and, assuming a square law approximation for the saturated MOS, is given by:

$$I_{wz} = (I\,w\,z+) - (I\,w\,z-) = \sqrt{k_w k_z}\; w\,z \tag{7}$$

where w and z are the voltages applied between w+, w- and z+, z- . k_w and k_z are the transconductance parameters for the upper two (equal) and the lower differential pairs respectively.

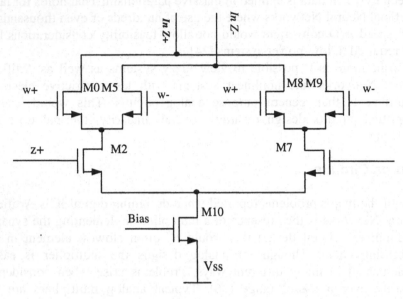

Fig. 8. NMOS-only Gilbert multiplier cell

The MOS resistive circuit is another very simple and linear multiplier [24] furnishing a differential output current proportional to the w and z voltage product. The basic principle is to use a triode biased MOS transistor ohmic characteristic. Major properties are its insensitivity to bulk effects and substrate noise and to parasitic high frequencies effects.

Diorio et al. [20] of the California Physics of Computation Laboratory, developed a floating-gate silicon MOS transistor for analog learning applications. This single-transistor learning device computers the product of the stored analog memory value and the applied input. In [7], Roche et al. proposes a set of synapses based on the summation of the input and weight rather than on multiplication. These are proven to solve the XOR problem.

Memories

The problem of efficiently storing analog signals is not truly resolved, yet. For this reason, the large part of intelligent systems hardware implementations is addressing the mixed analogue-digital approach. Examples are cited in [38] in the fuzzy-based domain and in [2], [24] in the artificial neural network domain. Digital memories consume more area than simple analog memories but are very useful in small systems that cannot tolerate the need for support hardware. The simplest method for storing an analog signal is using a capacitor read through a high impedance path. Leakage currents due to various parasitic couplings (primarily due to the sampling switch that provides the weight changing ability) are the major drawback of this method, thus always relying on some refreshing technique. The already cited floating-gate technology furnishers a special process feature for trapping a charge on the completely insulated (floating) gate of a MOS transistor, thus programming the threshold voltage allowing for both a non volatile analog memory storage and a local computation of the product between this value and the input [20].

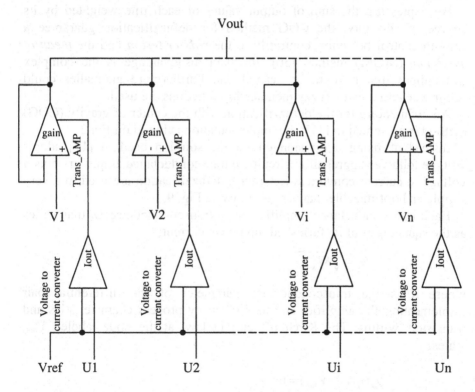

Fig. 9. A simple implementation of the COG defuzzifier method

Defuzzification

Defuzzification produces a non fuzzy action that best represents the inferred fuzzy output. Digital implementations involves arithmetic operations (including multiplications and divisions) on a large number of binary vectors. No single optimal algorithm exists and many not exist at all [27].

Practical algorithms are COG (center of gravity), HD (height defuzzification), COLA (center of largest area) and MOM (mean-of maxima).

$$COG = \frac{\sum_{i=1}^{n} \mu_i(z_i) \times z_i}{\sum_{i=1}^{n} \mu_i(z_i)} \tag{8}$$

where n is the number of quantization values used to discretize the output MF $\mu_i(...)$.

By expressing the sum of output values of each rule weighted by its degree of certainty, the COG method for defuzzification guarantee a smooth control behavior, contrarily to the *max criterion* and the *mean of maximum* (MOM) method [36]. Its main disadvantage is the complex calculations that have to be carried out. Furthermore anomalies could occur when no convex fuzzy membership functions are used.

An architecture for the defuzzification with the center of gravity (COG) method is presented in [17]: the implementation is based on Eq. 2.

Instead of using a division circuit the solution used in [17] adopts voltage follower-aggregation circuits: n transconductance amplifiers plus n voltage to current converters for n-term defuzzification are used in a very simple and optimizable manner, as shown in Fig. 9.

Each transconductance amplifier has a transconductance G_i that varies as the square root of its furnished input gain current:

$$G_i = \sqrt{KI_{gain}}$$

where K is the transconductance parameter of the differential pair implementing the amplifier and thus given by process characteristics and transistors widths. The Kirchhoff current law, at the node labeled V_{out}, states:

$$\sum_{i=1}^{n} G_i(V_i - V_{out}) = 0$$

by arranging the two equations we obtain:

$$V_{out} = \frac{\sum_{i=1}^{n} k_i V_i}{\sum_{i=1}^{n} k_i}$$

where the k_i terms varies as the square root of the single gain currents. A voltage to current converter, able to supply a current that is proportional to the squared value of its input, would then complete the picture leading to a straightforward implementation of Eq. 2. That is simply achieved by exploiting the properties of a saturated CMOS transistor pair.

Function generators

While most of the existing digital hardware realizations of fuzzy based systems are bounded to use only triangle or trapezoidal membership functions, analog systems can easily exploit the nonlinear characteristics of the active devices by using simple structures implementing a rather high variety of shapes. Membership function generators are usually part of the fuzzification of a fuzzy based design. In an analog implementation, usually this module transforms a sampled and helps input variable into a degree of membership.

An example of mixed analog-digital membership function circuit is the one discussed in [16] which implements two voltage-mode S- and Z-function generators sharing the same resistive load R (see Fig. 10). The circuit is able of generating trapezoidal shaped membership functions. Two differential pairs implement each one of the two fronts whose slopes are defined through the source resistance values. Such value is digitally controlled (4 bit code) via the switches P0 to P3 for the S-function and N0 to N3 for the Z-function. The position of the two generated functions could be translated over the universe of the discourse misbalancing the differential pair through the voltages Vr1 for the S-function and Vr2 for the Z-function. Again, these voltage levels are digitally coded in two 4-bit registers and then converted into analog reference voltages using D/A converters. Other fully analog implementations (see [38] for references) control this behavior via external pins.

4
Conclusions

The field of hardware implementations for advanced algorithms and computational intelligence is rapidly developing and the potential of some of the existing developments is difficult to assess. The hardware implementations described in this chapter exemplify a few of the current trends only. References to other trends can be found in the subsequent chapters of this volume, and in the related literature.

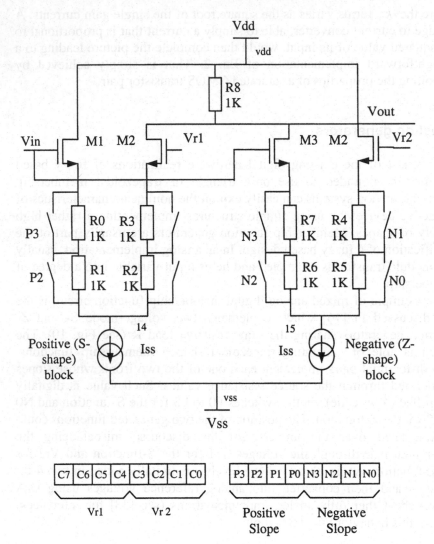

Fig. 10. Bell-shaped membership function example circuit

References

[1] De Gloria, A. Costa and M. Olivieri: Hardware design of asynchronous fuzzy controllers. *IEEE Transactions on Fuzzy Systems*, 4(3): 328-338, Aug. 1996.

[2] Y. Leblebici, A. Schmid and D. Mlynek: A mixed analog-digital artificial neural network architecture with on-chip learning. *IEEE Transactions on Very Large Scale Integration (VLSI) Systems*, 1999.

[3] G. Anzellotti, R. Battiti, I. Lazzizzera, G. Soncini, A. Zorat, A. Sartori, G. Tecchioli and P. Lee: A highly parallel chip for triggering applications with inductive learning based on the reactive tabu search. *International Journal of Modern Physics C*, 6(4): 555-560, 1995.

[4] G. Ascia, V. Catania, B. Giacalone, M. Russo and L. Vita: Designing for parallel fuzzy computing. *IEEE Micro*, 15(6): 62, December 1995.

[5] G. Ascia, V. Catania, M. Russo and L. Vita: Rule-driven VLSI fuzzy processor – implementing a scalable inference processor with analog fuzzy gates. *IEEE Micro*, 16(3): 62-74, June 1996.

[6] E. Avogadro, S. Commodaro, A. Costa, A. De Gloria, Faraboschi, F. Giudici and A. Pagni: An optimized risc instruction set for fuzzy applications. In *Proceedings of FUZZY-IEEE'94, Orlando, Florida*, pp. 133-137. IEEE, 1994.

[7] T. M. McGinnity, B. Roche and L. McDaid: A novel synapse design for digital VLSI implementation of neural networks. In *Irish Digital Signal Processing and Control Conference IDSPCC'96, Trinity College, Dublin*, pp. 290, 1996.

[8] R. Battiti, P. Lee, A. Sartori and G. Tecchiolli: Special-purpose parallel architectures for high-performance machine learning. In *Proc. Int.Conf. High-Performance Computing and Networking HPCN'95 Milan, Italy*. Springer-Verlag, May 1995.

[9] J. J. Blake, L. P. Maguire, B. Roche, T. M. McGinnity and L. J. McDaid: The implementation of fuzzy systems, neural networks and fuzzy neural networks using FPGAs. In *Neural Networks and Fuzzy Neural Networks using FPGAs*, Joint Conference on Information Sciences, *Durham, North Carolina*, Vol. 1, pp. 231-233, 1997.

[10] U. Cilingiroglu, B. Pamir, Z. Gunay and F. Dulger: Sampled-analog implementation of application-specific fuzzy controllers. *IEEE Transaction on Fuzzy Systems*, 5(3): 431-442, Aug. 1997.

[11] J. Chen and M. J. Patyra: VHDL modeling of a multivariable fuzzy logic controller hardware system. In *Proc. Third IEEE Int. Conf. On Fuzzy Systems, FUZZ-IEEE'94, Orlando, Florida*, pp. 129-132, 1994.

[12] W. D. Dettloff, K. E. Yount and H. Watanabe: A VLSI fuzzy logic controller with reconfigurable, cascadable architecture. *IEEE J. Solid-State Circuits*, 25(2): 376-382, April 1990.

[13] E. I. El-Masry, H.-K. Yang and M. A. Yakout: Implementations of artificial neural networks using current-mode pulse width modulation technique. *IEEE Transactions on Neural Networks*, 8(3): 532-548, May 1997.

[14] Gabrielli and E. Gandolfi: A fast digital fuzzy processor. *IEEE MICRO Chips, Systems, Software and Applications*, pp. 68-79, Jan./Feb. 1999.

[15] S. Guo and L. Peters: A reconfigurable analog fuzzy logic controller. In *The FUZZ-IEEE, Orlando, Florida*, pp. 124-128. IEEE, 1994.

[16] S. Guo and L. Peters: A high-speed fuzzy co-processor implemented in analog/digital technique. In *The 4th Int. Conf. on Soft Computing (IIZUKA'96)*, pp. 233-237, Sept. 30-Oct. 5, 1996.

[17] S. Guo and L. Peters: A new hardware implementation of the center of gravity defuzzification method. Technical report, Gesellschaft fur Methematik und Datenverarbeitung (GMD) and Institut fur Systementwurfstechnik (SET), 1994.

[18] T. Kunemund, H. Eichfeld and M. Menke: A 12b general-purpose fuzzy logic controller chip. *IEEE Transactions on Fuzzy Systems*, 4(4): 460-475, Nov. 1996.

[19] T. Hamalainen, J. Saarinen, P. Ojala and K. Kaski: Implementing genetic algorithms in a tree shape computer architecture. In J. T. Alander, (Editor): *Proceedings of the First Nordic Workshop on Genetic Algorithms and their Applications (1NWGA)* Vaasa (Finland), pp. 159-284, Jan. 1995.

[20] P. Hasler, C. Diorio, B. A. Minch, and C. Mead: A single-transistor silicon synapse. *IEEE Transactions on Electronic Devices*, 43(11), Nov. 1996.

[21] P. Ienne and G. Kuhn: *Digital Signal Processing Technology*, Vol. CR57 of *Critical Reviews Series*. Chapter: Digital Systems for Neural Networks, pp. 314-345. Society of Photo-Optical Instrumentation Engineers, 1995.

[22] N. Iijima, K. Koizumi, H. Mitsui and M. Sone: Fuzzy control design system based on dsp. In *Proceedings of FUZZ-IEEE'94, Orlando, Florida*, pp. 1786-1790. IEEE, 1994.

[23] R. Jager: *Fuzzy Logic Control*. Ph. D. thesis, Department of Electrical Engineering, Delft University of Technology, 1995.

[24] T. Lehmann: *Hardware Learning in Analogue VLSI Neural Networks*.PhD thesis, Technical University of Denmark – Lyngby, Sept. 1994.

[25] S. Lindsey, T. Lindblad, G. Sekniaidze, M. Minerskjold, G. Szekely and Age Eide: Experience with the IBM ZISC neural network chip. *Int. J. of Modern Physics C*, 6(4): 579-584, 1995.

[26] S. Lindsey and T. Lindblad: Survey of neural network hardware, invited paper. In *Proc. Of Applications and Science of Artificial Neural Networks Conference*, Vol. SPIE VOL. 2492, Part Two, pp. 1194-1205, Apr. 1995.

[27] J. L. Grantner, M. J. Patyra and K. Koster: Digital fuzzy logic controller: Design and implementation. *IEEE Transactions on Fuzzy Systems*, 4(4): 439-459, Nov. 1996.

[28] M. Marchesi, G. Orlandi, F. Piazza and A. Uncini: Fast neural networks without multipliers. *IEEE Trans. on Neural Networks*, 4(1): 53-62, Jan. 1993.

[29] G. M. Megson and I. M. Bland: Synthesis of a systolic array genetic algorithms. In *Proceedings of the 12th International Parallel Processing Symposium*, pp. 316-320, Apr. 1998.

[30] F. Piazza, M. L. Marchesi and A. Uncini: Backpropagation without multiplier for multilayer neural networks. *IEEE Proceedings Circuits, Devices and Systems*, 143(4): 229-232, Aug. 1996.

[31] M. Masetti, E. Gandolfi, A. Gabrielli, M. Cecchi, M. Russo and I. D'Antone: *Design and Realization of a 50 MFIPS Fuzzy Processor in 1.0 μ m CMOS VLSI Technology*, Vol. III of *Advances in Fuzzy Theory and Technology*, pp. 327-340. Duke University, Durham, North Carolina, USA, 1995.

[32] M. Russo: FuGeNeSys: A Genetic Neural System for Fuzzy Modeling. *IEEE Transactions on Fuzzy Systems*, 6(3): 373-388, Aug. 1998.

[33] M. Russo: Fuzzy Hardware Research from a Historical Point of View, pp. 1-25. In: Abraham Kandel and Gideon Langholz (Editors): *Fuzzy Hardware: Architectures and Applications*. Kluwer Academic Publishers, Boston, USA, 1998.

[34] M. Russo: GEFREX: a Genetic Fuzzy Extractor. *Int. J. of Knowledge based Intelligent Engineering Systems*, 2(1): 49-59, Jan.1998.

[35] M. Russo and L. C. Jain: *Introduction to Evolutionary Computing*, CRC Press, USA, 2000.

[36] D. Nauck, F. Klawonn and R. Kruse: Fuzzy sets, fuzzy controllers, and neural networks. *Wissenschaftliche Zeitschrift der Humboldt-Universitat zu Berlin, R. Medizin*, 41(4): 99-120, 1992.

[37] Patki: Fuzzy logic based hardware: Some experiences. In *Proc. International Discourse on Fuzzy Logic and Management of Complexity (FLAMOC'96)*, Sidney, Australia, Jan. 1996.

[38] L. Peters and S. Guo: *Three Generations of Fuzzy Hardware*, pp. 27-43. In "Fuzzy Hardware: Architectures and Applications" Kluwer Academic Pub., Boston, 1998.

[39] M. Russo: Fuzzy Hardware Research from a Historical Point of View, pp. 1-25. In A. Kandel and G. Langholz (Editors): *Fuzzy Hardware: Architectures and Applications*. Kluwer Academic Publishers, Boston, USA, 1998.

[40] L. Peters, S. Guo and H. Surmann: Design and application of an analog fuzzy logic controller. *IEEE Transactions on Fuzzy Systems*, 4(4): 429-438, Nov. 1994.

[41] J. Schwarz: Motorola microcontroller as the platform for fuzzy applications. In *Scientific International Conference on Communications, Signal and Systems CSS'96*, Brno, Czech Republic, Sept. 1996. AMSE.

[42] S. D. Scott, A. Samal and S. Seth Hga: A hardware-based genetic algorithm. In *Proc. Of the 1955 ACM/SIGDA Third Int. Symposium on Field-Programmable Gate Arrays, Monterey, CA*, pp. 53-59. ACM, Feb. 1995.

[43] S. D. Scott, S. Seth and A. Samal: *A hardware engine for genetic algorithms*. Technical Report UNL-CSE-97-001, University of Nebraska-Lincoln, Jul. 1997.

[44] M. J. S. Smith: *Application-Specific Integrated Circuits*. Addison Wesley, 1997.

[45] H. Surmann, A. Ungering and K. Goser: Optimized fuzzy controller architecture for field programmable gate arrays. In *Field-Programmable Gate Arrays: Architectures and Tools for Rapid Prototyping. Second Int. Workshop on Field Programmable Logic and Applications*, pp. 124-133, Vienna, Austria, August 1992.

[46] H. Surmann and A. P. Ungering: Fuzzy-rule-based systems on general purpose processors. *IEEE MICRO, Special issue on fuzzy systems*, pp. 40-48, August 1995.

[47] H. Surmann, A. P. Ungering, T. Kettner and K. Goser: What kind of hardware is necessary for a fuzzy rule based system. In *FUZZ-IEEE World Congress on Computional Intelligence, Orlando*, pp. 274-278, 26 June-2 July 1994.

[48] S. K. Halgamuge, T. Hollstein and M. Glesner: Computer-aided design of fuzzy systems based on generic vhdl specifications. *IEEE Transactions on Fuzzy Systems*, 4(4): 403-417, Nov. 1996.

[49] J. Tombs, A. Torralba and L. G. Franquelo: Design of a fuzzy controller mixing analog and digital techniques. In *Proceedings of FUZZ-IEEE'94, Orlando, Florida*, pp. 1755-1758. IEEE, 1994.

[50] M. Tommiska and J. Vuori: Hardware implementation of ga. In *Proceedings of the Second Nordic Workshop on Genetic Algorithms and their Applications (2NWGA) Vaasa (Finland)*, pp. 71-78, Aug. 1996.

[51] T. F. Colodro and L. G. Franquelo: A fuzzy-logic controller with on-chip learning, employing stochastic logic. In *Proc. FUZZ-IEEE'94, Orlando, Florida*, pp. 1759-1764. IEEE, 1994.

[52] H. Turton, T. Arslan and D. H. Horrocks: A hardware architecture for a parallel genetic algorithm for image registration. In *Proc. IEE Colloquium on Genetic Algorithms in Image Processing and Vision*, number 1994/193, pp. 11/1-11/6. IEE, Oct. 1994.

[53] T. Yamakawa and T. Miki: The Current Mode Fuzzy Logic Integrated Circuits Fabricated by the Standard CMOS Process. *IEEE Transactions on Computers*, c-35(2): 161-167, February 1986.

[54] P. Ungering, H. Bauer and K. Goser: Architecture of a fuzzy-processor based on an 8-bit microprocessor. In *Proc. Third IEEE Int. Conf. On Fuzzy Systems, FUZZ-IEEE'94, Orlando, Florida*, pp. 297-301. IEEE, Jun. 1994.

[55] H. Watanable: RISC approach to design of fuzzy processor architecture. In *IEEE International Conference on Fuzzy Systems*, pp. 431-440, Mar. 1992.

[56] J. Wawrzynek, K. Asanovic and N. Morgan: The design of a neuro-microprocessor. *IEEE Transactions on Neural Networks*, 4(3): 394-399, May 1993.

[57] Zorat, A. Sartori, G. Tecchiolli and L. T. Koczy: A flexible VLSI processor for fast neural network and fuzzy control implementation. In *Proc. 4th International Conference on Soft Computing (IIZUKA'96)*, Sep. 1996.

[58] Zorat, A. Sartori, G. Tecchiolli, I. Lazzizzera and P. Lee: Advances in the design of the totem neurochip. In *Proc. 5th International Workshop on Software Engineering, Artificial Intelligence and Expert Systems in High Energy and Nuclear Physics*, pp. 134-139. Elsevier North-Holland NIM, Apr. 1997.

Chapter 4

High Performance Fuzzy Processors

Gian Carlo Cardarilli, Roberto Lojacono, Marco Re

University of Rome "Tor vergata", Departament of Electronics, Via della Ricerca Scientifica, 1, 00133 – Rome, Italy

In this chapter, some methodologies for developing fuzzy hardware architectures are presented. The architectures can be grouped into two sets, namely general-purpose structures, and task oriented structures. We discuss the effectiveness of the task-oriented architectures for the implementation of fuzzy processors. We present an architecture exploiting the properties of the fuzzy processing in order to simplify and speed-up its basic blocks. In particular, the fuzzification unit is based on a suitable class of trapezoidal membership functions with power of two slopes for the oblique sides. The algorithm used for the defuzzification unit is based on the Center of Gravity (COG) method. It is implemented by a full look-up table approach in order to obtain the maximum speed. With respect to other look-up table approaches the architecture we propose uses less memory and is fully parallel. In addition, a divider that computes an approximate result has been added and further reduces the overall complexity of the circuit. The structure has been designed and simulated by using the *ES2* technology. We obtained a chip of 7 mm^2 for the core logic, and an external 10 Kbytes memory containing the output membership functions. The simulations have shown a speed over 100 KFLIPS for 2 inputs and 20 rules. The effectiveness of this architecture has been tested on a specific high-speed application, i.e. the radar target tracking. In this case, the simulation results give good performance in terms of target tracking capability and speed higher than 400 KFLIPS.

1
Introduction

The growing diffusion of fuzzy logic processing in complex and real time applications requires the development of more efficient implementations of fuzzy logic engines. Depending on the nature of the specific application we are dealing with, different implementation issues must be taken into account. Therefore, at system level design the right partition between hardware and software must be defined in order to obtain an efficient implementation of the inference engine. For example, by using general-purpose processors (i.e. personal computers and workstations with suitable hardware interfaces), the control of chemical and mechanical processes can be easily performed. This approach reduces the costs and the time connected with the development and implementation phases.

On the other hand, there are many applications where the cost and the speed are the main issues and that, therefore, require specialized hardware solutions. Frequently those applications need a real time evaluation of complex fuzzy sets and deal with high-speed processes. Automotive, speech and pattern recognition are examples of applications characterized by severe speed requirements. For these applications, a software implementation of the fuzzy logic algorithms on general-purpose processors is not suitable and the design constraints can only be matched by using application specific fuzzy processors, where fuzzy logic operators are implemented in hardware.

The hardware implementation of fuzzy processors can be performed either by using an analog or a digital approach. The digital approach offers some important advantages, if compared to the analog counterpart. Generally, it is more accurate and robust, and, moreover, it is easily reconfigurable. On the other hand, the digital solution may be more complex and expensive in terms of silicon area, with respect to an analog implementation.

The use of a digital architecture allows the direct mapping of the fuzzy inference into VLSI digital blocks by using standard libraries of components as, for example, arithmetic operators and memories. This direct translation (from the fuzzy algorithm to the digital architecture) preserves the accuracy of the processing but unfortunately does not optimize the final architecture, preventing the exploitation of the fuzzy properties. As a consequence, this methodology, that is quite general and suitable for general-purpose fuzzy processors, leads to relatively complex and slow structures. On the other hand, it is possible to take advantage of the properties of the fuzzy approach for developing a hardware structure that is effective in terms of speed and complexity. A possible solution is based on the exploitation of the structural robustness of the fuzzy approach, which is rather insensitive to the variations of the algorithm parameters and to the arithmetic errors. In the following of the chapter, after a classification of the different hardware implementations, we will show how these concepts can be exploited in an actual architecture.

2
Hardware Implementations Classification

As stated in the introduction, the digital approach spans from general purpose to dedicated fuzzy processors. In this section, we discuss the main characteristics of the hardware implementation of a fuzzy processor, comparing the different solutions and pointing out the fundamental processing blocks.

Different characteristics and performance indicators must be used in the classification of the different hardware implementation styles. The main elements of the analysis concern:

- the flexibility of the architecture to implement different fuzzy algorithms,
- its scalability for applications requiring more complex fuzzy processing,
- the maximum speed,
- prototyping, and production costs.

In the first item we include all the features that make a processor adaptable to different fuzzy algorithms, such as fuzzification and defuzzification methods, shapes of the input and output membership functions, inference techniques as MIN-MAX, product-sum etc.

The scalability concerns the possibility to use the same hardware structure for applications with different complexity. In this case, the key elements are the number of input variables, the number of input and output membership functions, and the rule-base size. Normally, in any hardware implementation, the above factors are limited to a maximum value. This limitation is related both to architectural and cost reasons. For example, a certain architectural choice can reduce the maximum number of inputs, while the amount of available memory affects the maximum number of rules that can be stored in the rule base.

With the extension of the fuzzy processing from the process control (generally dealing with systems characterized by slow dynamics) toward the product innovation (requiring the interaction with fast or very fast systems), the processing speed gained of importance. It becomes, together with the cost, one of the basic elements for the selection of a certain hardware approach. In this case, the obtainable speed must allow to solve in *real time*, that in practice means "an acceptable short time", the processing problem. Of course, the difficulty of finding a proper solution depends on the speed that must be assured, as well as on the complexity of the processing that must be implemented.

The last aspect of the hardware comparison regards the implementation costs. We have classified these costs in prototyping and production costs. In general, the prototyping costs are greater if an application specific hardware must be developed. In fact, that implies the need of a complete design of the hardware device and, usually, already developed systems or subsystems cannot be reused. On the other hand, this approach allows the reduction of the production costs, in particular when large volume production is required. Indeed, in this case, the cost increasing for the prototyping development is well compensated by the cost reduction of the production phase.

All the above factors must be carefully considered for the choice of the hardware implementation, realizing a trade-off between those different aspects. The classification elements discussed above lead to group the hardware implementations into two main categories:

1. application independent fuzzy processors,
2. application specific fuzzy hardware.

The application independent fuzzy processors are programmable structures based on general-purpose architectures. They might be either conventional processors, or processors with an extended set of instructions, which include the more frequent and expensive operations used in fuzzy algorithms. Moreover, we notice that the extended instructions set processors are usually developed following two different approaches. They can be either derived from general-purpose processors, such as microprocessors, microcontrollers, or digital signal processors, or can be specifically designed for general purpose fuzzy processing. With this approach, the resulting processor maintains the capability to efficiently perform non-fuzzy processing. The processor efficiently implements both the fuzzy flow and the conventional control flow.

On the other hand, processors designed for specific implementation of fuzzy processing are able to perform faster fuzzy processing, indeed they are suitable to be used in high speed systems, but they are characterized by a reduced flexibility, if compared to the general purpose derived processors. However, the main objective of the application independent fuzzy processors is to be the most general possible, allowing implementing any fuzzy processing strategies for any problem of interest. In the following we develop a specific taxonomy for such implementations.

The fuzzy logic implementations based on general purpose processors are named *Standard Hardware Fuzzy Processors* (SHFP), while those that use processors with a specific instruction set are named *Instruction Oriented Fuzzy Processors* (IOFP). Finally, the processors specifically developed for the implementation of fuzzy algorithms will be named *General Purpose Fuzzy Processors* (GPFP).

However, if the speed and the production costs are the pushing factors, the only possible solution for the fuzzy implementations is the use of *Application Specific Fuzzy Hardware* (ASFH). In this case the fuzzy processing blocks are designed for a specific application and the effects of the architectural choices on the final product must be carefully evaluated. With this kind of solution we are potentially able to reach very high performance, required for implementing real time solutions in critical applications, while the production costs are lower with respect to the above described approaches.

This class contains different hardware approaches. In our classification, all the hardware solutions that are designed for specific applications belong to this class. They span from the *Application Set Fuzzy Processors* (ASFP), which lack of generality but can be programmed for being used in a restricted class of fuzzy applications, to *Task Dedicated Fuzzy Processors* (TDFP). Another hardware methodology is based on look-up table (LUT) realization of fuzzy processor, the LUT being implemented on solid state memory. In Table 1, these methods are contrasted in terms of implementation issues.

Table 1. Hardware implementation comparison

Hardware Implementation	Flexibility	Scalability	Costs		Speed
			Prototype	Production	
Standard Hardware (SHFP)	very high	high	low	high	low
Instruction Oriented (IOFP)	very high	high	medium-low	high	medium-low
General Purpose (GPFP)	high	medium	high	medium	medium
Application Set (ASFP)	medium-how	low	very high	low	high
Task Dedicated (TDFP)	low	low	very high	low	very high
Look-up table (LUT)	low	very low	low	low	very high

As shown in Table 1, the advantages of a more efficient solution, as in the case of ASFP or TDFP, are counterbalanced by a smaller degree of flexibility. Moreover, these solutions require the introduction of a general-purpose processor to implement the non-fuzzy operations. However, this drawback is also present in the case of GPFP that are generally used as fuzzy coprocessors. For example, the TDFP approach, that allows obtaining the most efficient structures by exploiting the properties of the specific application, has the smallest flexibility degree.

In the subsequent sections of this chapter, we consider the implementation solutions related to the GPFP, ASFP, and TDFP approaches. The selection of a certain hardware approach for the solution of a given problem is obtained as a trade-off among different parameters, as the costs, the development time, and the performance. Consequently, the constraints imposed by a specific problem must be carefully evaluated in order to find the best solution.

The relation between application constraints (basically, the required speed and the algorithm complexity measured in terms of number of rules) and the possible hardware implementation styles is sketched in Fig. 1 (see [10] for more details). The figure shows that very complex fuzzy systems (above 100 rules) can only be implemented by using programmable systems. This fact is related to the capability of programmable systems to execute serially the inferences in the rule base. Instead, TDFP improves speed performance evaluating in parallel the rule base (in this way the control block of the processor is also simplified). This approach limits the dimension of the rule base that can be implemented.

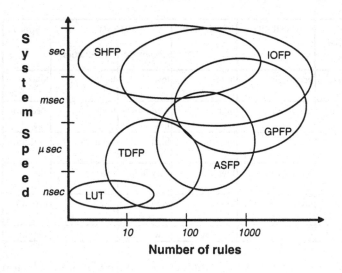

Fig. 1. Hardware selection

Approaches based on Look-Up Tables (LUT) have speed performance that is quite independent of the number of rules (actually an increase of the number of rules correspond to an increase of the memory size and, consequently, to a reduction of the memory speed). Unfortunately, since the memory size depends exponentially on the number of input bits, this method can be effectively applied only for very simple fuzzy systems.

In the following, we consider the main characteristics of the GPFP, ASFP and TDFP that affect the performance and the costs of the processors based on these approaches. The fundamental blocks that we discuss are:

- **Fuzzifier** - Starting from the crisp values, this block computes the activation degree α for each input membership function (IMF).
- **Inference Block** - This block uses the α values and the inference rules to compute the activation degree of the output membership functions (OMF).
- **Defuzzifier** - The defuzzifier computes the output crisp value. The output value can be computed starting either from the output membership function (OMF) weights or from the output possibility distribution.

In the next sections, the different approaches for the implementation of the above blocks are compared and an ASFP architecture we implemented is analyzed. The effectiveness of the obtained processor is tested on a radar target tracking application.

3
Fuzzification Block

The first block, at the input of the fuzzy processor, is the fuzzification block. This block computes the activation degree of a fuzzy rule antecedent. Normally, these degrees are then combined in the inference block to obtain the rule activation degree. The activation degree of an antecedent is obtained evaluating the corresponding input membership function with respect to the actual input value. There are several different methodologies to implement the fuzzification operation. The first one is based on the Look-Up Table. In the LUT-based approach, all the possible output values are stored as function of the different input values. This approach is very direct, but is unsuitable for implementing hardware fuzzy systems with large number of input variables and for those systems requiring a large number of bits for the representation of the internal and external signals.

For example, the defuzzifier of an 8 bits fuzzy processor based on LUT approach has been described in [3]. The 12-bit version of that processor is presented in [12]. However, in the latter processor, the authors did not use the LUT approach, due to the size of the required memories. For this kind of structures a more efficient solution is based on the computation of the membership functions. In this case, the value that the input membership function assumes for a given input value is computed starting from the parameters that describe the function itself. Normally, this approach is implemented assuming specific function shapes, as triangles or trapezoids. In [4], the admitted shapes are based on trapezoids. Six parameters, stored in a 16-bits word, are used to describe such functions. Moreover, the shape of the oblique sides can be modified from a straight line to S-shaped. In the latter case, a lookup table defines the shape of the oblique sides. The implementation of this method requires the memorization of the following parameters:

- f_n, specifies the position of the center of the membership,
- f_q, gives the length of the top side of the trapezoid,
- f_m, is the scaling factor of the horizontal direction,
- f_g, is used for the specification of the inclination,
- f_t, is used either for specifying the function shape or for modifying the inclination of the oblique sides, in the case of trapezoidal shape.

There is also an optional parameter f_e that is used for changing the shape of the oblique sides by referring to a look-up table.

Another possible approach to the fuzzifier implementation is proposed in [12], where the computation of the fuzzifier output is performed assuming a maximum overlapping factor (of four) among the membership functions (MOP). That means that any input value can belong to a maximum of four fuzzy set, i.e. for each input value only four membership functions can assume a value greater than zero. Moreover, the input domain is divided into a set of elementary intervals (EI), all having the same width. In each EI, there are a maximum of four active input membership functions. The membership functions organization is shown in Fig. 2. Each input membership function (quoted as IMF) is defined through the supporting point $SP(x_s, y_s)$ and the two gradients g_r and g_l. The output *alpha* value, corresponding to the membership degree, is computed by the following equations:

$$alpha = \begin{cases} min[1, \ y_s + (x - x_s) \cdot g_r] & for \quad (x - x_s) \geq 0, \quad g_r \geq 0 \\ max[0, \ y_s + (x - x_s) \cdot g_r] & for \quad (x - x_s) \geq 0, \quad g_r < 0 \\ max[0, \ y_s + (x - x_s) \cdot g_l] & for \quad (x - x_s) \leq 0, \quad g_l \geq 0 \\ min[1, \ y_s + (x - x_s) \cdot g_l] & for \quad (x - x_s) \leq 0, \quad g_l \geq 0 \end{cases} \tag{1}$$

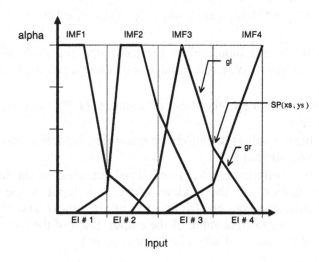

Fig. 2. Fuzzification procedure with EI [12]

The fuzzifier produces 16-bit output words. 4 bits provide the IMF number and 12 bits are used to represent the output *alpha* value. As a consequence, 15 different IMF are allowed for each input.

A major drawback of the methods based on the computational approach is the necessity of implementing one or more multipliers to evaluate the *alpha* value. This can be very expensive for TDFP architectures with parallel evaluation of two or more inputs. In this case a possible solution is that proposed in [15]. This architecture is based on piece-wise linear membership functions whose parameters are stored in a small memory. The arithmetic complexity of the evaluation is reduced by limiting the possible shapes of the membership functions.

Figure 3 depicts a typical membership function implemented by the architecture [15]. The slopes of the oblique sides are constrained to assume only power of two values. A first implementation of a fuzzifier based on this approach was presented in a preceding chapter [8]. The proposed implementation uses four parameters, P_1, P_2, NH_L and NH_R, for the specification of a membership function. In Fig. 3, the parameters P_1 and P_2 define the positions of the breakpoints of the membership function, while

$NH_L=N-H_L$ and $NH_R=N-H_R$ give, respectively, the exponents of the slope of the left and right sides of the trapezoid. Using this notation, the two straight lines are described in term of these parameters by the following equations

$$y_{r1} = 2^{NH_L}(x-P_1) \quad with \quad 0 \le (x-P_1) < 2^{H_L}$$
$$y_{r2} = 2^{NHr}(P_2-x) \quad with \quad 0 \le (P_2-x) < 2^{H_R} \tag{2}$$

where x is the current input value. Consequently, the evaluation of the membership function is obtained through the following algorithm:

- In the first step, the two differences $(x-P_1)$ and (P_2-x) are evaluated.
- The binary values of the above quantities are left shifted off NH_L and NH_R positions.
- The two differences $(x-P_1)$ and (P_2-x) are used in parallel for the identification of the region where the input value lays. In particular, the sign bits (S_1 and S_2) and the bits U_1 and U_2 are used to select the correct value of the output. Each of the two quantities U_1 and U_2 is set to 1 when $(x-P_1)$ or $(P_2-x)=0$.

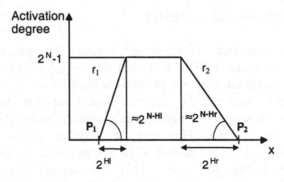

Fig. 3. Membership function shape

Starting from the above quantities, the identification of the region where the input lies and the computation of the output value can be done by selecting one of the following four cases.

1. $(x-P_1) \le 0$ *or* $(P_2-x) \le 0$. This case corresponds to an input x that is external to the interval $[P_1, P_2]$. Therefore, the output of the fuzzifier must be set to zero.

2. $x=P_1$ or $x=P_2$ and the slope of the corresponding oblique side is not infinite. In this case the output value is zero.
3. $x=P_1$ or $x=P_2$ and the slope of the corresponding oblique side is infinite. In this case the output value is $2^{(N-1)}$.
4. $(x-P_1)>0$ and $(P_2-x)>0$. This case corresponds to an input lying inside the trapezoid. If one of the shifted differences $(x-P_1)$ and (P_2-x), computed above, does not present overflow, it is taken as output. If both the shifted outputs present overflow, the input value x belongs to the horizontal part of the membership function. Consequently the maximum value $2^{(N-1)}$ is taken as output.

The above algorithm allows us a simple hardware implementation. A possible architecture is shown in Fig. 4.

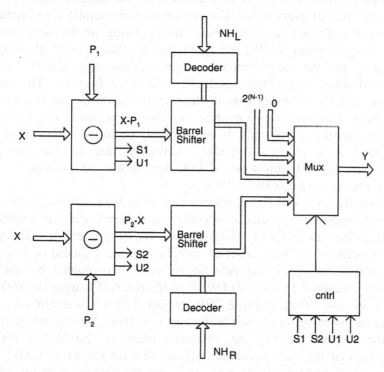

Fig. 4. Fuzzifier architecture [15]

The circuit uses two subtractors, which compute the two differences $(x-P_1)$ and $(x-P_2)$. The multiplications by 2^{NH_L} and 2^{NH_R} are implemented by two barrel shifters. The block CNTRL, according the rules described above performs the selection of the outputs.

The membership parameters are stored in an on-chip RAM. Each RAM location contains the parameters of a triangular membership function (namely, the two breakpoints and the two slopes of the oblique sides). Incrementing the memory address, we obtain the evaluation of the different membership functions. The connection between the RAM and the combinatorial block is presented later, inside the overall controller architecture.

4
Inference Block

The main task of the inference block is the computation of the rule activation degrees. The inputs of this block are the fuzzifiers outputs (i.e. the *alpha* value of every input with respect to each membership function). Furthermore, the activation degrees corresponding to the same output membership function (OMF) are aggregated to obtain the OMF weights. Depending on the implementation choices, this aggregation can be performed either in the inference block or in the defuzzifier. The typical operator used for the evaluation of the rule activation degree is the fuzzy *AND*, that corresponds to the evaluation of the minimum among the *alpha* values of the rule antecedents. In many cases, the fuzzy *AND* can instead correspond to a product operation. However, due to the multiplier implementation cost, this kind of inference should be avoided in high performance fuzzy implementations.

Normally, in a TDFP, the inference operator is chosen on the basis of the system simulation results. If possible, the simplest operator is selected. Instead, in the case of GPFP, since the best inference operator will depend on the specific application, a set of different operators should be foreseen. For example, in [12], the rule degree can be evaluated by using 6 inference operators: 1) *AND*, 2) *OR*, 3) *NOT*, 4) *LNOT* (linguistic *NOT*), 5) *INOR* (inclusive *NOR*), and 6) *EXOR* (exclusive *OR*). The operators 1) and 2) have two or more inputs, while the operators from 3) to 6) are one input operators. Again in [12], the inference block is responsible for the aggregation of the rule activation degrees that hit the same OMF. This aggregation is performed either by using the *MAX* operator or the *BSUM* (bounded sum) operator. In the latter case, the activation degrees of the rules that hit on the same OMF are added and the result is bounded at a given value. The above procedure is described by the expression:

$$WOMFk = max\left[1, \sum_{(n:S(R_n)=k)} D(R_n)\right] \tag{3}$$

where $D(R_n)$ denotes the activation degree of the rule n, and $S(R_n)$ is the number of the OMFs corresponding to the rule n.

The aggregation of the activation degree can also be performed in the defuzzifier. In [11], the processor scans the rule-base sequentially. As we explaine below, the activation degrees are sent to the defuzzifier that aggregates the rules having the same OMF.

5
Defuzzification Block

In defuzzification block is critical for the overall performance of a hardware fuzzy processor. Its task is the computation of the output crisp value considering the output possibility distribution, which has been obtained from the OMF weighted with the activation degrees. The defuzzification process can be implemented using different algorithms that have different characteristics in terms of performance and computational costs. Simple methods are those that evaluate the first maximum (*FM*) or the last maximum (*LM*) in the output possibility function. This method has been implemented in [12]. In the case sketched in Fig. 5, there are three OMFs whose weights are g_1, g_2 and g_3, respectively.

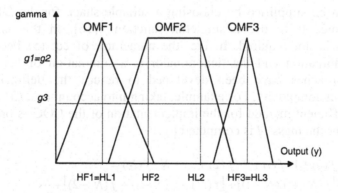

Fig. 5. Output possibility function

For this case, the crisp output y is obtained for *FM* and *LM* as:

$$\begin{aligned} y_{FM} &= inf\left(HF1, HF3\right) = HF1 \\ y_{LM} &= sup\left(HL1, HL3\right) = HL3 \end{aligned} \tag{4}$$

One of the most popular defuzzification methods is the "Center of Gravity" (COG). This method obtains the crisp output value by evaluating the center of gravity of the output possibility function. It is very robust with respect to small errors introduced in the output possibility distribution. On the other hand, its implementation requires iterative procedures that make the resulting hardware slow. In fact, it requires the integration of the mass and the area according to the expression:

$$\bar{y} = \frac{M}{A} = \frac{\sum_{k=1}^{N} f(y_k) \cdot y_k}{\sum_{k=1}^{N} f(y_k)} \tag{5}$$

where M is the mass, A is the area of the output possibility distribution, $N=2^{Nbit}-1$ is the output resolution, y_k is the k-th value of the output variable and $f(y_k)$ is the value of the output possibility distribution computed on the output value y_k. In general, an output value y_k represented with $Nbit$ bits lies in the range $[0, .., 2^{Nbit}-1]$, consequently we have

$$y_k = k \quad for \quad k = \left\{ 0, 1, \cdots, 2^{Nbit} - 1 \right\} \tag{6}$$

Eq. (5) can be simplified by choosing a suitable shape for the OMFs. A simple choice is to use a singleton function [16]. In this case, the integration is not required. In fact the numerator of eq. (5) becomes a linear combination and the denominator is a summation of few terms. Other approaches have been developed to reduce the defuzzification computation complexity. For example, taking into account eqs. (5) and (6), in [1] an efficient method for the implementation of the COG is proposed. In particular the mass M is computed by:

$$M = 0 \cdot f(0) + 1 \cdot f(1) + 2 \cdot f(2) + \ldots + N \cdot f(N) =$$
$$f(N) + [f(N) + f(N-1)] + [f(N) + f(N-1) + f(N-2)] + \cdots \tag{7}$$
$$+ [f(N) + f(N-1) + \cdots f(2) + f(1)]$$

The terms inside the square brackets correspond to the partial area. If we define the partial area A_j as the area in the output range $[j, N]$, we obtain:

$$A_j = f(N) + f(N-1) + \cdots + f(j) = A_{j+1} + f(j)$$
$$M = A_N + A_{N-1} + \cdots A_2 + A_1 \tag{8}$$

From eq. (8), we obtain that the mass can be computed during the area evaluation. Using this property, we can reduce the COG computation complexity. The properties of eq. (8) have been exploited for the COG implementation of the processor proposed in [4]. The resulting structure is shown in Fig. 6.

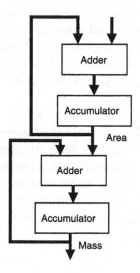

Fig. 6. Implementation of the COG proposed in [1]

The above integration may be time-expensive if hard constraints on the maximum computation delay are present. To overcome this problem, an adaptive integration has been proposed in [6]. This method avoids the iteration on the output intervals where the output possibility distribution is zero.

Despite the above simplification, in many cases the computational speed does not match the critical time constraints. This happens, in particular, for processors with a high output resolution. Two approximated evaluation techniques of the COG have been introduced in [12]. They were named *COG*1 and *COG*2. The first method deals with OMFs that are defined as singletons. If C_i is the center of the *i-th* OMF and g_i is the corresponding weight, we obtain:

$$\bar{y} = \frac{C_1 \cdot g_1 + C_2 \cdot g_2 \cdots + C_N \cdot g_N}{g_1 + g_2 \cdots + g_N} \qquad (9)$$

The *COG*2 method associates to the OMF an area A_i. Consequently, eq. (9) becomes:

$$\bar{y} = \frac{C_1 \cdot g_1 \cdot A_1 + C_2 \cdot g_2 \cdot A_2 \cdots + C_N \cdot g_N \cdot A_N}{g_1 \cdot A_1 + g_2 \cdot A_2 \cdots + g_N \cdot A_N} \qquad (10)$$

Different solutions have been proposed to speed-up this process, when unrestricted OMF are used. A first method is based on the use of a look-up table [2] that stores, for each rule activation degree, the partial contribution to the mass and the area of the output distribution. This approach is fast but shows some drawbacks. The corresponding architecture, in fact, requires a large amount of memory for the look-up table implementation and needs a large time for the serial computation in the regions where the membership functions overlap.

A method that overcomes these drawbacks has been presented in [11]. If compared with the other look-up table approaches, this method allows a higher computation speed with less memory usage. Subsequently, we describe the above method. Before the description of the defuzzification algorithm, it is useful to define some general elements of the data organization and processing. The defuzzification is based on a *min-max* inference method. In our approach, we assume that the rule base is composed by rules of the kind:

$$R_1 : IF \ x_1 = \ \cdots$$
$$\vdots \ \ :$$
$$R_n : IF \ x_1 = MF_{1j} \ AND \ \cdots x_k = MF_{kl} \cdots AND \ x_p = MF_{pi} \ THEN \ y = OMF_h$$
$$\vdots$$
$$R_N : IF \ x_1 = \ \cdots$$

The quantity x_k is the *k-th* input variable, MF_{kl} is the *l-th* input membership function corresponding to this variable, and OMF_h is the *h-th* output membership function, activated by the rule n. For the sake of simplicity, we introduce the operator $S(\cdot)$, defined as the operator that, for a given rule n, provides the number of the corresponding output membership function. For the above rule R_n we get $S(R_n)=h$. Furthermore, we will indicate with $D(R_n)$ the activation degree of the rule R_n. In addition, our defuzzification algorithm is based on the assumptions that:

- The Maximum Overlap Factor (MOF) among different output membership functions must be 2 (MOF=2).
- The pairs $S(R_n)$, $D(R_n)$ are sent serially to the defuzzification unit.
- The rule base is organized such that $S(R_{n+1}) \leq S(R_n)$. This means that the number of the rule consequent does not decrease along the rule base.

The complete algorithm is described in [15] and the resulting architecture, is shown in Fig. 7.

The algorithm uses two additional variables D'_{-1} and D'_{-2} that store the maximum value of the activation degrees of the two output membership functions S'_{-1} and S'_{-2}. These are the numbers indicating the two last OMFs that have been processed.

The algorithm uses two look-up tables. The first one contains the values of $Area(S'_{-1}, D'_{-1})$ and $Mass(S'_{-1}, D'_{-1})$, i.e. the values of the area and the mass of the output membership function S'_{-1}, evaluated for the activation degree D'_{-1}. In the following, we call these two quantities "Symbol" and "Degree".

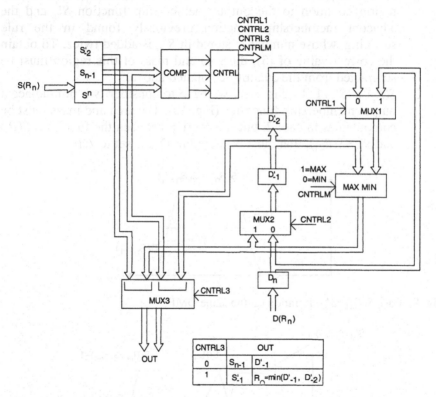

Fig. 7. Defuzzifier architecture

CNTRL3	OUT	
0	S_{n-1}	D'_{-1}
1	S'_{-1}	$R_n = min(D'_{-1}, D'_{-2})$

The second look-up table contains the values $A_\cap(S'_{-2}, R_\cap)$ and $M_\cap(S'_{-2}, R_\cap)$, corresponding to the area and the mass of the overlap region between the two adjacent output membership functions S'_{-2}, and S'_{-1}. The overlap look-up tables are addressed with the number of the membership function and with the degree $R_\cap$ corresponding to the minimum between the activation degrees of the two overlapping membership functions $min(D'_{-1}, D'_{-2})$. In general, when $S(R_n)$ is sent to the defuzzification unit, three different cases may occur:

1. $S(R_n)=S'_{-1}$. In this case, we are iterating on the same output membership function (Fig. 8), consequently we have to compute the maximum between the activation degrees D_{-1} and $D(R_n)$.

2. $S(R_n)=S'_{-1}+1$. In this case, we have to consider two adjacent output membership functions (Fig. 9). The area and the mass of the function S'_{-1} must be added to the denominator and the numerator of (5), respectively. With this procedure, the contribution of the region common to the output membership function S'_{-1} and the adjacent membership function previously found in the rule scanning, whose number is stored in S'_{-2}, is added twice. To obtain the correct value of (5), the area and mass of this region must be subtracted from the quantity computed above.

3. $S(R_n) > S'_{-1}+1$. In this case, we have to consider two non-adjacent output membership functions (Fig. 10). The area and mass must be computed as in case 2, but the overlap between the functions $S(R_n)$ and $S'_{-1}=S(R_{n-1})$, that must be stored in D'_{-2}, is set to zero.

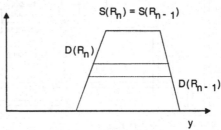

Fig. 8.   Case $S(R_n)=S'_{-1}$. Iteration on the same OMF

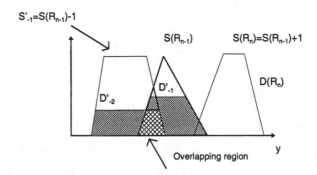

Fig 9. Case $S(R_n)=S'_{-1}+1$. Jump to an adjacent OMF

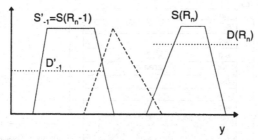

Fig. 10. $S(R_n) > S'_{-1}+1$. Jump to no adjacent OMF.

With this procedure, a final accumulation cycle relative to the symbol $S(R_N)$ must be performed to complete the accumulation process over the entire rule base. The amount of memory required by this method to store the area and mass information can be evaluated as follows. If N_{OMF} is the number of output membership functions, $N_{OMF}-1$ is the number of regions where an intersection is present and V_{Res} is the vertical resolution, the number of needed memory cells is given by:

$$N_{Cells} = 2 \cdot N_{OMF} \cdot V_{Res} + 2 \cdot (N_{OMF}-1) \cdot V_{Res} = (4 \cdot N_{OMF} - 2) \cdot V_{Res} \quad (11)$$

As shown in [11], our approach allows us a memory saving greater than 40% with respect to the memory required by the previously proposed implementation [2]. The hardware implementation of the above algorithm is quite straightforward. The architecture is that presented in Fig. 7.

The register S_n contains the symbol that the inference unit sends to the defuzzifier, for each step of the rule base scanning. The comparator $COMP$ and the control block $CNTRL$ generate the control signals activating the hardware resources that implement the different block of the algorithm. The MAX/MIN block, together with $MUX1$ and $MUX2$, computes the quantity $min(D'_{-1}, D'_{-2})$, if case 2 or 3 is detected, or the quantity $max(D'_{-1}, D(R_n))$, if the condition $S_n = S'_{-1}$ is true. Each time the condition $S(R_n) \neq S'_{-1}$ is detected, the shift register SR is activated. Consequently, the defuzzifier registers contain the three numbers (S_n, S'_{-1}, S'_{-2}), corresponding to the symbols of the three later output membership functions activated by the rules. At the same time, the three registers (D_n, D'_{-1}, D'_{-2}) memorize the activation degrees of the last three selected output membership functions. Every time the case $S(R_n) \neq S'_{-1}$ is detected, $MUX3$ sequentially gives the addresses for the intersections (Area and Mass) look-up table and for the area and mass look-up table.

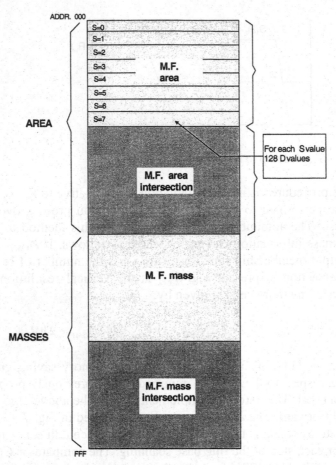

Fig. 11. External RAM organization

The final address is obtained from the values (S'_{-1}, S'_{-2}, D'_{-1}, D'_{-2}) by considering the particular organization of the memory module. In fact, the memory that stores area and mass information is organized in two banks (Fig. 11). The first bank contains the information regarding the mass. The values of the mass of the different output membership functions are allocated sequentially. The second bank contains the area information. These banks are stored in the same memory. In particular, the upper part of the memory stores the area of the output membership functions and of their intersections for each membership function and for all the possible activation degrees. The mass values are stored with the same structure in the lower part of the same memory. With this organization, the two most significant bits of the address are used to select the four memory banks containing the information about the area and the mass, and about intersections of the membership functions.

The final step of the defuzzification algorithm, the division, is implemented by a specific hardware structure. The divider has been simplified by accepting some approximations in the division algorithm. In particular, in our device, the division M/A is performed through the multiplication of the mass M by the reciprocal of the area A. Normally, all these reciprocals are stored in a look-up table. In our case, in order to reduce the complexity of the resulting architecture and taking advantage of the robustness of the fuzzy logic approach, we introduce some constraints on A. In particular a value $A \geq 256$ is assumed.

The structure has been greatly simplified by considering an approximated expansion of the reciprocal according with the above constraint. An exhaustive simulation that considers the actual values of M and A for a specific application has detected a maximum error $|E| \leq 2$ that is well tolerated by the robustness of the fuzzy approach. The resulting divider architecture requires only a 16×8 multiplier and a 256 bytes ROM.

6
General Architecture and Performance

The methods proposed in [11], [15] and presented in the previous sections have been used for realizing a high performance fuzzy processor. The general architecture of the processor is shown in Fig. 12. The processor has been implemented on a single chip, but can be used as a core cell in more complex systems [15]. The CMOS technology by $ES2$ (European Silicon Structures) has been used for the chip implementation and all the simulations have been performed with the parameters of the $ECPD10$ standard cell library.

The chip has been developed using the IC design tool CADENCE DFWII. The obtained circuit is quite inexpensive in terms of area: only 7mm^2 are required for the implementation of the logical circuit. Due to the limited performance of the available RAM generator, this chip uses an external memory for the COG look-up table implementation. A 10 Kbytes memory is connected to the chip to store the mass and the area of the output membership functions. Accurate simulation has been performed to characterize the pre- and post-layout performance. These simulations show that the most critical blocks, namely the fuzzifier and the defuzzifier, exhibit a delay time of about 20 ns. Taking into account the simulation results, a clock of 20 MHz was chosen for this implementation. Speed performance estimation requires evaluating, together with the clock frequency, the number of clock cycles needed for the completion of the inference computation. To perform a complete inference on a set of N rules with an input that activates only N_A rules, $K=14+8\ N_A+4N$ clock cycles are required.

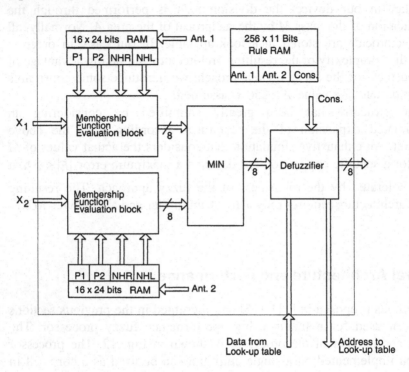

Fig. 12. Simplified architecture of the fuzzy processor

From Fig. 12, the main characteristics of the processor can be summarized as follows:
- number of parallel crisp inputs: 2;
- 8 bit of resolution for each input and, after fuzzification, 8 bit for the grade of truth;
- output resolution: 8 bits;
- up to 16 MF for each input and 7 MF for the output;
- maximum number of rules in the rule base: 256;
- fuzzification method: singleton based;
- defuzzification method: center of gravity implemented by an efficient look-up table approach and an approximated division;

- inference method: MIN-MAX with automatic skipping for zero value activation degrees;
- speed: over 100 KFLIPS with 20 active rules.

As described in [15], the overall structure was checked on a particular application, the radar target tracking. In this case, for 1 input and 4 rules we obtained a performance greater than 400 *KFLIPS*.

7
The Radar Target Tracking Application

The simplifications and approximations introduced in the processor blocks in order to lower the computational complexity, lead to a specific architecture that must be validated by extensive simulations considering the actual applications. In this section, we report the results obtained from the application of the processor to a radar target tracking application, as proposed in [9]. This application is interesting for two reasons:

1. The system simplicity allows an efficient evaluation of the overall behavior;
2. The system constraints require an efficient real time computation.

The Radar Target Tracking problem deals with the estimation of the target position, starting from the noisy radar measures. To this purpose, we use an α–β filter, which estimates at time step n the values of the two coordinates $x_f(n)$ and $y_f(n)$. This estimation is obtained from the measurements of the x and y positions at time n ($x_m(n)$ and $y_m(n)$), through a smoothing operation. The smoothing equations for the evaluation of the x-axis components of the above quantities are the following:

$$x_f(n) = x_p(n) + \alpha_m\left(x_m(n) - x_p(n)\right)$$
$$v_{xf}(n) = v_{xp}(n) + \beta_x\left(\frac{x_m(n) - x_p(n)}{T_c}\right) \qquad (12)$$

where T_c represents the time step length and the values ($x_p(n)$, $y_p(n)$) and ($v_{xp}(n)$, $v_{yp}(n)$) are, respectively, the position and the speed at time step n predicted in the time step n-1. They are obtained by:

$$x_p(n+1) = x_f(n) + T_c \cdot v_{xf}(n)$$
$$v_{xp}(n+1) = v_{xf}(n)$$

(13)

The terms α_x and β_x are the weighting coefficients of the α–β filter on the x-axis. Normally, in target tracking applications is assumed that $\alpha_x = \beta_x = C_x(n)$. The $C_x(n)$ value depends on the prediction error $e_x(n)=x_m(n)-x_p(n)$ normalized with respect to the white noise variance σ_x. In order to improve the system performance, a non linear function must be introduced for the $C_x(n)$ evaluation. In [9], this function is obtained by using a fuzzy approach with four input and four output membership functions, four rules and product-sum inferences. We have implemented this algorithm on our fuzzy processor, modifying the shape of the membership functions and introducing a min-max inference mechanism. The simulation results are shown in Fig. 11.

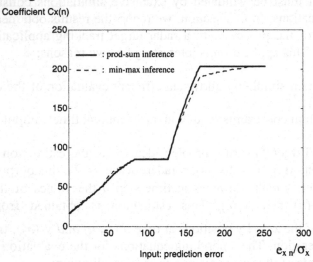

Fig. 11. Comparison of the $C_x(n)$ functions described in by [9] (prod-sum) and [15] (min-max)

In this figure, the input-output characteristic of the algorithm proposed in [9] (prod-sum inference) is compared with our implemented version. The output accounts for all the approximations and errors introduced by the processor, including the effects of the limited internal word-lenghts. As shown in [15], the overall processor input-output characteristic shows a good matching with respect to the results in [9]. But, compared with conventional methodologies as the Kalman approach, the fuzzy implementation is very simple and suitable for a real time high-speed application. A processing speed of over 400 KFLIPS is reached.

8
Conclusions

We have presented the architecture of fuzzy logic system based on the implementation of specific properties of the fuzzy processing. The proposed system is simpler and its basic blocks achieve higher sped. The fuzzification block uses a class of trapezoidal membership functions with power of two slopes for the oblique sides. The COG defuzzification algorithm is implemented by a full look-up table approach in order to obtain the maximum speed. With respect to other look-up table approaches the architecture we propose uses less memory and is fully parallel. In addition, a divider that computes an approximate result further reduces the overall complexity of the circuit. We obtained a chip of 7 mm^2 for the core logic, and an external 10 Kbytes memory containing the output membership functions. The simulations have shown a speed over 100 KFLIPS for 2 inputs and 20 rules. The tests in the radar target tracking application demonstrated the capability of the approach.

References

[1] Watanabe H., Dettloff W.D., and Yount K.E., "A VLSI Fuzzy Logic Controller with Reconfigurable, Cascadable Architecture," *IEEE J. on Solid State Circuits*, vol. 25, no. 2, pp. 376-382, 1990.

[2] Chiueh T., "Optimization of Fuzzy Logic Inference Architecture", *IEEE Computer*, pp.67-71, 1992.

[3] Eichfeld H., Lohner M., and Muller M., "Architecture of a CMOS Fuzzy Logic Controller with Optimized Memory Organization and Operator Design", *Proc. IEEE Int. Conf. Fuzzy System*, San Diego, CA, pp. 1317-1323, 1992.

[4] Nakamura K., Sakascita N., Nitta Y., Shimoumura K., and Tokuda T., "Fuzzy Inference and Fuzzy Inference Processor", *IEEE Micro*, pp.37-48, 1993.

[5] Eichfeld H., Klimke M., Nolles J., and Kunemund T., "A General-Purpose Inference Processor", *Proc. of Fourth Int. Conf. on Microlectronics for Neural Networks and Fuzzy Logic*, Turin, Italy, September 26-28, 1994.

[6] Eisele M., Hentschel K., and Kunemund T., "Hardware Realization of Fast Defuzzification by Adaptive Integration", *Proc. Fourth Int. Conf. on Microlectronics for Neural Networks and Fuzzy Logic*, Turin, Italy, September 26-28, 1994.

[7] Colodro F., Torralba A., and Franquelo L.G., "A Digital Fuzzy-Logic Controller with a Simple Architecture", *Proc. Intern. Conf. Circuits and Systems*, London, U.K., Vol. 2, pp.101, 1994.

[8]   Cardarilli G.C., Re M., and Salerno M., "Multiplierless Digital Architecture for Membership Function Evaluation", *Proc. Int. Conf. on Neural Information Processing*, Seoul, Korea, October 17-20, 1994.

[9]   D. Park, and E.W. Kang, "Radar Target Tracking with a Fuzzy Filter", ICONIP 1994 *Proc. Int. Conf. on Neural Information Processing*, Seoul, Korea, 17-20 October, 1994.

[10] Costa A., De Gloria A., Faraboschi P., Pagni A., and Rizzotto G., "Hardware Solutions for Fuzzy Control", *Proc. of IEEE*, vol. 83, no. 3, pp. 422-434, 1995

[11] Cardarilli G.C., Lojacono R., Re M., and Salerno M., "A VLSI Defuzzification Architecture for Real Time Fuzzy Processor", *Proc. Third European Congress on Intelligent Techniques and Soft Computing*, Aachen, Germany, August 28-31, 1995.

[12] Eichfeld H., Kunemund T., and Menke M., "A 12b General-Purpose Fuzzy Logic Controller Chip", *IEEE Trans. on Fuzzy Systems*, vol. 4, no. 4, pp. 460-475, 1996.

[13] Patyra M.J., Grantner J.L., and Koster K., "Digital Fuzzy Logic Controller: Design and Implementation", *IEEE Trans. on Fuzzy Systems*, vol. 4, no. 4, pp. 439-459, 1996.

[14] Cardarilli G.C., Lojacono R., Re M., and Carfagnini L., "High Speed Fuzzy Filter for Non-Linear Channel Equalizing", *Proc. Int. Symposium on Fuzzy Logic*, Zurich, Switzerland, February 13-14, 1997.

[15] Cardarilli G.C., Lojacono R., and Re M., "VLSI Implementation of a Real Time Fuzzy Processor", *J. of Intelligent and Fuzzy Systems*, IOS Press, n.6, pp.389-401, 1998.

[16] "ST52T301/E301, *Advanced Data Sheet*," STMicroelectronics, 1998

Chapter 5

A Digital Fuzzy Processor for Fuzzy-Rule-Based Systems

Davide Falchieri, Alessandro Gabrielli, Enzo Gandolfi

Department of Physics, University of Bologna, Viale Berti Pichat 6/2, 40127, Bologna, Italy

In this chapter, we describe a family of fuzzy processors oriented to physics experiments. We firstly present two fuzzy processors that have already been realized; the architectures are described in detail. Then, we present a new fast digital Fuzzy Processor that has been designed in 0.7 µm digital CMOS technology. The processor implements a set of fuzzy rules created by means of a genetic fuzzy rule generator. It can process ten 7-bit input variables and carries out one 7-bit output. It may be synchronized up to a 50 MHz clock signal for an estimated power consumption slightly more than 1 W. Moreover the processing rate depends on the number of fuzzy rule and, as a rule of thumb, it can be estimated by multiplying 20 ns, which is the clock period, for the number of fuzzy rules. Also, the inside parallel-pipeline architecture is described in detail. In addition, the architecture is described with layout and data flow simulation pictures. The fuzzy logic methodologies that have been adopted are justified in terms of hardware implementation feasibility and speed requirements.

1
Introduction

Fuzzy systems based on dedicated digital hardware can deliver much higher performance than those based on general-purpose computing machines. The simplicity and versatility of some successful fuzzy inference algorithms, the advent of high-density, user programmable logic devices, together with the powerful CAD tools, made dedicated digital fuzzy hardware a feasible solution for implementing high-performance fuzzy systems [1].

Recently, the fuzzy logic has become widespread due to the fact that computation with words represents the innovative feature of fuzzy theory. Fuzzy algorithms fit very well hardware capabilities and this has oriented a part of hardware research to fuzzy hardware processors.

Basically, fuzzy logic handles the classical operations that one should do for solving a problem with fuzzy rules: these rules are directly and easily generated using the verbal expressions describing processes. Namely, each quantitative word is connected with some numerical value, with some normalized distribution of uncertainty and with a scale function characterizing the reliability of the source of the verbal data.

In this chapter, we will explain the operation of a genetic fuzzy system on a hardware fuzzy processor. We describe the architecture of a 10 input fuzzy processor able to process a "genetic" fuzzy system. Firstly, a summary of the main features of a genetic fuzzy system is presented. In particular, the shape of Membership Function (MF) is oriented for fitting a genetic fuzzy system and this makes it different from a traditional fuzzy MF. In this case it is not possible to define a number of MFs per variable with the same shape for each rule, but each fuzzy rule has its own MFs. In a genetic fuzzy system, MFs lose the semantic meaning they had in traditional architectures and a human expert cannot generate them in a natural manner.

In the past, our group has designed and realized fuzzy processors [2], [3], that have a memory for storing both the fuzzy rules and, for each input variable, the MFs trapezoidal shapes or some MFs identification codes, such as starting and ending points, slopes, etc. In the processor presented in this chapter, there is only one memory in which all the fuzzy rules and the related MF shapes are coded. Since a genetic fuzzy system usually needs just a few rules, the rule memory allows up to 60 fuzzy rules and it is possible to store, one after the others, several fuzzy systems related to the same input data set. The architecture and the pipeline stages of the genetic fuzzy processor are described in detail subsequently.

It is worthwhile to emphasize that some applications in High Energy Physics Experiments (HEPE) require a very high processing rate: for instance some experiments require devices able to take a complex decision in less than a microsecond. Commercially available hardware is not able to match these kinds of constraints. We have proved [4] that a processor based on fuzzy algorithms can successfully apply to this target. We took the following decisions for designing the genetic fuzzy processor in order to reach the highest achievable processing rate:

1. A parallel and pipeline architecture is needed in order to increase the global throughput;

2. The weighted sum [5] and weighted mean defuzzification methods must be implemented in the circuit;
3. Active rule selection (the active rules are the ones that give a non-null contribution to the final result);
4. The design of the fuzzy processor must match the fuzzy systems obtained by a genetic rule generator, in case it is not possible to select the active rules.

2
Background: Fuzzy Hardware and Software

During the last 15 years, the number of hardware and software developments of fuzzy systems has been rather large. The following subsections give a brief overview on these arguments and some interesting references.

2.1
Fuzzy Hardware

There are a number of fuzzy hardware and software devices that can be used for easily implementing fuzzy systems. Hardware implementation is usually necessary where a high computation speed is required; otherwise a software implementation of a fuzzy system is a more convenient and cheaper solution. Three different implementations of fuzzy systems are available on the market:

- The fuzzy system can be developed using a high level programming language such as C or C++ and then it is run on a traditional microprocessor. This solution proves to be interesting when the main constraint is the system cost and not the computation speed.
- The fuzzy system can be run on a specific coprocessor designed and optimized for fuzzy computations (fuzzification, inference and defuzzification). This coprocessor, interfaced to a standard microprocessor for communication with external devices, significantly improves fuzzy processing speed.
- The fuzzy system can be run on specifically designed fuzzy hardware (analog, digital or mixed implementations). These are completely independent systems capable of interfacing with other devices without the help of standard microprocessors. This solution provides the best performance in terms of computational speed; in

fact the fuzzy chip architecture may be optimized on the particular fuzzy algorithm chosen.

The development of the first fuzzy chip is due to two research groups: Togai and Watanabe [5] for the digital fuzzy processor, and Yamakawa and Miki [6] for the analog one. The first digital processor has implemented 16 rules with an estimated speed of 80,000 FLIPS (Fuzzy Logic Inferences Per Second) without the defuzzification. The analog chip could reach an inference speed of 1 μs independent of the number of rules and the total area of the chip was smaller than the digital counterpart. Therefore, the first problem arising with the development of fuzzy systems was the choice between analog and digital implementations. In general, digital hardware is easier to design by using synthesizable HDL (Hardware Description Language): a great flexibility is reached through automatic synthesis of logic blocks starting from a behavioral description. Analog hardware design is more complex than the digital one and less flexible. For this reason Yamakawa [7] and Schumacher [8] suggested different programmable analog chips: Yamakawa programmed the membership functions and fuzzy rules through digital registers, whereas Schumacher proposed the generation of a layout from existing generic macrocells that are hardwired during the prototyping phase. We think, however, that as digital technologies shrink transistor sizes and improve propagation delays, the digital solution becomes more practical and feasible than the analog one; this is the solution we have chosen for the design of our fuzzy processors.

Today, fuzzy processors up to 20 MFLIPS are available on the market. Experts say that fuzzy microprocessor market is about to grow rapidly in the next few years and it is foreseen that at least the 50 % of microcontrollers will be equipped with fuzzy logic blocks.

A well-known example of this kind of applications is the fuzzy coprocessor WARP 2.0 [9] (WARP stands for Weight Associative Rule Processor). The chip has been designed to work as a coprocessor or as a stand-alone microcontroller. As a fuzzy coprocessor, WARP 2.0 can work together with standard micros, which perform normal control tasks such as A/D conversions, arithmetic calculus, interrupts and so on, while WARP 2.0 is independently responsible for all the related fuzzy computing. The WARP 2.0 chip includes fuzzification, I/O association and defuzzification blocks: it computes 32 rules with 5 inputs in 1.85 microseconds. Together with the chip, the manufacturer provides the software FUZZYSTUDIO 2.0 [10] for writing the fuzzy system. The software includes a variable editor for the definition of I/O variables and MFs, and a rule editor for the definition of the fuzzy rules. Using the editor, a file is created and downloaded into the WARP 2.0 memories and the processing phase starts.

Industrial applications of fuzzy processors are especially focused on the field of control and pattern recognition; both applications do not require a high speed. There are some specific applications that require a total computational speed much greater than the one available of fuzzy system application on the market.

For example, we tried to apply fuzzy logic to solve the problems related to trigger devices in High Energy Physics Experiments. A trigger is a device that has to recognize interesting events (such as particle-antiparticle collision) in the shortest possible time, and then it has to give the start to the acquisition system in order to record the event. It is easy to understand that the decision time available to the trigger is very short: some hundreds of nanoseconds. The next paragraphs show the solutions we propose for a fuzzy logic trigger. The solution is based on a family of fast fuzzy processors with a very high processing rate. An in-depth look will be provided for a 10-input fuzzy processor that is a combination of Fuzzy Logic and Genetic Algorithms.

2.2
Fuzzy Rule Generators: Neural and Genetic

The fuzzy set approach relies on the possibility of handling vague or uncertain information. Generally a fuzzy rule-based system interprets fuzzy rules such as the one shown below:

$$If\ (x\ is\ A)\ and\ (y\ is\ B)\ ...\ then\ (z\ is\ Z) \tag{1}$$

where x, y and z represent respectively the input and output variables while A, B and Z are the correspondent linguistic variables such as high, low, hot and fast.

As far as the fuzzy rule generation it can be said that the most simple and general fuzzy rule generator may be seen as a human expert that, on the basis of his/her own experience, writes down some logical rules to be converted into a set of fuzzy rules. On the other hand, for a human expert, it can be difficult to translate experience into logical or fuzzy rules; this is why generally the human expert knowledge may only be used in a first stage of features definition. For example the human expert could fix the number of linguistic variables, the shape of the MFs (gaussian, trapezoidal, etc.) and the maximum number of rules. Then, an automatic approach (DIRO: Data In Rule Out) may adapt and tune these features to fit a set of input – output patterns. Even on the market it is possible to find several software tools able to develop fuzzy rule generators.

Neural fuzzy systems are artificial neural networks able to tune fuzzy systems using a set of input – output pairs. This may be done be means of learning algorithms of feed-forward supervised multi-layer neural networks or Kohonen's algorithm for unsupervised learning. These approaches matched a large number of applications of neuro-fuzzy systems to diagnostics, control and decision. For example, the Artificial Neural Networks (ANNs) were applied to determining fuzzy rules for forecasting gas demand [11]. In this case a feed-forward back-propagation method uses a network with five layers of neurons. The input layer contains two nodes - temperature and the month and the output layer is the gas demand figure. The three hidden layers are used to represent possible fuzzy values of the input variable, significant AND combinations and fuzzy outputs respectively. After training, the weights and connections are analyzed properly. A system is developed based on the rules that are extracted directly from the network. We want to underline those neural networks and fuzzy systems support each other. In the above case, ANNs are used to learn the fuzzy rules.

Genetic Algorithms (GAs) are another well-known and widely used technique to explore and exploit a given operating space using available performance measures. In fact it could be said that GAs are used to find near optimal solutions in complex search spaces. This applies for example when the global space to investigate for finding the best set of fuzzy rules is too wide. In other words the space is divided into smaller parts, even slightly overlapping, and these sub-parts are investigated separately. As already mentioned, the knowledge of a system may be in form of linguistic variables, fuzzy membership function parameters, fuzzy rules and number of rules. The generic code structure and independent performance features of GAs make them suitable candidates for incorporating this kind of vague knowledge. The searching capabilities and its ability for incorporating a priori knowledge have extended the use of GAs in the development of a wide range of methods for designing fuzzy systems. Systems applying these design approaches have received the general name of Genetic Fuzzy Systems (GFSs) [12], [13].

Several researchers [14], [15], [16] have reported results using GAs to select fuzzy rules in classification. The problem is on using a set of numerical data to generate if-then rules for pattern classification. The approach in this work is similar and can be divided into a partition of the pattern space into smaller subspaces and an identification of the fuzzy rules for each subspace.

3
A Family of Fast Fuzzy Processors

We present two chips from the family of fuzzy processors; namely:

- a 4-input fuzzy processor [3];
- a 2-input fuzzy processor [17].

For the 2- and 4-input fuzzy chips, we adopted the strategy to process only the active rules, the rules that give a non-null contribution to the output. This solution allows reaching a very high processing rate (strictly determined by the number of active rules), but proves to be a feasible solution if the number of inputs and Membership Functions (MFs) per input is relatively low. For instance, in the 4-input fuzzy processor, up to 7 MFs are associated to each input: so far the total number of possible fuzzy rules is $7^4 = 2401$. This is still a reasonable number of rules that can be placed on a static on-chip memory. Taking also into account that the number of active rules is $2^4 = 16$ (if only two adjacent MFs can overlap), the strategy of active rules selection proves to be a very powerful one for increasing speed. On the other hand, it is not absolutely feasible to use the same strategy for the 10-input chip also. In this case, the total number of rules would grow to 7^{10} that is an enormous number to manage. Therefore, we used another strategy: while for the 2- and 4-input chip the knowledge base of the fuzzy system is given by an expert, for the 10-input one it is provided by a GAs based software rule generator. The number of rules is usually very low (10-20) if compared to the ones a human expert would give. This is good for what concerns speed even if with the introduction of the genetic algorithms we lose the transparency typical of fuzzy logic. The generated rule base is, however, difficult to understand intuitively. Consequently, it is very difficult to manually tune the fuzzy system.

3.1
The 4-Input Fuzzy Processor

The main feature of this design is the independence of the processing rate from the fuzzy system developed by the human expert. This has been obtained in the following way:
- Every fuzzy system is converted into a new one where all the rules are present and then downloaded into the internal RAM memories;
- Only the active rules are processed.

The main features of the chip are:

- four 7-bit inputs, one 7-bit output;
- 7 MFs for each of the inputs, only trapezoidal shapes are allowed;
- maximum overlapping of 2 adjacent MFs;
- 128 crisp MFs for the output variable;
- T-norm implemented by minimum or product;
- Sugeno order 0 inference and defuzzification method;
- 50 Mega Fuzzy Logic Inferences Per Second with a 50 MHz clock.

Given that a rule is processed in one clock period the total processing time is made up of the following contributions:
- 16 active rules times the clock period (20 ns) = 320 ns;
- pipeline stages delay = 240 ns;
- defuzzification division process: 90 ns.

So far, the total processing time is 650 ns, but the input set rate is 320 ns; that is, every 320 ns a valid value is given in output. The chip, realized using ES2 0.7μm technology, has a total area of 60 mm². One third of the total area is due to the RAM memories, that contain the fuzzy rules and input MFs. Area can be substantially reduced by reducing the total number of rules. Figure 1 shows the microphotograph of the 4-input fuzzy processor that shows the distribution of standard cells (logic gates AND, OR, NOT and so on) and RAM memories on the silicon area.

3.2
The Two-input Fuzzy Processor

The 2-input fuzzy processor is a reduced version of the 4-input one being able to process only two input variables at a time. Nevertheless since the number of active rules is reduced from $4^2 = 16$ to $2^2 = 4$ the input set rate is increased of a factor 4. Besides since the total number of rules is decreased from $7^4 = 2401$ to $7^2 = 49$ the chip dimensions become much smaller. A first version of the 2-input fuzzy chip has been realized using the ES2 0.7μm digital technology with the following performance:
- total area of 14 mm² (vs. 60 mm² of the 4-input chip);
- 50 MFLIPS with a 50 MHz clock;
- 80 ns for the processing rate.

Since our main goal is a high computational speed we decided to re-design the 2-input fuzzy chip using the more recent 0.35 μm Alcatel Mietec digital technology. This allowed us to reach the following results:

- total area of 3 mm^2;
- 133 MFLIPS with a 133 MHz clock;
- 30 ns for the processing rate.

This release of the 2-input fuzzy processor binds together the features of a very small area and a very high processing rate: the chip can take a decision every 30 ns. So far the chip can be applied in experiments requiring very smart triggers. This is mainly due to the constant progress in CMOS silicon technology: as transistor size keeps shrinking circuits become quicker and smaller. Moreover the task of re-targeting the chip on a newer technology is a highly automated one: in fact it is sufficient to synthesize the HDL code on the new technology without performing any structural changes to the old architecture.

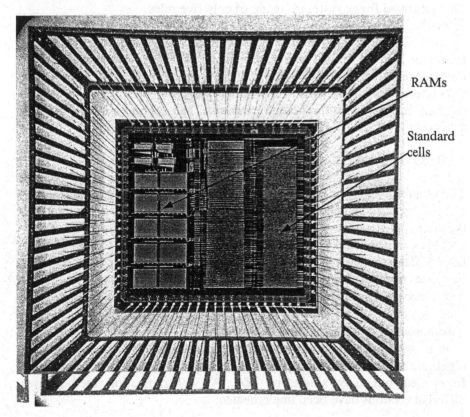

RAMs

Standard cells

Fig. 1. The 4-Input Fuzzy Processor Microphotograph

4
Genetic Rule Generator

In this section a rule generator based on genetic algorithms [18], [19] is described. The automatic learning of fuzzy rules allows applying fuzzy logic in fields where there is no human expert and transfers the tedious fuzzy rules and membership function tuning from a human designer to the computer itself. There are two hybrid techniques, which are mainly based on Genetic Algorithms (GAs). Even if these tools are built for approximation and classification tasks they can be used also for robotic applications. For example, genetic algorithms can be used in a motion-planning problem. It is to be considered the problem of mobile robot navigation in unknown 2D environments with obstacles. The robot is memory-less and, for example, 5 inputs and 2 outputs form a fuzzy control system that is trained starting from a few hundreds of learning patterns. The generated fuzzy system is made of only five rules.

In many developed applications the number of required fuzzy rules is very low. Typically this number has almost always been below a few tens even for ten or more inputs problems. Moreover, simplified fuzzy knowledge base can be generated; i.e. the tools are capable of eliminating the unnecessary antecedents in any rule. Finally, the tools can be used both in classification and interpolation problems. The generic r-th rule has the following form:

$$If\ (X1\ is\ A1r)\ AND\ ...\ AND\ (Xn\ is\ Anr)\ THEN\ (Zo\ is\ Zr) \tag{2}$$

The premise contains n antecedents and the conclusion one consequent.

In the generic antecedent $(Xn\ is\ Anr)$ there is the n-th crisp Xn input and the fuzzy set An, that is generally different from all the others. The fuzzy set MFs in the antecedents (Anr) can have a Gaussian, triangular or trapezoidal symmetric shape. For each antecedent it is therefore necessary to code two parameters in Gaussian and triangular cases or three parameters in the trapezoidal symmetric case. So, the genetic coding of the premise of a rule requires $2 \cdot n \cdot R$ or $3 \cdot n \cdot R$ parameters (genetic chromosomes), where R is the rule number.

It is assumed that all the connectors in the premise are ANDs. The algebraic minimum for this operator is used. In the consequent there is not fuzzy sets but only singletons (Zr). As defuzzification method two different versions have been implemented:

$$\text{Weighted Mean } Z0 = \frac{\sum_{r=1}^{R} \Theta r \times Zr}{\sum_{r=1}^{R} \Theta r} \qquad (3)$$

$$\text{Weighted Sum } Z0 = \sum_{r=1}^{R} \Theta r \times Zr \qquad (4)$$

Experiments have shown that the best results are reached using Weighted Sum in approximation problems and Weighted Mean in classification ones. In some genetic algorithms the genetic coding requires other R parameters, while in others no parameter is required for the consequent part of the rules. They are extracted in a robust manner solving an over-determined system. When the premises are fixed we can calculate the degrees of truth of each rule and each pattern. These values lead to a linear system in which we have more equations than the Zr variables.

Figure 2 gives a practical example of the inference rules [20]. It is a five input example. The MFs in the premise are triangular. As the reader can see, the width of the functions can be wider than the relative Universe of Discourse. Furthermore, the centers of the Gaussian functions can be outside the Universe of the Discourse. These two features permit to extract very compact fuzzy knowledge.

For this purpose, a continuous and fine grain evolution algorithm is used in order to allow choosing to slow down the process of genetic homogenization. In practice, the individuals are assumed to be on a rectangular grid and are selected from a deme with a user-defined radius. It has been adopted the so-called Roulette Wheel Selection [20] in which the individual's selection probability is proportional to its fitness normalized.

On the other hand, in fine grain models, there are two types of selection: global and local. In this case, global selection is fitness-proportional and identifies the center of the subpopulation deme; it also has a pre-established radius.

In a different way, local selection uses the same selection method but only in the subpopulation deme. Two parents generate a single offspring using a crossover operator with a single cut. Then the mutation operator is applied and the offspring generated in the deme goes to replace the individual with the lowest fitness value. Finally, a hill-climbing operator is introduced. It only starts whenever an individual is generated with a fitness value higher than the best one obtained so far. In a first step, the individual selected is transformed in a neuro-fuzzy system. That is, the equivalent neural network is built and all trainable weights are initiated. Then, the system is trained. In this phase it is possible that some neurons can be deleted, too. Finally, the trained system is re-transformed in a genetic individual and introduced in the genetic grid at the place of the starting individual selected.

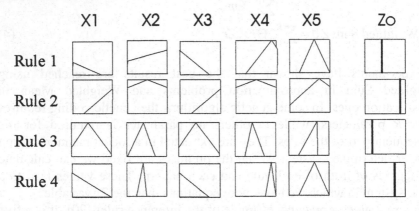

Fig. 2. A genetic fuzzy system

5
Ten-Input Fuzzy Processor Performance

We have presented (Figure 2) a typical five rule fuzzy system obtained by a genetic rule generator with five inputs and one crisp output. Figure 3 reports the trapezoidal symmetric MF shapes that will approximate, in our design, the gaussian one; of course our genetic rule generator will take this into account. Looking at Figure 2, we can conclude that, when we have a "genetic" fuzzy system:

- it is not worthwhile to improve the processing rate by selecting the active rules because most of them are active due to the MFs shape and width;
- the number of rules of the genetic fuzzy system may be much smaller than the number of rules written by an expert or obtained by neural rule generators;
- the number of MFs for each variable is generally equal to the number of rules of the fuzzy system, that is, each rule has its own MFs.

The main performance of the "genetic" fuzzy processor is:

- Maximum number of rules of the fuzzy system: 60 rules;
- 10 inputs, each of 9 bits, and one 9 bit output;

- MF shape: symmetrical and trapezoidal;
- 7 bits for the degree of truth and 512 crisp MFs for the output variable;
- 7 bits both for the antecedent and the premise degree of truth;
- T-norm implemented by Minimum;
- Weighted Sum and Weighted Mean defuzzification methods;
- 50 Mega Fuzzy Inference per second for a 50 MHz clock signal;
- Up to five different fuzzy systems can process the same input data set.

Therefore, the number of rules times 20 ns gives the processing rate. Moreover, two delays due to the number of pipeline stages (12) times 20 ns and due to the division process (240 ns) are included off-pipeline.

6
Processor Architecture

The first step to design this processor concerns the rule code. As described before we have coded in each fuzzy rule the MF parameters for each input variable. Consequently the MF shape:

- can be different from zero inside the whole Universe of Discourse of the input variable;
- can reach the '1' value outside the Universe of Discourse.

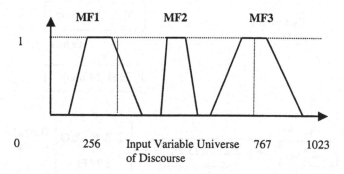

Fig. 3. Three typical MFs in the Universe of Discourse

To satisfy these requirements the MFs, which are trapezoidal and symmetrical, are identified by three parameters: the two 10-bit coordinates of the smaller base of the trapezium, and the 12-bit slope. The 9-bit input variables, before being processed, are shifted on the right of 256. In this way the input variable value is a 10-bit word which can span from 256 to 256+511 = 767, while the end points of the smaller base can span from 0 to 1023. In Figure 3 three typical MFs are reported. Therefore each rule will require 10×(10+10+12) = 320 bits for the premise code, 9 bits for the crisp output MF and one bit to recognize the last rule of each fuzzy system to be processed. The processor architecture has been divided in pipeline stages in order to reach the desired clock frequency that is 50 MHz, for High Energy Physics Experiments. Moreover the processor will be implemented within a printed circuit board that writes the 10 input variables serially, one by one, by means of an asynchronous strobe signal. Besides that, the processor has to provide an external synchronization signal for writing the fuzzy output variable into a post-processor device.

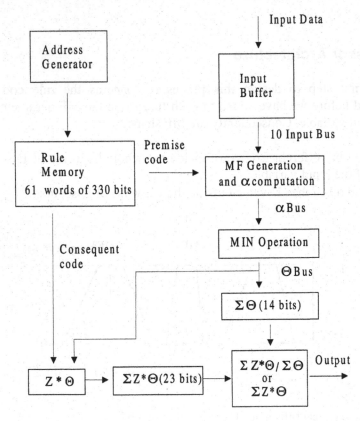

Fig. 4. The processor architecture

To meet these external constraints the processor firstly has an Input Buffer, as illustrated in Figure 4, which loads serially the 10 input variables and sets them for a parallel successive read stage. This step also requires an asynchronous to synchronous conversion of the input variables. From this point on, the variables and the signals have to be synchronized with the internal processor clock signal. After having loaded the input variables the processor provides a signal for disabling the external writing device for other writing cycles. At this stage, the processor, by means of the 6-bit counter Address-Generator, provides the first memory address for reading the first fuzzy rule from the Rule-Memory. Once the parameters for defining the membership functions for all the 10 input variables have been read and the input variables have been loaded, 10 MF-Generators start the input degrees of truth computation. After that, the premise degree of truth Θ is extracted from a tree architecture that computes the minimum between two input words at a time. At this stage two parallel fast adders add both $\Theta \times Z$ and Θ to obtain respectively the numerator and the denominator for the final division required by the Weighted-Sum defuzzification formula. The division starts when the end-of-fuzzy system signal is read from one of the rule memory words. Then the process just described may restart from the degrees of truth computation for another, if present, fuzzy system that may follow the first one inside the rule memory. The processor, in this way, may process up to 5 different fuzzy systems. In fact, since the number of pipeline stages, as below described, is 12, five fuzzy systems require at least 60 fuzzy rules. Finally, after having processed all the fuzzy systems, there is a last coded rule for stopping the fuzzy processor and enabling a signal to let the external device write a new input data set. In parallel to the new input loading phase process the final off-pipeline division takes place and when the output fuzzy variable is ready another signal is enabled.

7
Layout Design

This processor layout is completed and is ready to be sent to the silicon foundry. The estimated power consumption is about 1 W and the time required to process a complete fuzzy rule set is about 1 microsecond. The computations have been made after the post-layout simulation phase. A final layout design is shown in Figure 5. The Figure shows the first block subdivision. It is clear that most of the layout area is covered by the membership generators and by the memories used to store the fuzzy rules. The long wide horizontal and vertical lines, close to the boundary, are the power and ground supply wires to allow up to 200 mA of global core current. The global silicon area is 75 mm^2 and the rectangular shape has been provided with 4 17-pad sides. Five couples of pads for core and three couples for peripheral supply have been used. Finally it has been designed for a realization with ES2 0.7 µm digital technology.

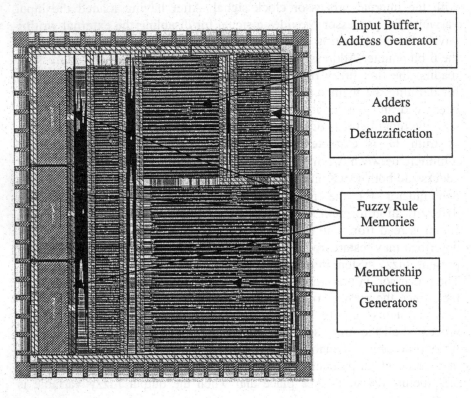

Fig. 5. The 10-Input Fuzzy Processor Layout

8
Conclusions

The fuzzy processor has met the constraints for which it has been designed in terms of speed and flexibility. It satisfies the requirements for applications to advanced physics experiments (typically, in high-energy physics experiments), where a high computation speed is needed. Nevertheless, due to the implemented features for making it configurable in different ways, it may be applied as a general-purpose fuzzy processor too. In fact, the input-output configurable mapping makes the processor useful for a much wider application field than it was designed to.

The fuzzy processor architecture is configurable in different ways in terms of number of fuzzy systems and shape of input membership functions. Moreover, since most of the fuzzy processor – apart from the memory blocks – has been designed by means of VHDL language, it can easily be readapted for new dedicated applications.

References

[1] D. L. Hung, "Dedicated Digital Fuzzy Hardware", *IEEE Micro*, Vol. 15, No. 4, August 1995.

[2] Gabrielli, E. Gandolfi and M. Masetti, "Design of a Family of VLSI High Speed Fuzzy Processors", *IEEE Fuzz'96*, New Orleans, September 8-11 1996.

[3] Gabrielli, E. Gandolfi, "A Fast Digital Fuzzy Processor", *IEEE Micro*, vol. 19, No. 1, pag. 68-79, Jan/Feb 1999.

[4] Y. Lin and G.A. Cunningham III, "A New Approach to Fuzzy-Neural System Modeling", *IEEE Transactions on Fuzzy Systems*, Vol. 3, pp. 190-198, May 1995.

[5] M. Togai and H. Watanabe, "A VLSI Implementation of a Fuzzy Inference Engine: Toward an Expert System on a Chip", *Information Science*, Vol. 38, pp. 147-163, 1986.

[6] T. Yamakawa and T. Miki, "The Current Mode Fuzzy Logic Integrated Circuits Fabricated by the Standard CMOS Process", *IEEE Transactions on Computers*, Vol. C-35, No. 2, pp. 161-167, 1986.

[7] T. Miki and T. Yamakawa, "Silicon Implementation for a Novel High-Speed Fuzzy Inference Engine: Mega-FLIPS Analog Fuzzy Processor", *Intelligent & Fuzzy Systems*, Vol. 1, No. 1, pp. 27-42, 1993.

[8] T. Kettner, K. Schumacher and K. Goser, "Realization of a Monolithic Analog Fuzzy Logic Controller", *Proc. of the 20th European Solid State Circuit Conference*, Sevilla, pp.. 66-69, 1993.

[9] Pagni et al., "Automatic Synthesis, Analysis and Implementation of a Fuzzy Controller", *IEEE Int. Conf. On Fuzzy Systems*, San Francisco CA, pp. 105-110, 28 March 1 April, 1993.

[10] FUZZYSTUDIO TM 2.0:
     http://www.st.com/stonline/products/support/fuzzy.

[11] N. K. Kasabov, "Learning Fuzzy Rules through Neural Networks", *Proc. of the First New Zealand Intl. Conf. on Artificial Neural Networks and Expert Systems, ANNES'93*, Dunedin, IEEE Computer Society Press, pp. 137-140, 1993.

[12] O. Cordon et al., "Selecting Fuzzy-Rule-Based Classification Systems with Specific Reasoning Methods Using Genetic Algorithms", *Proc. Seventh IFSA World Congress*, pp. 424-429, Prague 1997.

[13] Y. Yabuchi and J. Watada, "Switching Regression Model Based on Genetic Algorithms", *Proc. Seventh IFSA World Congress*, pp. 113-118, Prague 1997.

[14] H. Ishibuchi, K. Nozaki and H. Tanaka, "Distributed Representation of fuzzy rules and its application to pattern classification", *Fuzzy Sets and Systems*, 52:21--32, 1992.

[15] H. Ishibuchi, K. Nozaki and N. Yanamoti., "Selecting Fuzzy Rules by Genetic Algorithms for Classification Problems", *Proc. Second IEEE Intl. Conf. on Fuzzy Systems*, vol. 2, pp. 1119--1124, 1993.

[16] H. Ishibuchi and K. Moriaka, "Determination of Type II Membership Functions by Fuzzified Neural Networks", *Proc. EUFIT'95 Conf.*, pp. 529-533, 1995.

[17] D. Falchieri, A. Gabrielli, E. Gandolfi and M. Masetti, "A 2 Input Fuzzy Chip Running at a Processing Rate of 30 ns Realized in 0.35 μm CMOS Technology", *Proc. Conf. on Circuits Systems Communications and Computers'99*, pp. 203-210, 4 - 8 July 1999, Athens.

[18] M. Russo, "FuGeNeSys: SW and HW Implementation", *Proc. IEEE First International Conference on Conventional and Knowledge based Intelligent Electronic System*, Adelaide, Australia, pp. 209-218, May 1997.

[19] M. Russo, "FuGeNeSys: A Genetic neural System for Fuzzy Modeling", to appear on *IEEE Transactions on Fuzzy Systems* 6(3), pp. 373-388, 1998.

[20] D. E. Goldberg, *"Genetic Algorithms in Search, Optimization and Machine Learning"*, New York, Addison-Wesley, 1989.

Part 3

Neural Networks Hardware Implementations

Chapter 6

Optimum Multiuser Detection for CDMA Systems Using the Mean Field Annealing Neural Network

Po-Rong Chang, Bor-Chin Wang, and Tan-Hsu Tan

Department of Communication Engineering,
National Chiao-Tung University, Hsin-Chu, Taiwan

In this chapter, we investigate the application of Mean Field Annealing (MFA) neural networks to the optimum multiuser detection in a direct-sequence code-division multiple-access (DS/CDMA) system over the additive white Gaussian noise (AWGN) channel. Although the optimum receiver for multi-user detection is superior to the conventional matched filter receiver when the relative powers of the interfering signals are large, the optimum receiver obtained by the maximization of a log-likelihood function has a complexity that is exponential in the number of users. This prohibitive complexity has spawned the area of research on employing neural network techniques to develop an optimum detector with moderate complexity. In this chapter, it is shown that the energy function of the neural network can be derived from and is then expressed in terms of the likelihood function of the optimum multi-user detection for both the synchronous and asynchronous CDMA systems. An MFA network, which combines characteristics of the simulated annealing algorithm and the Hopfield neural network is proposed to seek out the global optimum solution of this energy function. Additionally, MFA exhibits the rapid convergence of the neural network while preserving the solution quality afforded by the stochastic simulated annealing algorithm. This would lead to a cost-effective and efficient minimization mechanism for CDMA multiuser detection. Computer simulation carry out performance comparisons among optimum detection, matched filter detection and MFA detection.

1
Introduction

Spread spectrum communications are currently under development for wireless mobile communication applications due to their efficient utilization of channel bandwidth, the relative insensitivity to multipath interference, and the potential for improved privacy [1]. In addition to providing multiple accessing capabilities and multipath rejection, spread spectrum communications also offer the possibility of further increasing overall spectrum capacity, by overlaying a Code Division Multiple Access (CDMA) network over narrowband users [1]. CDMA is a promising technique for radio access in variety of cellular mobile and wireless personal communication networks. In an SS-CDMA system, several independent users share simultaneously a common channel using spreading code waveform. In addition, it offers some attractive features such as high flexibility, high capacity, simplified frequency planning and soft capacity. For example, CDMA provides up to about four to six times more capacity than first generation TDMA, Cellular systems, mobile satellite networks, and personal communication networks (PCN) that use CDMA have been proposed and are currently under design, construction, or deployment [1], [2]. Moreover, networks of LEO (Low Earth Orbit) and MEO (Medium Earth Orbit) satellites for world-wide (global) communications such as Loral/Qualcomm's Globalstar and TWR's Odyssey that employ CDMA have been developed [1], [2].

The conventional method of detecting a spread-spectrum signal in a multiuser channel employs a filter matched to the desired signal [1], [2]. This conventional single-user detector ignores the presence of interfering signals, or equivalently, ignores the cross-correlation between the signals of different users. Therefore, the performance of the single-user detector severely degrades when the relative received power of the interfering signal becomes large, i.e. the near-far effect [1]. To tackle this difficulty, there has been an interest in designing optimum detectors for various multiuser CDMA communication systems [2], [4], [7]. The optimum multiuser detection can be carried out by the maximization of a log-likelihood function. Although the optimum multiuser detection is superior to the conventional single-user detector, Verdu [6] showed that these optimum detectors require computational complexity, which grows exponentially with increasing the number of users. Since a CDMA system could potentially have a large number of users, it may be impractical to implement the optimum detection unless the number of users is quite small. For instance, a 10-user CDMA system operating with a bit rate of 100 kbits/s using QPSK signaling would require up to 10^5 million computations of the likelihood function per second [5].

Hence, there is a need for suboptimum receivers that are robust to near-far effects with a reasonable computational complexity to ensure their practical implementation. Lupas and Verdu [4] introduced a class of suboptimum detectors that are based on linear transformations of a bank of matched filter outputs. Recently, Aazhang, Parisi, and Orsak [7] published the first paper that considered the applicability of multilayer perceptron (MLP) neural networks to multiuser detection. However, there are some problems when the MLP network is used for the multiuser detection. Firstly, it is not known how many neurons in the hidden layer are needed, where the number of neurons grows exponentially with the number of users. Secondly, it is not clear that how many symbols are needed for training. Lastly, the well-known backpropagation training algorithm for the MLP is very time-consuming, and is not guaranteed to find the global minimum of its decision error surface. More recently, Mitra and Poor [8] applied a single-layer radial-basis-function neural network to the multiuser detection. The number of neurons is exponential with the number of users, and the decision statistics is a linear combination of nonlinear transformations of observable. Thus, the use of a RBF network detector may not be desirable if there is a significant number of active users in a CDMA system.

Miyajima et al. [9], and Kechriotis and Manolakos [10] proposed a Hopfield neural network for synchronous CDMA multiuser detection using the log-likelihood function as the energy function to be minimized. The synaptic weights of the networks are nonadaptive and equal to the cross-correlation times the corresponding amplitudes, both of which are assumed known. When the true minimum of the function is found, the decisions are optimum. However, the network does not always converge to the global minimum. Moreover, it is shown empirically in [9] that the probability of convergence to spurious local minimum increases with the number of users, the channel noise level, or when the interfering signals are weak. To overcome this major limitation of the Hopfield network, in this chapter, we employ a mean-field annealing (MFA) machine, which merges many features of Hopfield neural network and simulated annealing technique [12] to minimize the energy function. The main advantage of using the MFA method lies in the fact that the search for optima is parallel in the global sense, and hence the execution time is shorter than other stochastic hill-climbing methods [12], [13]. Moreover, the MFA was recently found to be an efficient global minimization method in solving a large scale combinatorial optimization problem in which the energy function to be optimized is a function of discrete variable [17], [19].

Recently, Alspector et al. [24] described a microchip implementation of a MFA machine. The chip contains 32 neurons with 992 connections. They showed that these microchip analog circuits for MFA machines are able to speed up the converge rate of solving optimization problems by orders of magnitude, and can seek out the optimal solution in submicrosecond intervals. Our MFA method is not only suitable for synchronous CDMA multiuser detection but also valid for the asynchronous detection since Lupas and Verdu [3] showed a fact that a K-user asynchronous CDMA system can be converted into an equivalent synchronous CDMA system with MK users where M denotes the packet length of data. It should be mentioned that the similar works could be found in [25], [31].

The chapter is organized as follows. In Section 2, we briefly describe the CDMA multiuser detection problem, and map it onto a neural network framework. A set of mean field equations is derived by the saddle point method in Section 3 to solve the multiuser detection problem. A fixed-point iteration implementation for MFA machine is proposed in Section 4. Moreover, in Section 5, an analog MOS VLSI hardware is proposed to realize the MFA machine in order to seek out the optimal solution in real time manner. The numerical calculations and simulation results are discussed in Section 6.

2
Mapping the Optimum CDMA Multiuser Detection Problem onto a Mean-Field Annealing Network

In the multiple-access system for data transmission of interest, transmitters are assumed to share a radio band in a combination of the time and code domains. One way of multiple accessing in the code domain is spread spectrum, which is a signaling scheme that uses a much wider bandwidth than necessary for a given rate. Our model is based on an SS-CDMA system with binary phase shift keyed (BPSK) signaling [1], [2]. There are a total of K users transmitting over a common wireless channel. Associated with each user $k \in 1,2,\cdots,K$ is a data signal $b_k(t)$ and a signature code waveform $a_k(t)$, which are functions of time. If we assume that the period of the spreading code is equal to duration of a data bit, the signature waveform for the k-th user may be expressed as:

$$a_k(t) = \sum_{i=0}^{N_c-1} a_{k,i} \prod_{T_c} (t - iT_c), \quad 0 \le t \le T \tag{1}$$

where $\{a_{k,i}, 0 \le i \le N_c - 1\}$ is a random signature code sequence assigned to the k-th user with each chip $a_{k,j}$ independent and equiprobably distributed on +1, -1, and $\prod_{T_c}(\cdot)$ is the unit pulse function of duration T_c, defined by:

$$\prod_{T_c}(t) = \begin{cases} 1 & t \in [0, T_c) \\ 0 & \text{elsewhere} \end{cases} \tag{2}$$

The duration of each data bit is T, while the duration of each chip in the signature code signal is T_c. As a result, the number of chips per bit is $N_c = T / T_c$, where N_c is an integer and usually called the length of the spreading sequence.

For simplicity, it is convenient to consider the transmission of a packet of bits of a length, M. Then, the data packet from the k-th user is:

$$b_k(t) = \sum_{j=0}^{M-1} b_{k,j} \prod_T (t - jT) \tag{3}$$

where $b_{k,j} \in \{+1, -1\}$ denotes the k-th user's information bit in the j-th time interval.

The equivalent lowpass transmitted signal is given by:

$$s_k(t) = \sqrt{\varepsilon_k} \sum_{i=1}^{M} b_{k,i} a_k(t - iT) \tag{4}$$

where ε_k is the signal energy per bit for the k-th user.

A receiver receives the signal $r(t)$ which is the sum of delayed versions of all transmitted signals and thermal noise. The received signal $r(t)$ is:

$$\begin{aligned} r(t) &= \sum_{k=1}^{K} s_k(t - \tau_k) + n(t) \\ &= \sum_{k=1}^{K} \sqrt{\varepsilon_k} \sum_{i=1}^{M} b_{k,i} a_k(t - iT - \tau_k) + n(t) \end{aligned} \tag{5}$$

where $n(t)$ is a white Gaussian channel noise with two-sided power spectral density $N_0 / 2$, and τ_k denotes the relative time delay between the k-th user and base station.

In addition to the general system, symbol-synchronous CDMA systems will be also considered. Synchronous systems find applications in time slotted channels with a base station transmitting to remote mobile units and also in relays between control stations. The K users maintain time synchronism, therefore, in the model described above, the relative time delays associated with all users are assumed to be zero, i.e., $\tau_k = 0$. The synchronous problem will also be constructed for providing a manageable setting to better understand the issues in the more general and difficult asynchronous scenario. In the chapter, we are particularly interested in the synchronous CDMA multiuser detection systems. Moreover, in subsection B, we will show that the neural network approach is still valid for asynchronous CDMA multiuser detection.

Since the received power of the signal waveform for each user is affected by path loss and shadowing; e.g., a shadowing phenomenon due to physical structure blocking the transmission path between a transmitter and a receiver, the received signal via a synchronous CDMA channel of (5) would become

$$r(t) = \sum_{k=1}^{K} \sum_{i=1}^{M} \sqrt{\varepsilon_k \alpha_k} \, b_{k,i} a_k (t - iT) + n(t)$$

$$= \sum_{k=1}^{K} \sum_{i=1}^{M} \sqrt{E_k} \, b_{k,i} a_k (t - iT) + n(t)$$

(6)

where α_k and $E_k (= \varepsilon_k \alpha_k)$ are the power loss factor and the received energy per bit for the k-th user's signal respectively.

A Formulation of Neural-Based Energy Function for Synchronous Maximum-Likelihood CDMA Multiuser Detection

In optimization problems, one needs to formulate a particular objective function incorporating with a number of constraints, which is to be optimized. This constrained optimization problem is then mapped onto the energy function of a Hopfield-like network. The energy function consists of two terms: the cost term and the constraint term. The cost term is the optimization cost function that is independent of the constraint term. This constraint term is the penalty imposed that for violating the constraints. Thus, $E = cost + \lambda \times penalty$, where λ is a penalty parameter. Usually, the energy function of a Hopfield-like network of K neurons can be characterized by a simple Ising-Hamiltonian of K spins [26] as follows:

$$E = -\frac{1}{2} \sum_{i=1}^{K} \sum_{j=1}^{K} w_{ij} s_i s_j - \sum_{i=1}^{K} I_i s_i$$

(7)

where w_{ij} represents the synaptic weight of the connection from neuron j to neuron i, I_i is an input bias or threshold applied to neuron i from an external source, and s_i denotes the state of neuron i or the i-th spin. The state space of each neuron or spin is $s_i \in \{-1,1\}$, $1 \leq i \leq K$. In addition, Hopfield and Tank [11] have shown that in the case of symmetric connections, this network always leads to a convergence to stable states. Moreover, this network with vanishing diagonal connection ($w_{ij} = 0$) have minim only at the corners of the K-dimensional hypercube $[-1,1]^K$ [11], [15].

In synchronous transmission, the optimum maximum-likelihood receiver computes the log-likelihood function over a specific data symbol interval, i.e., $[0,T]$,

$$\Lambda(\mathbf{b}) = -\int_0^T \left[r(t) - \sum_{k=1}^K \sqrt{E_k} b_{k,0} a_k(t) \right]^2 dt \tag{8}$$

where $\mathbf{b} = [b_{1,0}, b_{2,0}, \cdots, b_{K,0}]^T$.

Since the integral involving $r^2(t)$ is common to all possible sequences $\{b_{k,0}\}$ and is of no relevance in determining which sequence was transmitted, therefore the optimum decision rule can be expressed as a constrained integer quadratic optimization problem and given by

$$\underset{\mathbf{b}}{Max} \left[2\sum_{k=1}^K \sqrt{E_k} b_{k,0} \int_0^T r(t) a_k(t) dt - \sum_{j=1}^K \sum_{k=1}^K \sqrt{E_j E_k} b_{j,0} b_{k,0} \int_0^T a_j(t) a_k(t) dt \right] \tag{9}$$

subject to $b_{k,0} \in \{-1,1\}, 1 \le k \le K$.

Equation (9) can be rewritten in form of correlation matrix

$$\underset{\mathbf{b}}{Max} \left[2\mathbf{y}^T \mathbf{b} - \mathbf{b}^T H \mathbf{b} \right] \tag{10}$$

subject to $b_{k,0} \in \{-1,1\}, 1 \le k \le K$ where $\mathbf{y} = [y_1, y_2, ..., y_k]^T$ is the vector of sufficient statistics

$$y_k = \int_0^T r(t) \left(\sqrt{E_k} a_k(t) \right) dt = < r(t), \sqrt{E_k} a_k(t) > \tag{11}$$

Here, y_k represents the cross-correlation or matched filter output of the received signal with the k-th spreading code times its received amplitude over an interval $[0, T]$. Notice that $< \cdot, \cdot >$ denotes the inner product.

Further, the (j, k)-th entry of the matrix of cross-correlation, H, is defined as:

$$\begin{aligned} h_{jk} &= \int_0^T \left(\sqrt{E_j} a_j(t) \right) \left(\sqrt{E_k} a_k(t) \right) dt \\ &= < \sqrt{E_j} a_j(t), \sqrt{E_k} a_k(t) > \end{aligned} \tag{12}$$

The constrained maximization problem of (10) can be converted into its equivalent constrained minimization problem with neural variables $s_i s$ as follows:

$$\underset{\mathbf{s}}{Min} \left[\frac{1}{2} \mathbf{s}^T H \mathbf{s} - \mathbf{y}^T \mathbf{s} \right] \tag{13}$$

subject to $s_i \in \{-1,1\}, 1 \le k \le K$ where $\mathbf{s} = [s_1, s_2, ..., s_K]^T = \mathbf{b}$.

To solve the constrained quadratic programming problem defined in Equation (13), we convert it to an equivalent unconstrained problem. The way to do this is to define a general energy function (pseudo-cost function):

$$E = \frac{1}{2}\mathbf{s}^T H \mathbf{s} - \mathbf{y}^T \mathbf{s} + \sum_{k=1}^{K} \lambda_k (1 - s_k)(1 + s_k) \tag{14}$$

where the last term of the energy function is referred to as the penalty function used to ensure the minimum point towards the corners of the hypercube, $[-1,1]^K$ and λ_k is the penalty parameter for neuron k. If the value of λ_k is chosen as $\frac{1}{2} < \sqrt{E_k}a_k(t), \sqrt{E_k}a_k(t) > \left(= \frac{1}{2}h_{kk}\right)$, $1 \le k \le K$, thus the diagonal elements of the synaptic connection weight matrix vanish. By neglecting the constant $\left(\sum_{k=1}^{K} \lambda_k\right)$ in Eq. (14), Equation (14) can be expressed as the form of a standard energy function

$$E(\mathbf{s}) = -\frac{1}{2}\mathbf{s}^T W \mathbf{s} - \mathbf{I}^T \mathbf{s} \tag{15}$$

where $W = -\tilde{H}$, $\mathbf{I} = \mathbf{y}$ denotes the input bias vector, and

$$\tilde{H} = H - diag\left(< \sqrt{E_k}a_k(t), \sqrt{E_k}a_k(t) >, 1 \le k \le K\right) = H - diag\left(h_{11}, h_{22}, \cdots, h_{KK}\right)$$

denotes a zero-diagonal matrix.

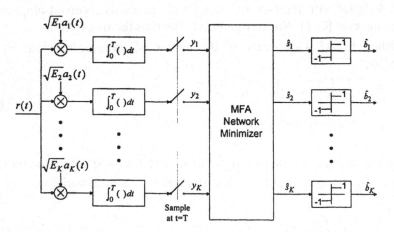

Fig. 1. Structure of a MFA neural network multiuser receiver for a K-user synchronous CDMA system.

Figure 1 shows the optimum neural-based receiver for symbol-synchronous transmission that consists of a bank of K correlators or matched filters followed by a Hopfield-like mean field annealing network detector that minimizes the energy function given by Eq. (15). Then the detector selects the sequence corresponding to the smallest energy or the largest log-likelihood metric. Moreover, Lupas and Verdu [3] showed that the optimum asynchronous maximum-likelihood CDMA receiver can be converted into an equivalent optimum synchronous CDMA receiver with MK users, where M denotes the packet length of data. Let $\mathbf{b}$ represent the data sequences from the K users and be equal to a $MK \times 1$ vector, $\mathbf{b} = \left[\mathbf{b}^T(1), \mathbf{b}^T(2), \cdots, \mathbf{b}^T(M) \right]$, and $\mathbf{b}(i) = \left[b_{1,i}, b_{2,i}, \cdots, b_{K,i} \right]^T$, $1 \le i \le M$. Without loss of generality, it is assumed that the users are numbered such that their transmission delays satisfy $0 \le \tau_1 \le \tau_2 \le \cdots \le \tau_K \le T$. Moreover, we assume that the receiver knows the received signal powers $\{E_k, 1 \le k \le K\}$ for the K users and their delays $\{\tau_k\}$. Clearly, the users via control channel must measure these parameters at receiver as side information.

Similarly, from the above derivation for synchronous CDMA, the optimum decision on $\mathbf{b}$ can be characterized by the following integer quadratic optimization problem:

$$\underset{\mathbf{b}}{Max} \left| 2\mathbf{y}^T \mathbf{b} - \mathbf{b}^T H_a \mathbf{b} \right| \tag{16}$$

subject to $b_{k,i} \in \{-1, 1\}, 1 \le i \le M, 1 \le k \le K$, where H_a is a $MK \times MK$ symmetric block-Toeplitz matrix given by:

$$H_a = \begin{bmatrix} H_a(0) & H_a(-1) & 0 & 0 & \cdots & 0 \\ H_a(1) & H_a(0) & H_a(-1) & 0 & \cdots & 0 \\ 0 & H_a(1) & H_a(0) & H_a(-1) & \ddots & 0 \\ \vdots & \vdots & \ddots & 0 & \ddots & 0 \\ 0 & 0 & 0 & \cdots & H_a(1) & H_a(0) \end{bmatrix} \tag{17}$$

and $H_a(m)$ is a $K \times K$ matrix with elements

$$h_{ij}(m) = \int_{-\infty}^{\infty} \left(\sqrt{E_j} a_j \left(t - \tau_j \right) \right) \left(\sqrt{E_k} a_k \left(t + mT - \tau_k \right) \right) dt \tag{18}$$

It should be noted that $H_a(-m) = H_a^T(m)$ and $H_a(m) = 0, \forall m > 1$ since the spreading code waveforms are zero outside [0, T]. In [16], $\mathbf{y}$ denotes the MK correlator or matched filter outputs and can be expressed by a $MK \times 1$ vector

$$\mathbf{y} = \left[\mathbf{y}^T(1), \mathbf{y}^T(2), \cdots, \mathbf{y}^T(M) \right]^T \tag{19}$$

where $\mathbf{y}(i) = [y_{1,i}, y_{2,i}, \cdots, y_{K,i}]^T$, is the vector of K matched filter outputs, $i = 1, 2, \cdots, M$. The sampled output of the matched filter for the i-th bit of the k-th user, $i = 1, 2, \cdots, M$, $k = 1, 2, \cdots, K$, is

$$y_{k,i} = \int_{iT+\tau_k}^{(i+1)T+\tau_k} r(t) \left[\sqrt{E_k} \, a_k (t - iT - \tau_k) \right] dt \qquad (20)$$

Using vector notation, it can be shown that the MK matched filter outputs can be expressed in the form

$$\mathbf{y} = H_a \mathbf{b} + \mathbf{n} \qquad (21)$$

where $\mathbf{n} = \left[\mathbf{n}^T(1), \mathbf{n}^T(2), \cdots, \mathbf{n}^T(M) \right]^T$ is an $MK \times 1$ Gaussian noise vector and the $K \times 1$ Gaussian noise vectors $\mathbf{n}^T(i)$, $i = 1, 2, \dots, M$ have zero mean and autocorrelation matrix

$$E\left[\mathbf{n}(i) \mathbf{n}^T(j) \right] = \frac{1}{2} N_0 H_a(i - j) \qquad (22)$$

and $\frac{1}{2} N_0$ denotes the power spectral density of AWGN channel noise.

Equation (21) can be interpreted as an equivalent synchronous problem where the whole-transmitted sequence is considered to result from MK users, labeled as shown in Figure 2, during one transmission interval of duration $T_a = M \times T + \tau_k - \tau_1$.

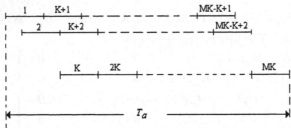

Fig. 2. Equivalent MK-user synchronous transmitted sequence for a K-user asynchronous CDMA system with a transmission time interval $T_a = MT + \tau_K - \tau_1$

Then the results presented here for finite transmission length can be derived via analysis of synchronous multiuser communication. Hence, we are able to derive the energy function for the asynchronous CDMA multiuser detection via the same procedure discussed in previous subsection as follows:

$$E(\mathbf{s}) = -\frac{1}{2} \mathbf{s}^T W_a \mathbf{s} - \mathbf{I}_a^T \mathbf{s} \qquad (23)$$

where $W_a = -\tilde{H}_a$, $\mathbf{I}_a = \mathbf{y}$, and $\tilde{H}_a = H_a - diag\left(h_{kk}(0), 1 \le k \le MK \right)$.

In asynchronous multiuser communication, the neural-based receiver consists of a bank of MK matched filters. The neural detector determines the optimum decision on **b** by minimizing the energy function of Eq. (23).

3
Equations of Motion for Hopfield-Like Mean Field Annealing Networks

In the previous section, the CDMA multiuser detection problem has been mapped onto the Hopfield-like mean field annealing neural network framework, and its associated energy function has been formulated. The remaining task is to employ a robust method to minimize the energy function. Prior to introducing those possible robust methods, we would like to examine the computational complexity of optimum multiuser detection. Verdu [6] showed that the problem of optimum multiuser detection is nondeterministic polynomial time hard (NP-hard) in the number of users and therefore does not admit polynomial time algorithms. The mathematical expression of the above discussion can be expressed as:

Lemma 1 [6] Given $K \in Z^+$, $y \in R^K$, and a nonnegative definite matrix of cross-correlation between the spreading code waveforms with the received amplitudes, $H \in R^{K \times K}$. The optimum multiuser detection is to find $b^* \in A^K$ that maximizes $\left(2b^T y - b^T H\, b\right)$ where K represents the number of users (or MK for asynchronous CDMA), and A denotes the finite alphabet used to generate the data symbols $b_1, b_2, \cdots, b_K$ and $b = [b_1, b_2, \cdots, b_K]^T$. This optimum detection problem can be solved in $O\left(|A|^K\right)$ operations. Note that the time complexity of BPSK CDMA multiuser detection is $O\left(2^K\right)$ since $A = \{-1, 1\}$.

While the exponential complexity of multiuser detection may be acceptable in CDMA systems with a small number of users, it is prohibitive in large CDMA systems with the number of users in excess of 10 or 20, depending on the transmission rate, the available computing power, and the alphabet size. For example, a 10-user 100 kb/s system with QPSK signaling (i.e. $|A| = 4$) would require up to 10^5 million computation of the likelihood function per second.

In order to solve such a NP-hard combinational optimization in a reasonable time, the Hopfield-like neural network is one of the possible candidates for tackling this difficulty. However, conventional Hopfield networks based on the gradient method [11] are local in scope and may be trapped in local minimum. Recently, several robust methods such as simulated annealing (SA) [12] and genetic algorithm [13] have been proposed to solve large scale problems; however, not every problem can be mapped onto the framework suitable for these methods. In addition, these methods may take an excessive computation time to reach the global minimum. To overcome this major limitation, we use a mean-field approximation, according to which the stochastic, binary-state neurons of the Boltzmann machine based on simulated annealing are replaced by deterministic, analog ones [14], [15]. Mean-field annealing machine [16], [17], [18], [19] is derived from the stochastic simulated annealing by incorporating the annealing mechanism with the Hopfield energy function. In SA, there are two conceptual operations involved: a thermostatic operation that schedules the decrease of the temperature, and a random relaxation process that searches for the equilibrium solution at each temperature. The random relaxation allows the search to climb uphill, thus providing the SA a mechanism to escape from local minimum. In MFA, these two operations are still needed. The main difference between SA and MFA is that the relaxation process in searching for the equilibrium solution in a stochastic manner has been replaced by searching for the mean value of the solutions. MFA has been shown to be robust in solving large-scale problems, and more efficient than SA. Equilibrium can be reached faster by using mean [19], and thus the MFA speed up several tens to hundreds times over the SA.

A Determination of Mean Field Equations for the Optimum CDMA Multiuser Detection Using the Saddle-Point Method

In this section, we would like to derive the mean-field equations for optimum CDMA multiuser detection in a more rigorous manner using the saddle-point method. It should be noted that the original derivation of the mean-field equation for a number of specific optimization problems, such as graph partition problem and travelling salesman problem (TSP), was proposed by Peterson [17] according to the assumptions of $s \in \{0,1\}^K$. However, the mean-field equations for CDMA multiuser detection should be derived based on the different assumptions of $s \in \{-1,1\}^K$. Here, we would like to modify Peterson's derivation [17] to meet the new assumptions. The relaxation in SA is made according to Boltzmann distribution [12]

$$P(\mathbf{s}) = e^{-E(\mathbf{s})/T} / Z \tag{24}$$

where $s \in \{-1, 1\}^K$ is any one of the possible configurations specified by the corresponding neuron set, $E(s)$ is the energy of the corresponding configuration, s, T is the parameter called temperature, Z is the Potts glass model partition function [27] given by

$$Z = \sum_{s \in \{-1,1\}^K} e^{-E(s)/T}$$ (25)

and the summation covers all possible neuron configurations. Note that this temperature is analogous to the gain of the neurons in a neural network and may be used to tune such networks for better performance.

In the mean field theory, instead of concerning the neuron variables directly, we shall investigate their means by defining

$$V = <s>$$ (26)

where V is a $K \times 1$ vector with elements V_i, $1 \le i \le K$ which are called the mean-field variables.

By introducing the other mean-field variables, U_i, $1 \le i \le K$ to Eq. (25), the discrete sum in Eq. (25) can be replaced by multiple nested integrals over the continuous mean-field variables V_i and U_i, $1 \le i \le K$ [15], [16]

$$Z = \sum_s \int_{R^K} e^{-E(V)/T} \delta(s - V) dV$$

$$= \left(\frac{1}{2\pi j}\right)^K \sum_s \int_{R^K} dV e^{-E(V)/T} \int_{I^K} dU e^{U^T(s-V)}$$ (27)

$$= \left(\frac{1}{\pi j}\right)^K \prod_{i=1}^K \int_{-\infty}^\infty \int_{-\infty}^\infty \exp\left(-\frac{1}{T} E_{eff}(V, U, T)\right) dV_i dU_i$$

where I denotes the imaginary axis, i. e., $(-j\infty, j\infty)$, $\delta(\cdot)$ represents the vector-valued Dirac delta function, and $E_{eff}(V, U, T)$ is the effective energy defined by

$$E_{eff}(V, U, T) = E(V) + T \sum_{i=1}^K [U_i V_i - \ln(\cosh U_i)]$$ (28)

It has been indicated by Peterson [15], [16] that the partition function Z is actually dominated by the saddle point, i.e.,

$$Z \approx C e^{-\frac{1}{T} E_{eff}(V_0, U_0, T)}$$ (29)

where C is a constant, and (V_0, U_0) is the saddle point of Eq. (28). Thus, the mechanism of the MFA is likewise governed by the mechanism of the saddle point. Moreover, the saddle point of the partition function Z will be found among the roots of the equations:

$$\frac{\partial}{\partial U_i} E_{eff}(\mathbf{V}, \mathbf{U}, T) = 0 \tag{30}$$

$$\frac{\partial}{\partial V_i} E_{eff}(\mathbf{V}, \mathbf{U}, T) = 0 \tag{31}$$

From Eq. (28), (30), and (31), it yields:

$$V_i = \tanh U_i = \tanh\left(-\frac{1}{T}\frac{\partial E(\mathbf{V})}{\partial \mathbf{V}_i}\right), \quad 1 \le i \le K \tag{32}$$

where $\tanh V_i$ is the hyperbolic tangent that results from the differentiation of $\ln(\cosh U_i)$. Equation (32) is known as the general mean-field equations for $s \in \{-1,1\}^K$, sometimes called the mean-field theory Potts neural network equations.

Substituting Eq. (15) into Eq. (32), we obtain the mean-field equations for the synchronous CDMA multiuser detection problem as follows:

$$V_i = \tanh\left[\frac{1}{T}\left(\sum_{j=1, j\neq i}^{K}\left(w_{ij}V_j + I_i\right)\right)\right], 1 \le i \le K \tag{33}$$

Equation (33) represents the steady state solution to the system differential equations

$$\frac{dV_i}{dt} = -\eta\left\{V_i - \tanh\left[\frac{1}{T}\left(\sum_{j\neq i}^{K} w_{ij}V_j + I_i\right)\right]\right\}, 1 \le i \le K \tag{34}$$

where $\eta = RC$ is a time constant.

Equations (33) and (34) are also valid for the asynchronous CDMA multiuser detection when the number of users is replaced by MK which is the number of users for its equivalent synchronous CDMA system.

4
Numerical Implementation for Mean-Field Annealing Machines

When implementing the MFA Equations (33) numerically, a fixed-point iteration or relaxation process is used at each temperature to obtain the steady state neuron values

$$V_i^{(l+1)} = \tanh\left[\frac{1}{T}\cdot\left(\sum_{j=1}^{K} w_{ij}V_j^{(l)} + I_i\right)\right], \quad 1 \le i \le K \tag{35}$$

The superscript i indicates the iteration index. Note that for a temperature T close to zero, Eq. (35) closely approximates the following equation:

$$V_i^{(l+1)} = sgn\left[\sum_{j=1}^{K} w_{ij}V_j^{(l)} + I_i\right] \tag{36}$$

Note that Eq. (36) corresponds to the discrete Hopfield neural model [11]. But this model takes us to the closest local minimum rather than the global minimum.

For each iteration, there are many neurons to be updated. We can either update all neurons synchronously or one after another asynchronously. In practice, it is found that asynchronous updating has a better performance. In MFA, there are two nested loops involved in its algorithm. The inner loop is the relaxation process of (35). The outer one is a temperature decrement procedure according to the linear annealing schedule starting from the critical temperature, T_c,

$$T(m+1) = 0.9 \cdot T(m) \tag{37}$$

where $T(0) = T_c$ and m is the index of the iteration for the outer loop.

The critical temperature is the highest temperature at which one neuron V_i reaches -1 or 1 from its original trivial state, i.e. 0. The value of T_c is determined by the eigenvalue distribution of the connection weight matrix W and may be set to $\lambda_{\max}(W)$, which is the largest absolute eigenvalue or dominant eigenvalue of W [17]. The value of $\lambda_{\max}(W)$ can be found by the power method [20] or neural network [21]. To avoid the excessive computation and hardware implementation, Peterson [17] have proposed an efficient method to estimate $\lambda_{\max}(W)$ in low computation complexity.

The stopping criterion for the annealing procedure is defined by the temperature at which the network is saturated. The network is saturated if the following conditions are met:

(i) Endpoint criterion: all neuron values fall within the range [-1.0, -0.8] or within the range of [0.8, 1.0] without any exception, i.e., $0.8 < |V_i| < 1$, $1 \le i \le K$.

(ii) The saturation parameter $\sum_s = \frac{1}{N_s}\sum_{i=1}^{K}(V_i)^2 > 0.9$, where N_s is the number of neurons that have values within the range of [-1.0, -0.8] or [0.8, 1.0].

The procedure to perform the CDMA multiuser detection using MFA is summarized below:

Step 0: [Initialization]
(i) For a given cross-correlation matrix, H and a given vector of sufficient statistics, y in CDMA multiuser detection problem, establish the synaptic matrix W and the bias vector $\mathbf{I}$;
(ii) Determine the critical temperature T_c by a simple low-complexity approximation formula (A. 41) that appears in appendix of [17].
(iii) $m = 0$ and $T(0) = T_c$.

Step 1: [Start the temperature decrement procedure]
WHILE (The network is not saturated)
BEGIN
Step 2: [Initialize neurons with random numbers]
$for(i \leftarrow 1; i \leq K; i \leftarrow i+1)$

$$V_i \leftarrow 0.1 \times rand[-1, 1] \tag{38}$$

Step 3: [Start the relaxation process to reach the equilibrium point]
$l \leftarrow 0$
Do until (Equilibrium conditions are satisfied)
BEGIN
$for(i \leftarrow 1; i \leq K; i \leftarrow i+1)$

$$V_i^{(l+1)} = \tanh\left[\frac{1}{T(m)} \cdot \left(\sum_{j=1}^{K} w_{ij} V_j^{(l)} + I_i\right)\right] \tag{39}$$

$l \leftarrow l+1$
End Do-Block of Step 3
Step 4: [Anneal the network using cooling schedule]
$T(m+1) \leftarrow 0.9T(m)$

$m \leftarrow m+1$
End Do-Block of Step 1

Note that $rand[-1, 1]$ denotes a uniform distribution used to generate a random value within $[-1, 1]$. It should be mentioned that the condition of reaching an equilibrium point at the $(l+1)$-th iteration could be determined by the following equation:

$$\frac{1}{K} \cdot \sum_{i=1}^{K} \left|V_i^{(l+1)} - V_i^{(l)}\right| < \Delta \tag{40}$$

where the value of Δ is chosen within $[10^{-3}, 0.05]$ (for details, see [17], [19]).

5
Programmable Analog VLSI Implementation of Mean-Field Annealing Machines

For the VLSI implementation of neural systems, analog approach seems to be extremely attractive in terms of hardware size, power, and speed [28]. Unlike digital approach, the analog VLSI implementation would operate at a much higher speed and it requires less hardware than a digital implementation [27]. In addition, mean-field annealing process can be easily applied to the VLSI design by changing the gain of the output neuron amplifier. Alspector et al. [24] have proposed an analog VLSI implementation to achieve the mean-field annealing machine in real time manner (submicrosecond interval). In this chapter, we present a more compact analog CMOS circuit for the implementation of MFA machine. Figure 3 shows an example of the complete circuit schematic for realizing the system dynamics differential equation shown in Eq. (34) for the first neuron (amplifier) with an adjustable gain $\beta = 1/T$.

Rather than the temperature T being gradually lowered, the amplifier gain, β, is increased from near zero to a high value. It should be noted that the proposed CMOS circuit is also valid for the other neurons, $2 \leq i \leq K$. Furthermore, the implementation of the synaptic weights, w_{ij}, for the MFA machine is achieved via an adaptation of the vector multipliers with the programmable capability, where the weights are assigned as positive or negative voltage levels according to CDMA cross-correlation matrix via dynamic environment.

The neurons are realized by a number of gain-adjustable CMOS amplifiers, which are interconnected through the MOS vector multipliers. Each multiplier implements the scalar vector product of the vector of neuron outputs, V_i, $1 \leq i \leq K$, and the vector of the synaptic weights, w_{ij}, $1 \leq i, j \leq K$. For a network of K neurons, there is K such scalar vector products. Each scalar product is achieved using only one operational amplifier and $4(K+1)$ MOS transistors of two K-tuple vector inputs resulting in an economic analog MOS VLSI implementation using depletion transistors. Gates of MOS transistors can be connected to ground resulting in a special case of the vector multiplier that allows the multiplication of voltages that are referred to ground. Positive or negative levels can be assigned to the synaptic weights connected to the first neuron, w_{1j}, $1 \leq j \leq K$.

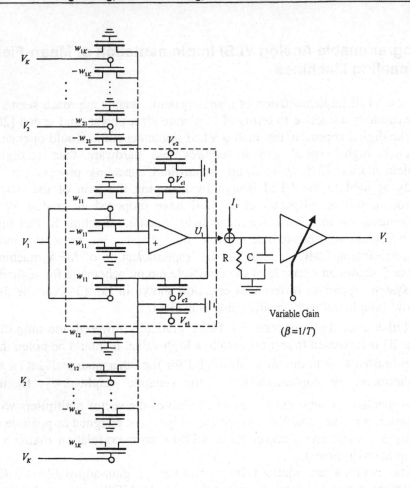

Fig. 3(a). A CMOS circuit for the VLSI implementation of MFA neural network for the first neuron with the capability of programmable weights and adjustable gain.

The outputs of K neurons, V_j, are feedback as inputs to the j-th analog scale multiplier, $1 \le j \le K$. For instance, the output of the two-input scalar multiplier shown in the dotted subsection in Figure 3(a) is proportional to $(w_{11} \times V_1)$, where V_1, the output of neuron 1, and w_{11}, its associated weights are voltages referred to ground. Thus, the overall output of the vector multiplier, U_1 is given by

$$U_1 = \sum_{j=1}^{K} c \times w_{1j} \times V_j \tag{41}$$

where c is the constant that depends on the characteristics of MOS implementation. It is interesting to note that the constant could be compensated by absorbing its value into w_{1j}. For example, one may precompute the new weights, $\hat{w}_{1j}$ as $c^{-1} \times w_{1j}$. The input-output compatibility of the overall MOS implementation is of particular interest because the relatively high output impedance node of the double inverter is connected to the almost no restriction on the fan-in/fan-out capability. More details about the analog MOS vector multiplier are given by Mead [28]. The MFA neuron transfer function in numerical software computation is specified as an exact mathematical equation, which is able to decide the direction of seeking out the global optimal solution during the cooling process. In our CMOS VLSI implementation, the MFA neuron transfer function is realized by Lee and Sheu's gain-adjustable amplifier [29] illustrated in Figure 3(b).

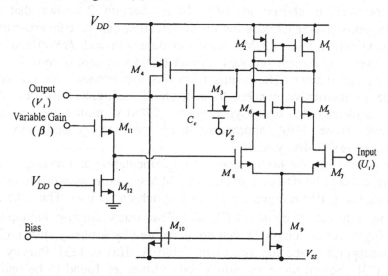

Fig. 3(b). A CMOS circuit for the VLSI implementation of gain-adjustable neuron amplifier

In Figure 3(b), transistors M_5 and M_6 form an improved cascade stage to increase the voltage gain and M_3 operates in the triode region to provide the frequency-stabilization resistance. The amplifier voltage gain can be changed by externally applied gain control voltage, which adjusts the drain-to-source resistance ratio of transistors M_{11} and M_{12}. If the gate voltage of M_{11} is below transistor threshold voltage, the amplifier operates in the open-loop high-gain configuration (lowest near zero temperature).

When the gate voltage of M_{11} increases above the threshold voltage, the closed-loop gain of the amplifier decreases. In other words, the values of its corresponding temperature are increasing. The gain-adjustable amplifiers are able to execute the cooling process in MFA machines. More details about the function of the other transistors $M_1, M_2, M_4, M_7, M_8, M_9$ and M_{10} can be found in [29].

6
Computer Simulation Results

Performance comparison of the conventional matched filter, optimum and MFA network multiuser detections for a CDMA AWGN channel are carried out via Monte Carlo simulations. The termination criterion, Δ, for MFA network is chosen as 10^{-2}. Since Section 2 shows that any asynchronous K-user CDMA multiuser detection can be converted to its equivalent synchronous CDMA multiuser detection with MK effective or virtual users, only a synchronous six-user CDMA system is considered in computer simulations. The results from this synchronous system would provide an instructive concept to understand the applicability of MFA neural networks to the asynchronous CDMA multiuser detection. Moreover, these MFA approaches lend itself to generalization for asynchronous CDMA systems.

In our simulations for both numerical implementation and analog CMOS circuits, the data bit rate of a practical CDMA system is assumed to be 100 Kbits/sec using BPSK signaling for each synchronous user. Thus, the data bit time interval T equals 10^{-5} sec. The users employ autooptimal spreading codes of length 31 that are generated by a binary shift register and correspond to the top entries in Table A. 1(a) in [23]. Pursley and Roefs [23] showed these spreading code sequences found to be optimal with respect to certain peak and mean square correlation parameters which play an important role in the bit error rate analysis of the conventional detector. Then, the chip interval, T_c, equals $\left(\frac{1}{31} \times 10^{-5}\right)$ sec. It is assumed that this synchronous six-user CDMA channel is in a severe near-far condition with five equal energy interferes where $E_i / E_1 = 6\,\mathrm{dB}$ for $2 \leq i \leq 6$. In other words, the users except the desired first user have equal larger received energy level and provide the interfering signals to the desired user. In Figure 4, the average bit-error rate (BER) of the first user for each of the three detectors (matched filter, optimum, and MFA) is plotted versus the signal-to-noise ratio of the first user (the weakest user), i.e., E_1 / N_0. The value of each average bit-error probability was computed from an ensemble of 10^6 transmitted symbols for each value of the E_1 / N_0. The BER of the matched filter detector is worse than that of the optimum detector because of the severe near-far problem. Since MFA network always converges to the global minimum, the BER of the MFA multiuser detector is nearly equal to that of the optimum one over the range of E_1 / N_0. Next, we would like to consider the near-far effect in the six-user CDMA channel.

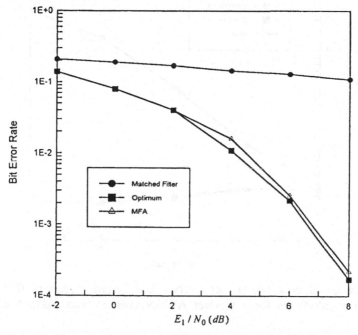

Fig. 4. Average bit error rate versus SNR of user 1, E_1/N_0 for a six-user AWGN channel with five active equal energy interferers, $E_i/E_1 = 6$ dB, $2 \leq i \leq 6$, and $N_c = 31$.

In Figure 4, the BER of the first user for each of the detectors is depicted as a function of the near-far ration (NFR), E_i / N_1 ranging from -10 to 10 dB corresponding to the i-th interfering signal being a tenth of the desired signal power to ten times that level under $E_1 / N_0 = 6$ dB . For simplicity, all the interfering signals are assumed to have identical energy level.It is clearly from this figure that the performance of the matched filter detector becomes worse as the energy level of the interfering signal increases. Since the matched filter ignores the multiple-access interference, it has an acceptable performance only for very low values of E_i / N_1, and degrades exponentially as this ration increases. On the other hand, the optimum detector is able to eliminate the multiple-access interference over the range of E_i / N_1. The BER performance of the optimum detector is almost not affected by and remains invariant with the interfering signal strength. From Figure 5, the performance of the MFA multiuser detector closely tracks that of the optimum detector over the range of E_i / N_1.

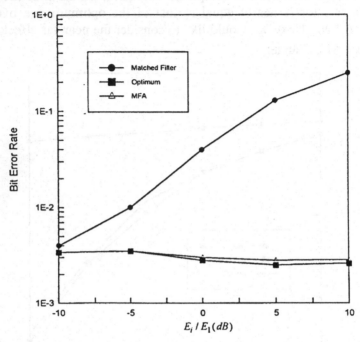

Fig. 5. Average bit error rate of user 1 versus near-far ratio E_i/E_1 with five active equal energy interferers for a six-user AWGN channel with E_1/N_0=6 dB and N_c=31.

It is interesting to examine the computational efficiency of both numerical implementation and the analog CMOS VLSI circuit. For numerical implementation, its computational load is in terms of the average number of iterations to reach steady state (relaxation process in the inner loop) and the average number of iterations in annealing process (outer loop) over 10^6 transmitted symbols for six different values of E_1 / N_0 from -2dB to 8 dB. The average numbers of iterations involved in both the inner and outer loops are found to be 31 and 22, respectively. Next, we would like to estimate computation time of the analog CMOS VLSI implementation for MFA-based CDMA detection. For a fixed amplifier gain corresponding to a temperature determined by the annealing process in the outer loop, the convergence time for the analog CMOS circuit implementation for the relaxation process in the inner loop is within the RC time constant of the circuit. A continuous-time Hopfield network can actually realize this analog relaxation process. Culhane, Peckerar and Marrian [30] showed that Hopfield-like analog neural circuit designed to perform the quadratic nonlinear programming would lead to a steady state solution in a time determined by its RC time constant, not by algorithmic time complexity. Their argument is also valid for our analog implementation for the quadratic nonlinear programming shown in either Equation (15) or (23).

We use an advanced CMOS family called the ACT (Advanced CMOS TTL Compatible) to implement the analog MFA circuit proposed in Section 5. This family is very fast, comparable to the ALS (Advanced Low-power Schottky) TTL, and they can source or sink gobs of current, more than most TTL circuits can [31], [32]. For example, the propagation delay of an ACT-based NAND gate is identified as 4.75 ns compared to 4 ns for ALS TTL NAND gate. The amount of time that the output of the ACT-based MFA circuit takes to change from one state to another (equilibrium state) when its associated gain (temperature) is fixed during the transition is called the transition time. This transition time is actually identical to the convergence time for the ACT-based circuit implemented for the analog computation of the relaxation process or Hopfield network. It should be mentioned that the MFA machine becomes purely a Hopfield network when its temperature is fixed. From Figure 3 (a) and (b), the transition time depends mainly on four factors, the load resistance R, load capacitance C, the "on" transistor resistance R_{on}, and the stray capacitance, C_s. In other words, the transition time is in proportional to the RC time constant resulted from these four factors. Nevertheless, to avoid excessive evaluation of both the "on" transistor resistance and stray capacitance, the values of load resistance and capacitance could be chosen appropriately, and then become the dominant parameters in determination of RC time constant for the analog MFA circuit. Therefore, the transition time is purely dependent on the time constant, $\eta = RC$. In our experiments, the value of η is chosen as 300 ns. Figure 6 shows an example of the time evolution of the reduction of energy by performing the proposed CMOS analog circuit on HSPICE simulation package when all neuron amplifier gains β's are assigned to be 10^3.

Energy

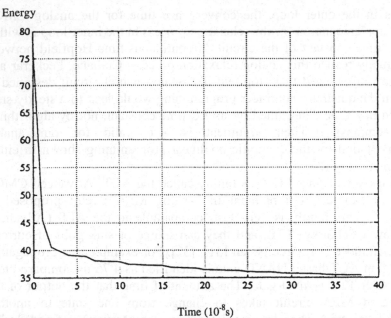

Time (10^{-8}s)

Fig. 6. The time evolution of the reduction of energy for 6-user CDMA detection when all neuron amplifier gains (β's) are equal to 10^3, E_1/N_0=4 dB and E_i/E_1=6 dB, $2 \leq i \leq 6$.

The energy has reached the equilibrium state after 380 ns. Moreover, it is found that the transition time is almost fixed for different values of neuron amplifier gains since it is mainly in proportion to the RC time constant only. For an ensemble of 10^6 transmitted data for six different values of E_b/N_0, average transition time is found to be 387.462 ns. As shown above, the average iteration number of annealing process (or gain-adjustable process) is 22. Thus, the average convergence time for the ACT-based MFA circuit for the six-user CDMA detection is estimated to be 8.524 μs.

7
Conclusions

This chapter has introduced multiuser detection based on MFA neural networks, which is capable of optimally demodulating spread-spectrum signals in a multiple-access AWGN channel. It was shown that the energy function of the network could be expressed in terms of the log-likelihood function of the optimum CDMA multiuser detection. The mean field equations for the multiuser detection problem are derived from the energy function using the saddle point method. A cost-effective relaxation process based on these mean field equations has been conducted to efficiently seek out the global optimum solution of this energy function. The bit-error probability of MFA multiuser detector was compared with the conventional and optimum receivers. The BER performance of the MFA receiver is independent of the strength of the interfering users and is better than the matched filter detector by a few orders of magnitude over a wide range of signal-to-noise ration for the weakest user. Moreover, the simulation results indicate that the MFA detector is able to achieve the near-optimum BER performance, which is comparable to that of the optimum detector even in a severe near-far condition. Finally, an ACT-based VLSI implementation has been proposed to realize the MFA-based CDMA detector in a real time manner.

References

[1]   A. J. Viterbi: "CDMA, Principle of Spread Spectrum Communication", Addison-Wesley Company, NY, 1995.
[2]   A. Duel-Hallen, J. Holtzman, Z. Zvonar: "Multiuser detection CDMA systems", *IEEE Personal Communication*, vol. 2, no. 2, pp. 46-58, April 1995.
[3]   R. Lupas, S. Verdu: "Linear multiuser detectors for synchronous code-division multiple access channels", *IEEE Trans. Inform. Theory*, vol. 35, no. 1, pp. 123-136, Jan. 1989.
[4]   R. Lupas, S. Verdu: "Near-far resistance of multiuser detectors in asynchronous channels", *IEEE Trans. Commun.*, vol. 38, no. 4, pp. 496-508, April 1990.
[5]   M. K. Varanasi, B. Aazhang: "Near-optimum detection in synchronous code-division multiple-access systems", *IEEE Trans. Commun.*, vol. 39, no. 5, pp. 725-736, May 1991.
[6]   S. Verdu: "Computational complexity of optimum multiuser detection", *Algorithmica*, vol. 4, no. 3, pp. 303-312, 1989.
[7]   B. Aazhang et al.: "Neural networks for multiuser detection in code-division multiple-access communications", *IEEE Trans. Commun.*, vol. 40, no. 7, pp. 1211-1222, July 1992.
[8]   U. Mitra, H. V. Poor: "Neural network techniques for adaptive multiuser demodulation", *IEEE J. Select. Areas on Commun.*, vol. 12, no. 9, pp. 1460-1470, Dec. 1994.
[9]   T. Miyajima et al.: "On the multiuser detection using a neural network in code-division multiple-access communications", *IEICE Trans. Commun.*, vol. E76-B, no. 8, August 1993.
[10] G. Kechriotis, E. S. Manolakos: "Implementing the optimum CDMA multiuser detector with Hopfield neural networks", *Proc. of the Int'l Workshop on Applications of Neural Networks to Telecommunications*, pp. 60-67, Princeton, NJ, Oct. 1993.

[11] J. J. Hopfield, D. W. Tank: "Neural computation of decisions in optimization problems", *Biol. Cybernetics*, vol. 52, pp. 141-152, 1985.

[12] P. J. M. Van Laarhoven, E. H. L. Arts: "Simulated Annealing: Theory and Application", Dordrecht, Holland: Reidel, 1987.

[13] D. E. Goldberg: "Genetic Algorithms in Search, Optimization, and Machine Learning", Reading, MA: Addison-Wesley, 1989.

[14] D. E. Van den Bout, T. K. Miller III: "Graph partition using annealing networks", *Complex System*, vol. 1, no. 2, pp. 192-203, June, 1990.

[15] C. Peterson: "A mean field theory learning algorithm for neural networks", *Complex System*, vol. 1, pp. 995-1019, 1987.

[16] C. Peterson: "Neural networks and NP-complete optimization problem: a performance study on the graph bisection problem", *Complex System*, vol. 2, pp. 59-89, 1988.

[17] C. Peterson: "A new method for mapping optimization problem onto neural networks", *Int'l J. Neural System*, vol. 1, no. 1, pp. 3-22, 1989.

[18] C. Peterson, E. Hartman: "Explorations of the mean field theory learning algorithm", *Neural Networks*, vol. 2, pp. 475-494, 1989.

[19] G. Bilbro, R. Mann et al.: "Optimization by mean field annealing", *Advances in Neural Information Processing System 1*.

[20] G. H. Golub, C. F. V. Load: "Matrix Computation", 2nd edition, The Johns Hopkins University Press, Baltimore, 1989.

[21] A. Cichocki, R. Unbenauen: "Neural Networks for Optimization and Signal Processing", John Wiley & Son, NY, 1993.

[22] W. C. Y. Lee: "Power control in CDMA", *Proc. Veh. Technol. Conference*, 1991, pp. 77-80.

[23] M. B. Pursley, H. F. Roefs: "Numerical evaluation of correlation parameters for optimum phases of binary register sequences", *IEEE Trans. Commun.*, vol. COM-27, pp. 1593-1604, Oct. 1979.

[24] J. A. Alspector et al.: "Experimental evaluation of learning in a neural microsystem", in *Advances in Neural Information Processing System 1*. (J. E. Moody et al. ed.), pp. 871-878, San Mateo CA, Morgan Kaufmanns, 1992.

[25] T. Miyajima, T. Hasegawa: "Multiuser detection using a Hopfield network for asynchronous code-division multiple-access systems", *IEICE Trans. on Fundamentals*, vol. E-79 A, no. 12, Dec. 1996.

[26] R. J. Glauber: "Time-dependent statistics of the Ising model", *Journal of Mathematical Physics*, vol. 4, pp. 481-485, 1963.

[27] M. Mezard, G. Parisi, M. Virasoro: "Spin glass theory and beyond", Singapore: World Scientific, 1987.

[28] C. Mead: "Analog VLSI and VLSI system", New York: Addison-Wesly, 1989.

[29] B. W. Lee, B. J. Sheu: "General-purpose neural chips with electrically programmable synapses and gain-adjust neurons", *IEEE Journal of Solid-State Circuits*, vol. 27, no. 9, pp. 1299-1302, Sept. 1992.

[30] A. D. Culhane, M. C. Peckerar, C. R. K. Marrian: "A neural net approach to discrete Hartley and Fourier transform", *IEEE Trans. on Circuits and Systems*, vol. 36, pp. 695-702, May 1989.

[31] J. F. Wakerly: "Digital Design, Principles and Practices", 2nd edition, New Jersey: Prentice-Hall Inc., 1994.

[32] N. H. E. Weste, K. Eshraghian: "Principles of CMOS VLSI Design", 2nd edition, MA: Addison-Wesley, 1993.

Chapter 7

Analog VLSI Hardware Implementation of a Supervised Learning Algorithm

Gian Marco Bo, Daniele Caviglia, Hussein Chiblé, and Maurizio Valle

Department of Biophysical and Electronic Engineering, University of Genoa, Italy

In this chapter, we introduce an analog chip hosting a self–learning neural network with local learning rate adaptation. The neural architecture has been validated through intensive simulations on the recognition of handwritten characters. It has hence been mapped onto an analog architecture. The prototype chip implementing the whole on–chip learning neural architecture has been designed and fabricated by using a 0.7 µm channel length CMOS technology. Experimental results on two learning tasks confirm the functionality of the chip and the soundness of the approach. The chip features a peak performance of 2.65×10^6 connections updated per second.

1
Introduction

Artificial neural networks (ANNs) are strongly inspired by models of biological neural systems. They are regarded as networks consisting of highly interconnected simple and similar processing units, usually with adaptation (i.e. learning) capabilities, [1–3]. They are useful in applications demanding a non–linear mapping between two data sets. Typical examples are pattern recognition (i.e., handwritten and voice recognition, quality analysis, etc.), optimization (i.e., process control), identification, etc. During the 1980's, the interest in ANNs grew and, at the same time, the research in the microelectronic implementation of ANNs became a hot topic as well. A debate was raised about which implementation approach (i.e., digital, analog, or hybrid) would be most effective. Nevertheless, we believe that a debate in these terms is meaningless. It is not possible to identify a unique implementation approach as "optimum" but different solutions can be envisaged depending on specific application demands (e.g., precision, speed, size, etc.).

The aim of our work is the analog VLSI implementation of ANNs with supervised on–chip learning capabilities. To this aim, we developed an analog architecture and a learning algorithm which greatly increases the locality of the computation and which are particularly suited for the on–chip implementation. The learning algorithm increases the convergence speed and classification accuracy. We designed a prototype chip implementing a Multi Layer Perceptron (MLP) network with 8 inputs, 16 hidden neurons and 4 output neurons. The on–chip learning algorithm is based on the by–pattern Back–Propagation with a local learning rate adaptation rule [1], [2]. The prototype chip was fabricated through the Europractice service by using the ATMEL CMOS 0.7 μm channel length technology. Its functionality has been successfully verified through two learning experiments: the exclusive OR function and a simple classification task. The resulting computational power [4] is 2.65×10^6 CUPS (connection updated per second).

The chapter is organized as follows. In Section 2, the main features and issues of the analog VLSI implementation of ANNs will be introduced and discussed and a brief review of the state of the art will be presented. In Section 3, the feed–forward architecture and the learning algorithm will be introduced and discussed together with a local learning rate adaptation technique. Section 4 will deal with the on–chip learning architecture: this section will present the mapping of the feed–forward and learning algorithms onto an analog VLSI architecture (*SLANP*: Self–Learning Analog Neural Processor). The main features of the circuit implementation through standard CMOS sub micron technology, together with the experimental chip, will be described in Section 5. The experimental results will be presented in Section 6. Finally, conclusions are drawn in Section 7.

2
Analog VLSI for Neural Computation

2.1
Hardware Implementation of Neural Networks

When attempting to implement ANNs through dedicated VLSI circuits, one should take inspiration from the biological neural systems borrowing the principles and the structures. Consequently, the essential concepts in designing VLSI neural systems are:

- Massive parallelism: a neural system is composed of a large number of highly interconnected processing elements (neurons) working in parallel;
- Collective computation: the information is distributed over the whole neural system through the processing elements that collectively perform the computation;
- Adaptation: the neural system adapts its processing tasks according to the evolution of its input stimuli (i.e., the "environment");
- Exploitation of physical properties of the computing structures: in many applications, hardware neural systems must feature low power consumption, small area, and do not need large signal to noise ratio (S/N) or high precision to accomplish the task.

In Table 1 a comparison between the digital and analog VLSI technology is reported. The main characteristics of digital VLSI technology are easy signal regeneration, capability of high–precision computation (i.e., number of bits) and, thanks to the recent developments in CAD tools, relative simplicity in designing and testing. Nevertheless, it is difficult to integrate massively parallel systems on a single chip: even if sub–micron technologies are used, only few neurons can be integrated on a chip, while neural systems need thousands of neurons working in parallel.

Table 1. Digital vs. analog VLSI technology

	digital technology	analog technology
Signal representation	numbers	physical values (e.g., voltages, currents, charges, etc.)
Time	sampling	continuous/sampling
Signal amplitude	quantized	Continuous
Signal regeneration	along path	Degradation
Precision	cheap and easy	Expensive
Area per function	large	Small
Transistor mode of operation	switch mode	all modes
Architecture	low degree of parallelism	high degree of parallelism
Design and test	easy	difficult/expensive

Moreover, in digital implementations, silicon area is mainly occupied by interconnections between neurons.

On the other hand, analog VLSI technology looks attractive for the efficient implementation of artificial neural systems for the following reasons:

- Massively parallel neural systems are efficiently implemented in analog VLSI technology, thus allowing high processing speed: the neural processing elements are smaller than their digital equivalent, so it is possible to integrate on the same chip ANNs composed of a large number (thousands) of interconnections (synapses);
- To ensure fault tolerance to the hardware level it is necessary to introduce redundant hardware and in analog VLSI technology the cost of additional nodes is relatively low;
- The use of weak inversion operated MOS transistors reduces the synaptic and neuron power consumption, thus offering the possibility of low–power neural systems;
- Analog neural networks eliminate the need for analog–to–digital and digital–to–analog converters and can be directly interfaced to sensors and actuators: this advantage is evident when data are given in input to the neural network in a massive parallel way.

The analog designer has usually to trade–off silicon area–power consumption against S/N ratio (i.e., precision of computation in terms of equivalent number of bits): small silicon area and low power consumption imply low precision. In the analog implementation of ANNs, one must minimize both area and power of neuron and synapses to integrate on–chip large networks. However, this is not a problem since in a neural system the overall precision of computation is not determined by the precision of the single computational nodes (neurons and synapses), but by the collective computation of the whole network [5]. The design on analog ANNs must then trade off silicon area–power consumption of the whole network against signal–to–noise ratio.

2.2
Analog On–chip Learning Implementation

In the following we will refer to a feed–forward architecture as the MLP network [1], [2] due to its wide usage in real world applications [6–9] and to its reliability.

The advantages of on–chip learning implementation are not evident when the considered task requires a small network (i.e., a small number of neurons and synapses) and the training set is composed of few examples. In this case, networks without on–chip learning circuitry can be considered and the learning can be implemented by a host computer (e.g., a PC IBM compatible) using a chip–in–the–loop technique [10].

When large networks with thousands of synapses and large training sets consisting of thousands of examples are considered, the training phase takes a lot of time when performed by a host computer and a chip–in–the–loop technique. High–speed neural hardware is then needed.

Analog on–chip learning MLP networks feature high processing speed since the weights are updated by analog parallel computation. Thus, training of large networks with large databases can be performed very quickly. On–chip learning implementations are also best suited when continuously adaptive neural systems are considered.

The main drawback of the on–chip learning implementation is that the circuitry needed to perform the weight adjustment is used only during the training phase. During the classification, the silicon area occupied by learning circuits is not used (this is not true if continuously adaptive neural systems are considered).

Analog MLP neural networks can be trained by using a supervised algorithm [11] where the training set is composed of exemplary network input patterns and desired network output patterns (i.e., targets). The weights are adjusted until the target output is generated for the corresponding network input. To accomplish this task, we use a gradient–descent algorithm [3]. One of the most widely used is the Back Propagation (BP) algorithm [1], [2]. Other learning approaches have been presented in the literature [12], [13] where model–free algorithms are used to perform the training operations. The BP algorithm updates the weight values according to the gradient of an error cost function with respect to the weight values.

We pursued the analog VLSI implementation of a MLP network with on–chip BP learning. The adaptation capability of the neural network is further increased by considering a local adaptation of the learning parameters (i.e., learning rates, [2], [14]), thus increasing the training convergence speed. It has also been demonstrated that the adaptation of the learning parameters improves the fault tolerance [15].

Some examples of analog implementation of ANNs with on–chip learning capability have been presented in literature. In [16], a $4 \times 3 \times 2$ MLP network with on–chip BP learning is presented. The neurons and synapses feature very low power consumption; moreover, the non–volatile UV–light programmable analog floating gate storage looks to be an attractive way to implement the weight adaptation and long term storage. The main drawback is that the weight update operations, i.e., the write operation on a floating gate cell, takes a lot of time, i.e., each input pattern is presented to the network at intervals of 10s.

In [17] a multi chip analog implementation is considered. A scaleable 8 × 4 synaptic chip and a 4–neuron chip with learning capabilities have been presented. Larger networks can be realized by connecting together several neuron and synaptic chips. This multi–chip approach does not seem the best solution for the integration of analog on–chip learning networks. Better results could be achieved by considering scaleable chips integrating both synapses and neurons (with the learning circuitry). Other examples of analog implementations and design issues can be found in [14], [18–29].

3
Neural Network and Learning Algorithm

3.1
The Feed–Forward Network

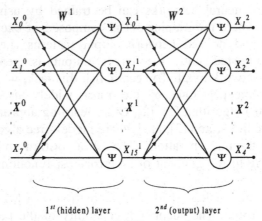

1st (hidden) layer   2nd (output) layer

Fig. 1. Architecture of the 2–layer MLP network: the arrows represent the synapses while the Ψ blocks represent the neurons. The vector X^0 is the network input. The vector X^1 is the output of the first neuron layer; the matrix W^1 contains the weight strength values of the synaptic array between the inputs and the first neuron layer. The vector X^2 is the output of the second neuron layer (network outputs), the matrix W^2 contains the weight strength values of the synaptic array between the first and the second neuron layer.

The architecture of the feed–forward 2–layer MLP network [1], [2] that has been implemented on the experimental chip is shown in Fig. 1. The first layer is made of a matrix of 8×16 synaptic multipliers (i.e., in Fig. 1 the synapses are indicated by arrows) and a vector of 16 neurons (i.e., in Fig. 1 the neurons are indicated by the Ψ blocks); the second layer is made of a matrix of 16×4 synaptic multipliers and a vector of 16 neurons.

The neurons implement the linear summation of the synaptic outputs and the non–linear activation function $\Psi(\cdot)$. The neurons usually have output values in the range $[-1 \div +1]$ and the non–linear activation function is: $\Psi(a) = \tanh(a)$. Nevertheless, in some cases the output range is $[0 \div +1]$, and the non–linear activation function is: $\Psi(a) = \dfrac{1}{1+e^{-a}}$ [1], [2].

Taking into account the hyperbolic tangent function, $\Psi(a) = \tanh(a)$, the computation performed by the network of Fig. 1 is:

$$\begin{aligned}
a_j^1 &= \sum_{i=0}^{7} W_{j,i}^1 \cdot X_i^0 \\
X_j^1 &= \tanh\!\left(a_j^1\right) \\
a_k^2 &= \sum_{j=0}^{15} W_{k,j}^2 \cdot X_j^1 \\
X_k^2 &= \tanh\!\left(a_k^2\right) \\
i &\in [0 \div 7],\; j \in [0 \div 15],\; k \in [0 \div 3]
\end{aligned} \tag{1}$$

where X_j^1 is the output of the j–th neuron of the first layer, X_i^0 is the i–th network input, the term a_j^1 (usually called activation) is the sum of the outputs of the synapses of the first layer which are connected to the j–th neuron of the first layer, and $W_{j,i}^1$ is the weight of the synapse connecting the j–th neuron of the first layer and the i–th network input (please note that the neuron layer 0, called input layer, does not perform any computation but only feeds the input signals X_i^0, $i \in [1 \div 8]$ to the network). Similar definitions apply to X_k^2, a_k^2, and $W_{k,j}^2$ in the second layer.

The bias terms [1], [2], not explicitly shown in Fig. 1 and Eq. (1), are usually considered as weight connections between each neuron and an input whose value is held fixed at 1, so the previous formulation can be considered fairly general.

3.2
The Learning Algorithm

The synaptic weight values, together with the network topology, determine the network function, i.e., the non–linear mapping between the input and output data spaces. Their values are the result of the training phase which is computed as follows: given a training set, i.e., a set of exemplary patterns made by network input/target output pairs, the training phase consists in determining the weight values for all synapses such that the target output is generated for the corresponding input [1]. The synaptic weight values are usually obtained by minimizing an error function E computed on the difference between the target and actual network outputs, summed over all the pattern examples of the training set.

We define the error function E_p for the p–th pattern example as the square of the difference between the target network output $\overline{X}_k^2$ and the actual network output X_k^2 (the index k runs over the output layer neurons):

$$E_p = \frac{1}{2} \sum_{k=0}^{3} \left[\overline{X}_k^2 - X_k^2 \right]^2 \qquad (2)$$

The error function E is computed as the average of the error functions E_p over all the exemplary patterns of the training set (N_p is the number of exemplary patterns of the training set):

$$E = \frac{1}{N_p} \sum_{p=1}^{N_p} E_p \qquad (3)$$

The training is achieved by minimizing the total error function E with respect to the weight values.

In general, the BP algorithm is operated by following either the *by–pattern* or the *by–epoch* pattern example presentation approaches [1], [2]. We adopted a by–pattern approach: starting from an initial random weight guess configuration, at each pattern presentation (i.e., *learning iteration* in the remainder of the chapter) the weights values are updated according to the following rule [1–3]:

$$\Delta W_{k,j}^2 = -\eta \frac{\partial E_p}{\partial W_{k,j}^2}$$
$$j \in [0 \div 15], k \in [0 \div 3] \qquad (4)$$

for the output layer and:

$$\Delta W_{j,i}^1 = -\eta \frac{\partial E_p}{\partial W_{j,i}^1}$$

$$i \in [0 \div 7], j \in [0 \div 15]$$

(5)

for the hidden layer.

The positive parameter η is called learning rate and, for the moment, we leave it equal for all the synapses. The value of η heavily affects the learning procedure: if η is "sufficiently small," the procedure deals to a (local) minimum of the total error function E [1,3]. By applying the chain rule to Eqs. (4) and (5), we obtain:

$$\Delta W_{k,j}^2 = -\eta \frac{\partial E_p}{\partial W_{k,j}^2} = -\eta \frac{\partial E_p}{\partial X_k^2} \cdot \frac{\partial X_k^2}{\partial a_k^2} \cdot \frac{\partial a_k^2}{\partial W_{k,j}^2}$$

$$\Delta W_{j,i}^1 = -\eta \frac{\partial E_p}{\partial W_{j,i}^1} = -\eta \sum_{k=0}^{3} \left[\frac{\partial E_p}{\partial X_k^2} \cdot \frac{\partial X_k^2}{\partial a_k^2} \cdot \frac{\partial a_k^2}{\partial X_j^1} \right] \cdot \frac{\partial X_j^1}{\partial a_j^1} \cdot \frac{\partial a_j^1}{\partial W_{j,i}^1}$$

(6)

$$k \in [0 \div 3], j \in [0 \div 15], i \in [0 \div 7]$$

Let us define the neuron error terms. For the k–th neuron of the output layer the error term δ_k^2 is:

$$\delta_k^2 \equiv -\frac{\partial E_p}{\partial X_k^2} \cdot \frac{\partial X_k^2}{\partial a_k^2} = \left[\overline{X}_k^2 - X_k^2 \right] \cdot D_k^2$$

$$k \in [0 \div 3]$$

(7)

and the error δ_j^1 at the j–th neuron of the hidden layer is:

$$\delta_j^1 \equiv -\sum \left[\frac{\partial E_p}{\partial X_k^2} \cdot \frac{\partial X_k^2}{\partial a_k^2} \cdot \frac{\partial a_k^2}{\partial X_j^1} \right] \cdot \frac{\partial X_j^1}{\partial a_j^1} = \left[\sum_{k=0}^{3} \delta_k^2 \cdot W_{k,j}^2 \right] \cdot D_j^1$$

$$j \in [0 \div 15]$$

(8)

where D_k^2 and D_j^1 are the derivatives of the neuron activation function (i.e., the hyperbolic tangent) with respect to a_k^2 and a_j^1 respectively:

$$D_j^1 = \frac{\partial X_j^1}{\partial a_j^1} = 1 - \tanh^2\left(a_j^1\right) = 1 - \left(X_j^1\right)^2$$

$$D_k^2 = \frac{\partial X_k^2}{\partial a_k^2} = 1 - \tanh^2\left(a_k^2\right) = 1 - \left(X_k^2\right)^2$$

(9)

$$k \in [0 \div 3], j \in [0 \div 15]$$

Starting from the output layer, the terms δ_k^2 are computed and propagated backward to the hidden layer, to compute δ_j^1. By substituting

Eqs. (7) and (8) in Eq. (6), we obtain the weight update rule for the output and the hidden layers:

$$\Delta W_{k,j}^2 = \eta \cdot \delta_k^2 \cdot X_j^1$$
$$\Delta W_{j,i}^1 = \eta \cdot \delta_j^1 \cdot X_i^0 \qquad (10)$$
$$k \in [0 \div 3], j \in [0 \div 15], i \in [0 \div 7]$$

The by–pattern BP algorithm so far described is summarized in Table 2.

Table 2. The *by–pattern* BP algorithm

1   Initialize the synaptic weights to small random values.
2   Present to the network an input example (chosen randomly way out of the training set) and compute the neuron outputs [Eq. (1)].
3   Present the corresponding target output and compute the error terms for all neurons [Eqs. (7), (8), and (10)].
4   Update the synaptic weight values [Eq. (10)].
5   Go back to step 2 until the error E is acceptably low (i.e., the given termination condition is satisfied).

3.3
Improvements in the Learning Convergence Speed

The local learning rate adaptation rule we adopt here is derived from [29] and it is based on the use of specific learning rate for each synapse. It can be described as follows:

$$\text{if } S_{j,i}^l(t) = S_{j,i}^l(t-1)$$

$$\eta_{j,i}^l(t+1) = \eta_{j,i}^l(t) \cdot \left[\frac{\eta^{max}}{\eta_{j,i}(t)} \right]^{\gamma}$$

$$\text{else} \qquad (11)$$

$$\eta_{j,i}^l(t+1) = \eta_{j,i}^l(t) \cdot \left[\frac{\eta^{min}}{\eta_{j,i}(t)} \right]^{\gamma}$$

where, taking into account the generic synapse connecting the j-th neuron of the l-th layer (l=1, 2) and the i-th neuron of the (l-1)-th layer, $s^l_{j,i}(t)$ is the sign of the gradient component $\dfrac{\partial E_p(t)}{\partial w^l_{j,i}}$, and $\eta^l_{j,i}$ is the learning rate value at the t-th learning iteration; η^{max} and η^{min} are respectively the maximum and minimum values of the learning rate and γ is the learning rate adaptation coefficient ($\gamma \in [0\div1]$).

The rationale of the adaptation rule described by Eq. (11) is:

• each synapse has its own learning rate $\eta^l_{j,i}$ locally adapted according to the variation of the sign $s^l_{j,i}(t)$ of the gradient component $\dfrac{\partial E_p(t)}{\partial w^l_{j,i}}$;

• the computation of Eq. (11) is local (it is performed on local information at the synaptic site) so it is easily mapped onto analog circuits;

• the adaptation rule can be extended to many other learning algorithms to train feed—forward and recurrent neural networks (see, among others, [12,13] where model—free learning algorithms have been introduced).

The learning rate adaptation rule is applied at each learning iteration between steps 3 and 4 of the learning process in Table 2.

4
Analog On—chip Learning Architecture

This section presents the mapping of the feed—forward and learning algorithms onto an analog VLSI architecture that we called Self Learning Analog Neural Processor (SLANP).

The analog architecture of the $8 \times 16 \times 4$ MLP neural network with on—chip BP learning with local learning rate adaptation is shown in Fig. 2 [14].

The number of neuron layers is 2, since it has been demonstrated that the MLP network is able to perform every non—linear mapping between two data spaces if the network has a proper number of neuron in the first layer [1], [2]. The proposed architecture can be easily extended to the case of a higher number of neuron layers and neurons per layer.

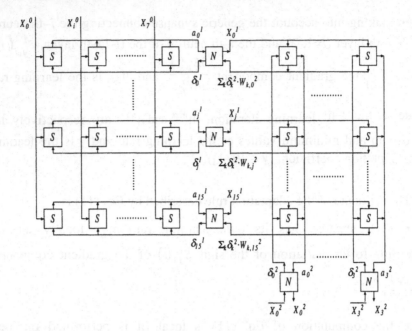

Fig. 2. The analog on–chip BP learning MLP architecture.

The hardware architecture consists of two matrices of synaptic modules (indicated by S) and two arrays of neuron modules (indicated by N). We refer to the synapses in the first layer as hidden synapses and those in the second layer as output synapses. In the same way we refer to neurons in the first and second layer as hidden and output neurons respectively.

The output (hidden) synaptic module has four (three) terminals: the synaptic input X_j^1 (X_i^0 for the hidden synaptic modules), the synaptic output $W_{k,j}^2 \cdot X_j^1$ ($W_{k,j}^2 \cdot X_j^1$ for the hidden synaptic modules), the input error term δ_k^2 (δ_j^1 for the hidden synaptic modules) and the back–propagated error term $\delta_k^2 \cdot W_{k,j}^2$ (not required in the hidden synaptic modules since they do not back–propagate any error term).

The output (hidden) neuron module has also four terminals: the neuron input a_k^2 (a_j^1 for the hidden neuron modules), the neuron output X_k^2 (X_j^1 for the hidden neuron modules), the target $\overline{X}_k^2$ ($\sum_{k=1}^{4} \delta_k^2 \cdot w_{k,j}^2$ for the hidden neuron modules), and the error terms δ_k^2 (δ_j^1 for the hidden neuron modules).

We can identify in Fig. 2 two different signal paths (highlighted in Fig. 3), orthogonally placed, which correspond respectively to the feed–forward and learning (or backward) phases.

- Feed–forward path (see Fig. 3a): the signals X_i^0 are applied to the hidden synapses and forward propagated through the hidden neurons, the output synapses, and the output neurons.

- Learning path (see Fig. 3b): the signals $\overline{X}_k^2$ are applied to the output neurons and back propagated through the output synapses, the hidden neurons, and the hidden synapses.

The structure of the synaptic and neuron modules is discussed in the following sub–sections.

4.1
The Synaptic Module

The block diagram of the synaptic module is shown in Fig. 4. Since the output and hidden synaptic modules differ only for the B1 block (not present in the hidden synaptic modules as explained below), the layer index is not shown for the sake of simplicity. It contains the following blocks:

- F, is the feed–forward four–quadrant multiplier which performs the multiplication between the synaptic input X_j, and the weight value W_{kj} (i.e., $W_{k,j} \cdot X_j$).

- B1, is the backward four–quadrant multiplier that performs the multiplication between the error term δ_k and the weight W_{kj} (i.e., $\delta_k \cdot W_{k,j}$).

- B2, is the weight update four–quadrant multiplier which performs the multiplication between the synaptic input X_j, the error term δ_k, and the learning rate η_{kj}, thus generating the weight update signal ΔW_{kj} (i.e., $\eta_{k,j} \cdot \delta_k \cdot X_j$). B2 also generates the sign S_{kj} of the corresponding component of the gradient of E_p, $S_{k,j} = sign\left(\dfrac{\partial E_p}{\partial W_{k,j}}\right) = -sign(\Delta W_{k,j})$.

- H, is the local learning rate adaptation circuit block, which adapts the value of η_{kj} according to the sign of two consecutive weight update values [see Eq. (11)].

- WU, is the weight block which updates the weight values $W_{k,j}$: $W_{k,j}^{new} = W_{k,j}^{old} + \Delta W_{k,j}$. The WU performs also the short–term storage of the weight value.

As stated before, in the hidden synaptic modules the multiplier B1 is not required since they do not back–propagate any error signal.

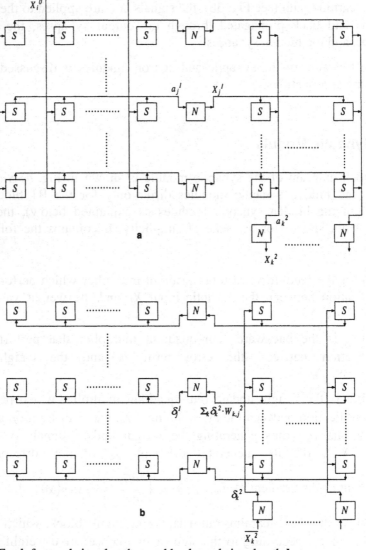

Fig. 3. Feed–forward signal path **a** and backward signal path **b**.

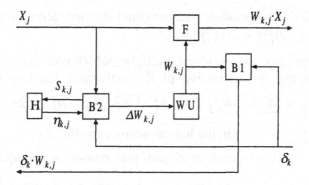

Fig. 4. Block diagram of the synaptic module.

4.2
The Neuron Module

The structure of the neuron module is shown in Fig. 5. The structure of the output neuron module (Fig. 5a) is slightly different with respect the one of the hidden neuron modules (Fig. 5b).

The neuron module contains the following blocks:

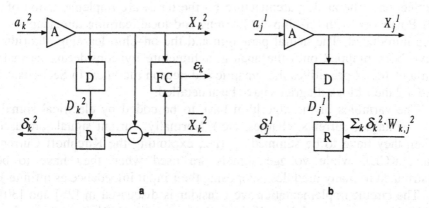

Fig. 5. Output neuron module block diagram **a** and hidden neuron module block diagram **b**.

- A, activation function module which implements the activation function $\Psi(a)$ (i.e., $X_{k(j)}^{2(1)} = \Psi\left(a_{k(j)}^{2(1)}\right)$).

- D, derivative module that computes the derivative of the activation function (i.e., $D_{k(j)}^{2(1)} = 1 - \left(X_{k(j)}^{2(1)} \right)$).

- R, the error two quadrant multiplier which computes the error term by multiplying the derivative of the activation function by the term $\left(\overline{X}_k^2 - X_k^2 \right)$ or $\sum_k \delta_k^2 \cdot W_{k,j}^2$ (i.e., $\delta_k^2 = \left(\overline{X}_k^2 - X_k^2 \right) \cdot D_k^2$ in the output neuron and $\delta_j^1 = \left(\sum_k \delta_k^2 \cdot W_{k,j}^2 \right)$ in the hidden neuron, see Fig. 5).

- FC, the cost function circuit that computes the quadratic error between the target $\overline{X}_k^2$ and the network output X_k^2, i.e., $\varepsilon_k = \left(\overline{X}_k^2 - X_k^2 \right)^2$. The total error function can be obtained by summing the quadratic error related to all the output neurons, i.e., $\sum_{k=1}^{4} \varepsilon_k$.

5
Analog CMOS Implementation

5.1
SLANP Circuit Implementation

In Section 4 the analog architecture for the hardware implementation of a MLP network with on–chip BP learning and local learning rate adaptation was introduced. The neural paradigm and the on–chip learning algorithm have been mapped onto the analog architecture by considering as main computational primitives the synaptic and neuron modules. In Sections 4.1 and 4.2 their block diagrams have been detailed.

The variables of the algorithm have to be coded by electrical signals (i.e., voltages, currents, charges, etc.). Normally, current signals are used when they have to be summed up (i.e., exploiting the Kirchhoff Current Law, KCL), while voltage signals are used when they have to be distributed to many modules (supposing their input impedance as infinite).

The circuit implementation we consider is discussed in [28] and [30], and represents an evolution of the one proposed in [27]. To achieve low voltage and low power functionality, we design the MOS circuits using a submicron CMOS technology to work (when possible) in the weak inversion region of operation [5, 31].

Low values of bias currents for the neural circuits (e.g., less than 200 nA) reduce the power consumption and the sizes of MOS transistors working in weak inversion [5]. Nevertheless, a degradation of the circuit response time is obtained. On the other hand, high values of bias currents for the neural circuits (e.g., higher that 5 μA) improve the circuit response time, but also increase the power consumption and the sizes of MOS transistors working in weak inversion [5].

Bias current values govern then the trade–off between response time and area/power consumption. We choose to design the neural computational circuits by considering bias current values in the order of 10^{-6} A.

The supply voltage was set to 5 V, and the signal ground was set to 2.5 V, thus when a voltage is equal to 2.5 V, the corresponding neural variable is null. It is worth noting that all the neural signal voltages have a limited range (i.e., $V \in [2.4V + 2.6V]$) to force the analog circuits implementing the neural modules to work in the desired region (see [28] and [30] for details).

Synaptic weight values are stored at each synapse as voltages across capacitors. The weight voltages are updated at each learning iteration by charging/discharging for a fixed time duration the capacitors through currents coding the weight update values.

During the recall phase a medium/long term storage of the weight values is needed. When the training process is stopped, the weight values are externally accessed and converted in digital values (8 bits) and stored in an off–chip RAM. The digital weights are then periodically loaded in the chip through a digital–to–analog converter, thus refreshing the voltage values across the capacitors.

5.2
The Physical Design and Implementation

A prototype chip implementing the proposed on–chip neural architecture with local learning rate adaptation (SLANP) has been designed and fabricated through the ATMEL ES2 ECPD07 CMOS technology available through the Europractice Service. This is a digital single–poly, double metal CMOS process with 0.7 μm of minimum channel length.

The chip photograph and layout floorplan are shown in Fig. 6. S1 and N1 are the synaptic and the neuron arrays related to the first (i.e., hidden) layer, while S2 and N2 are the synaptic and the neuron arrays related to the second (i.e., output) layer. The block B contains the circuits needed to generate and distribute the bias voltages and currents to all the circuits on the chip. The block CU contains some digital logic needed to address and to access the weight voltages of the synaptic modules when the learning phase has been completed. The chip features an area of about 3.5 mm × 3.5 mm and contains about 22×10^3 transistors.

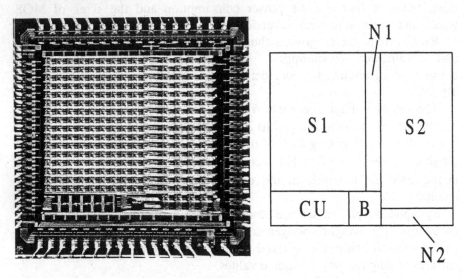

Fig. 6. Chip microphotograph and layout floorplan. The prototype chip implements the MLP neural network with 8 inputs, 16 hidden neurons, and 4 output neurons; each neuron is provided by an extra synapse implementing the bias unit [1], [2]. Globally the chip implements 212 synaptic modules and 20 neuron modules. The chip has the 8 MLP inputs and the 4 MLP outputs (the outputs of the four output neurons) directly accessible, while the outputs of the 16 hidden neurons are multiplexed onto a single signal.

6
Experimental Results

A test board hosting the SLANP chip was developed and the chip functionality has been experimentally verified. In particular, the on–chip learning has been validated through two learning experiments: the learning of the two input exclusive OR function (the XOR2 experiment) and of a simple classification task (referred to as the Classification experiment).

6.1
XOR2 Experiment

We trained the MLP chip to learn the two–bit exclusive OR function (the two–input XOR function) We connected 6 of the 8 MLP inputs to the signal ground (2.5 V) and we considered as network inputs the last two MLP inputs (let us say X_0^0 and X_1^0). Only one output neuron (let say X_0^2) is fed by the target signal (let say $\overline{X}_0^2$). Moreover, only two of the 16 hidden layer neurons were biased, so the network was configured as a $2 \times 2 \times 1$ MLP (the hidden neurons not biased were off). The training phase of the two input XOR function has been performed also activating the local learning rate adaptation circuits. The minimum and maximum learning rate control voltages were set to 0.4 V and 0.7 V respectively: this corresponds to a ratio between η_{max} and η_{min} of about one thousand [14], [30]. The duration of the learning iteration was 200 µs.

The results of the training procedure are reported in Fig. 7. The various signals are shown at the end of the training process: it can be seen how the network has learned the two–input XOR function.

6.2
Classification Experiment

We trained the MLP chip to recognize four different input patterns which are illustrated in Table 3. To implement this task we configured a $8 \times 16 \times 4$ MLP, thus using the whole network implemented by the chip; all the learning rates were locally adapted and the minimum and maximum learning rate control voltages were again 0.4 V and 0.7 V. The learning iteration time was 80 µs.

Despite its simplicity, the training problem has two important advantages:

- the learning procedure is anyway fast (i.e., few learning iterations);
- all the circuitry integrated on the chip is involved in performing the training: we could then verify the behavior of the whole MLP chip.

The results of the training procedure are reported in Fig. 8. The network correctly classifies the training set patterns shown in Table 3.

Table 3. Training set for the Classification problem.

Input Pattern	Target
11001100	0001
10011001	0010
00110011	0100
01100110	1000

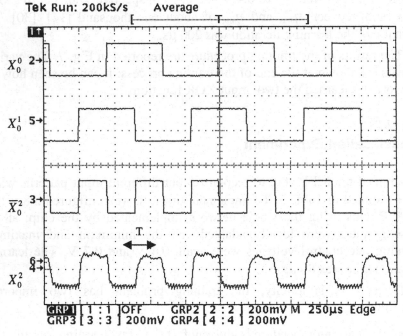

T=Learning iteration time = 200 μs

Fig. 7. Training of the 2 input XOR function. The two input signals (first and second traces), the target signal (third trace) , and output signal (fourth trace) at the end of the training process. The network was configured as a 2 × 2 × 4 MLP and all the learning rates were locally adapted. The learning iteration time was 200 μs.

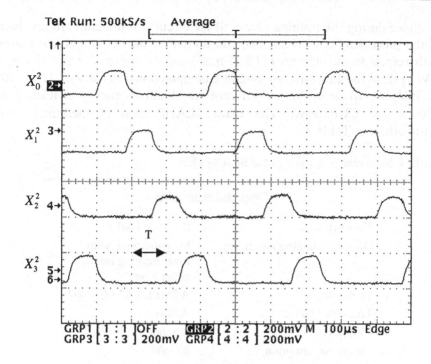

T=Learning iteration time = 80 μs

Fig. 8. The four output neuron signals at the end of the learning process for the learning experiment described in Table 3. The network was configured as an $8 \times 16 \times 4$ MLP and all the learning rates were locally adapted. The learning iteration time was 80 μs.

6.3
Discussion

The experimental results presented in the previous Sections confirm and validate the chip functionality and allow us to estimate the chip performances.

The computational power is determined by the number of weight updates performed per seconds. For the Classification problem we considered a learning iteration time duration of 80 μs. This corresponds to a computational power of 2.65×10^6 CUPS (connection updated per seconds) [4].

Since during the training phase all the circuits of the chip are involved in the processing operations, one can normalize the computational power with respect to the chip area (12.25 mm^2) and the power consumption (25 mW) [4]. In the first case we obtain a computational density of 216×10^3 CUPS/mm^2, while in the second case we obtain an energy efficiency of 106×10^3 CUPS/mW. The main SLANP chip characteristics are summarized in Table 4.

Table 4. Main characteristics of the SLANP chip

Chip characteristics	
Network size	$8 \times 16 \times 4$ MLP
On–chip learning algorithm	by–pattern BP with local learning rate adaptation
Technology	ATMEL ES2 ECPD07
Transistor count	22000
Chip size	3.5 mm × 3.5 mm
Power consumption	25 mW
Computational power	2.65×10^6 CUPS
Computational density	216×10^3 CUPS/mm^2
Energy efficiency	106×10^3 CUPS/mW

7
Conclusions

This chapter reports on the analog VLSI implementation of a multi layer perceptron neural network with on–chip back propagation learning. The reasons for the choice of this network rely on its ability to be successfully employed as a classifier (see among others [6–9]).

The training phase is performed by using a by–pattern variant of the back propagation algorithm. To increase the training performance, a local learning rate adaptation technique has also been adopted. This technique improves the convergence speed as well.

The rationale of the proposed learning rate adaptation technique is:

i)   the rule is local, i.e., each synapse has its own learning rate adapted according to local information;

ii) the rule is suited for the analog VLSI implementation;

iii) the adaptation rule can be extended to many other learning algorithms to train feed–forward and recurrent neural networks (see, among others, [12,13] where model–free learning algorithms are used to perform the training operations).

The neural paradigm and the learning rule have been validated on the recognition of hand–written digits.

The neural architecture has been mapped onto an analog architecture. The structure of the synaptic and neuron modules has been presented and some issues about the mapping of the neural variables onto electrical signals have been discussed. The analog circuits implementing the neural computational modules have been introduced. The circuit implementation has been developed by using the ATMEL ECPD07 CMOS technology, a digital single–poly, double metal CMOS process with 0.7 μm of minimum channel length. A prototype chip implementing the on–chip neural architecture with local learning rate adaptation (SLANP) has been designed and fabricated. The chip implements a MLP neural network with 8 inputs, 16 hidden neurons, and 4 output neurons. Learning experimental results confirm the chip functionality and the soundness of our approach.

In Table 5 the SLANP chip performances are compared to other analog implementations presented in literature.

Table 5. Comparison between the SLANP chip and other analog implementations of on–chip learning networks presented in literature.

Chip	Computational Power [CUPS]	Computational Density [CUPS/mm²]	Energy Efficiency [CUPS/mW]
Lehmann 1994 [17] (two chips)	0.27×10^6	22.5×10^3	13.5×10^3
Berg et al. 1996 [16]	4.6	1.15	92
Cauwenberghs 1996 [18]	42×10^3	8.7×10^3	35×10^3
SLANP Chip (this work)	2.65×10^6	216×10^3	106×10^3

References

[1]   D. E. Rumelhart, and J. L. McClelland. *Parallel Distributed Processing.* Cambridge, USA, MIT Press, 1986.

[2]   J. Hertz, A. Krogh, and R. G. Palmer. *Introduction to the Theory of the Neural Computation.* Addison–Wesley Publishing Company, 1981.

[3]   A. Cichocki and R. Unbehauen. *Neural Networks for Optimization and Signal Processing.* John Wiley & Sons, 1993.

[4]   A. H. Kramer. "Array–Based Computation: Principles, Advantages and Limitations", in *Proc. of Microneuro'96*, pp. 68–79, 1996.

[5]   E. A. Vittoz, "Analog VLSI Signal Processing: Why, Where and How", *J. of VLSI Signal Processing*, Vol. 8, pp. 27–44, 1994.

[6]   G. M. L. Sarnè and M. N. Pastorino, "Application of Neural Networks for the Simulation of theTraffic Flows in a Real Transportation Network", *Proc. of the Int. Conf. on Artificial Neural Networks ICANN94*, pp. 831–833, Sorrento, Italy, 1994.

[7]   G. M. Bo, D. D. Caviglia, e M. Valle, "An Analog VLSI Neural Architecture for Handwritten Numeric Character Recognition", in *Proc. of the Int. Conf. on Artificial Neural Networks ICANN95 – Industrial Conference*, Paris, France, 1995.

[8]   H. Bourlard and N Morgan, "Hybrid Connectionist Models for Continuous Speech Recognition", in C. Lee, F. K. Soong, and K. K. Paliwal editors, *Automatic Speech and Speaker Recognition*, pp. 259–283, Kluwer Academic Publishers, 1996.

[9]   D. Baratta, G. M. Bo, D. D. Caviglia, M. Valle, G. Canepa, R. Parenti, e C. Penno, "A Hardware Implementation of Hierarchical Neural Networks for Real–Time Quality Control Systems in Industrial Applications", in *Proc. of the Int. Conf. on Artificial Neural Networks, ICANN'97*, pp. 1229-1234, Lausanne, Switzerland, 1997.

[10] A. J. Annema. *Feed–Forward Neural Networks.* Kluwer Academic Publisher, 1995.

[11] R. P. Lippmann, "An Introduction to Computing with Neural Nets", *IEEE ASSP Magazine*, Vol. 4, No. 2, pp. 4–22, 1987.

[12] J. Alspector, R. Meir, B. Yuhas, A. Jayakumar, and D. Lippe, "A Parallel Gradient Descent Method for Learning in Analog VLSI Neural Networks", in *Advances in Neural Information Processing Systems* 5 (NIPS5), pp. 836–844, 1993.

[13] G. Cauwenberghs, "A Fast Stochastic Error–Descent Algorithm for Supervised Learning and Optimization", in *Advances in Neural Information Processing Systems* 5 (NIPS5), pp. 244–251, 1993.

[14] G. M. Bo, D. D. Caviglia, H. Chiblé, M. Valle, "A Circuit Architecture for Analog On–Chip Back Propagation Learning with Local Learning Rate Adaptation", *Analog Integrated Circuits and Signal Processing*, Kluwer Academic Publisher, Vol. 2/3, pp. 163-173, 1999.

[15] P. J. Edwards, and A. F. Murray. *Analogue Imprecision in MLP Training.* World Scientific Publishing Co. Pte. Ltd., 1996.

[16] Y. Berg, R. L. Sigvartsen, T. S. Lande, and A. Abusland, "An Analog Feed–Forward Neural Network with On–Chip Learning", *Analog Integrated Circuits and Signal Processing*, Kluwer Academic Publisher, Vol. 9, pp. 65–75, 1996.

[17] T Lehmann. *Hardware Learning in Analog VLSI Neural Networks.* Ph.D. Thesis, Electronics Institute, Technical University of Denmark, 1994.

[18] G. Cauwenberghs, "An Analog VLSI Recurrent Neural Network Learning a Continuous–Time Trajectory", *IEEE Transaction on Neural Networks*, Vol. 7, No. 2, pp. 346–361, 1996.

[19] L. M. Reyneri, and E. Filippi, "An Analysis on the Performance of Silicon Implementations of Backpropagation Algorithms for Artificial Neural Networks", *IEEE Trans. on Computers*, Vol. 12, pp. 1380-1389, 1991.

[20] T. Shima, T. Kimura, Y. Kamatani, T. Itakura, Y. Fujita, and T. Iida, "Neuro Chips with On–Chip Back–Propagation and or/Hebbian Learning", *IEEE Journal of Solid State Circuits*, Vol. 27, No. 12, pp. 1868-1876, 1992.

[21] Y. Arima, M. Murasaki, T. Yamada, A. Maeda, and H. Shinohara, "A Refreshable Analog VLSI Neural Network Chip with 400 Neurons and 40K Synapses", *IEEE Journal of Solid State Circuits*, Vol. .26, No. 12, pp. 1854-1861, 1992.

[22] L. Tarassenko, J. Tombs, and G. Cairns, "On–Chip Learning with analog VLSI Neural Networks", *Int. J. of Neural Systems*, Vol. 4, No. 4, pp. 419–426, 1993.

[23] Y. Wang, "A Modular Analog CMOS LSI for Feedforward Neural networks with On–Chip BEP Learning", in *Proc. of the IEEE International Symposium on Circuits and Systems ISCAS 1994*, Vol. 4, pp. 2744–2747, 1994.

[24] H Withagen, "Implementing Backpropagation with Analog Hardware?", in *Proc. of the Int. Conf. on Neural Networks ICNN*, 1994.

[25] J. Cho, Y. K. Choi, and S. Lee, "Modular Analog Neuro–Chip Set with On–Chip Learning by Error Back–Propagation and/or Hebbian Rules", *Proc. of the Int. Conf. on Artificial Neural Networks ICANN'94*, Sorrento, Italy, Vol. 2, pp.1343, 1994.

[26] T. Morie and Y Amemiya, "An All–Analog Expandable Neural–Network LSI with On–Chip Back Propagation Learning", *IEEE Journal of Solid State Circuits*, Vol. 29, No. 9, pp. 1086-1093, 1994.

[27] M. Valle, D. D. Caviglia, and G. M. Bisio, "An Analog VLSI Neural Network with On–Chip Back Propagation Learning", *Analog Integrated Circuits and Signal Processing*, Kluwer Academic Publisher, Vol. 9, pp. 231–245, 1996.

[28] H. Chiblé. *Studio e Progetto di Architetture Microelettroniche Analogiche di Tipo Neurale con Capacità di Apprendimento Autonomo*. Ph.D. Thesis, DIBE, University of Genoa, 1997.

[29] M. Valle, D. D. Caviglia, G. Donzellini, A. Mussi, F. Oddone, and G. M. Bisio, "A Neural Computer based on an Analog VLSI Neural Network", in *Proc. of Int. Conf. on Artificial Neural Network, ICANN94*, Vol. 2, pp. 1339-1342 1994.

[30] G. M. Bo, *Microelectronic Neural Systems: Analog VLSI for Perception and Cognition*. Ph.D. Thesis, DIBE, University of Genoa, 1998.

[31] C. A. Mead. *Analog VLSI and Neural Systems*. Addison–Wesley, Reading, 1989.

Chapter 8

pRAM: The Probabilistic RAM Neural Processor

Trevor G. Clarkson

Department of Electronic Engineering, King's College London, Strand
London WC2R 2LS, United Kingdom

The pRAM has been implemented as a VLSI processor incorporating 256 neurons with on-chip learning. Several such processors may be connected to form larger networks. The pRAM was originally conceived to model the noisy release of neurotransmitter vesicles in synaptic connections. In a network, it forms n-tuples and may operate as a noisy lookup table with generalization. The reinforcement training used is also biologically realistic and has a scope ranging from a single neuron to the whole network, the architecture being user-defined.

1
Introduction

The pRAM artificial neuron model was inspired by the quantal release of neurotransmitter at the synapses of biological neurons. The biological neuron's probability of firing is related to the release of neurotransmitter and its synaptic efficiency can be modified through training. The pRAM's weights can be changed during the training process to model synaptic efficiency and the pRAM's firing behavior is probabilistic. The pRAM is a non-linear, stochastic model of an artificial neuron.

The pRAM generates an output in the form of a spike train. This differs from "pulse-stream" neurons in that no arithmetic is performed on the spike trains themselves (for example - to achieve multiplication). Synaptic weights are instead realized by multiple joints firing probabilities in the pRAM. The different mean firing frequencies of the spike trains arriving at the multiple pRAM inputs mean that there is also a set of probabilities determining which weight will be accessed.

The pRAM can learn non-linear binary functions and can generalize after training. The intrinsic noise is present at the synaptic level and not merely superimposed on the output as with some other models. This corresponds to the quantal release of neurotransmitter at each synapse. Biologically-realistic features are expected to become increasingly advantageous in the applications of neural networks.

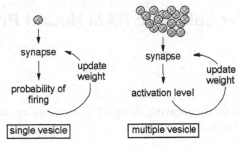

Fig. 1. The pRAM models the probability of firing of a neuron for the arrival of a single neurotransmitter vesicle at the synaptic cleft; many other neural models operate at the multiple vesicle and multiple action potential level.

The pRAM models neuronal behavior at a much lower level than models such as the Perceptron. The pRAM's weights are its firing efficiency for each permutation of the input activity. Whereas the pRAM's firing efficiency can be trained on the basis of a single output firing event (either an action potential or no firing activity), most other models have weights which are the average required response for a given synapse. For this reason, the pRAM can store a highly non-linear set of responses to its binary inputs and most other artificial neural models can only implement linearly-separable functions of the inputs.

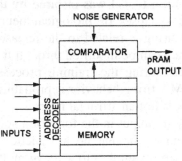

Fig. 2. The pRAM neural model

The structure of a pRAM neuron is shown in Figure 2 and the typical output of pRAM neurons can be seen to be in the form of spike trains (Figure 3). Since the pRAM output is probabilistic, a single firing event has limited significance. In most cases, a pRAM network will be operated for many cycles and the average output, in the range 0 to 1, will be used to represent the confidence of the network's decision.

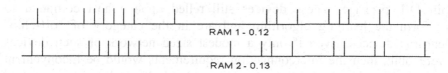

Fig. 3. Two output traces from a network of coupled pRAMs showing the mean output firing frequencies. In the example shown, the neurons are connected to perform mutual excitation and a biologically-realistic response can be seen.

The simple RAM neuron model has been called 'weightless' (Aleksander [1]) since the output state is related to one of an array of stored conditions, selected by the input vector. A simple RAM neuron can implement any arbitrary function, but does not generalize unless additional units and layers are provided. RAM-based networks normally have limited fan-in at each node so that a neuron in the input layer only sees a sub-set of *n* bits, or an n-tuple, of the total number of bits in the input vector. The n-tupling gives a form of generalization as it can perform partial matches to new patterns. Since the pRAM clearly has trainable weights, it is not normally described as weightless, but is classed as a RAM-based neural model.

2
pRAM Development

Four generations of pRAM hardware have been developed; three of which are in VLSI [2,3, 4]. In 1988, the first hardware pRAMs were constructed using LSI logic parts. Two of these simple 2-input devices were made as demonstrators. A small net, comprising two of these devices, was shown to give results that agreed well with an earlier theoretical analysis. Tasks such as mutual inhibition or mutual excitation (Fig. 3) were successfully learned. The training was achieved by running the pRAM hardware for a single iteration on a PC interface card and the output of the pRAMs was then read. A reinforcement learning rule was applied in software on the PC and the updated weights were written back to the hardware before the next iteration was started. This form of learning, whilst versatile, is quite slow and on-chip learning is desirable.

Following the success of the 2-input neurons, the VLSI design of a 4-input pRAM was completed in early 1990. Each pRAM was held in a 40-pin DIL package. These devices still relied upon a host computer to perform the learning algorithm and are in the category of "off-chip" learning devices. Even if only a modest sized network of such devices were built, then the interconnection requirements would be inconvenient and any reconfiguring of the network could only be achieved by rewiring. It was necessary to provide each pRAM neuron in a network with its own noise generator to avoid unwanted correlations between neuronal signals. This was achieved by the external selection of one of sixteen maximal length sequences; each pRAM was configured to generate a different sequence. There are clearly limits to this approach if large-scale nets are envisaged.

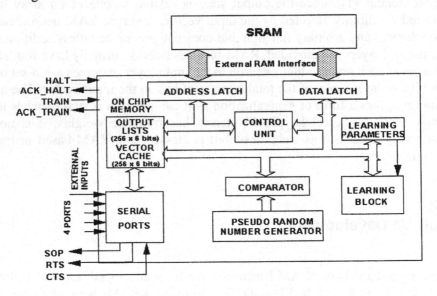

Fig. 4. The pRAM-256 modular architecture. The weight memory is held in external SRAM chips connected to the Address and Data Latches shown. The pRAM interconnection information is also held in this SRAM.

The fourth generation pRAM module was designated the pRAM-256 (Fig. 4). This allows a number of learning techniques to be used, all of which are based on reinforcement training. This has been achieved by allowing the reward and penalty inputs for each neuron to be reconfigurable by an extension of the look-up table. For example, a reward input to a neuron may either be connected to external pins on the chip which receive a global reward or penalty signal, or to the output of another pRAM. The number of inputs per pRAM was increased to six. Thus pRAM modules now contain 256, 6-input pRAMs, where the input connectivity is fully reconfigurable (Fig. 5 and Fig. 6).

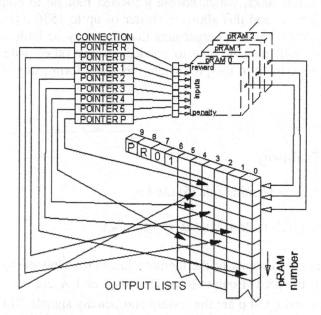

Fig. 5. The Output Lists are on-chip and hold the immediate firing history of all pRAMs in this chip (column 0) and in adjacent pRAM-256 chips (columns 1 to 5). pRAM inputs are connected to any other pRAM output held in the Output List or to a logic 1, logic 0 or Global Reward or Global Penalty signals. The Connection Pointer table is held in external SRAM and may be reconfigured at any time.

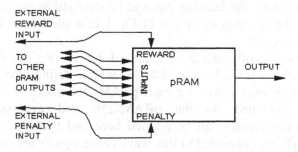

Fig. 6. One of 256 nodes in a pRAM-256 chip showing that all inputs including reward and penalty can be connected to any source.

In the pRAM-256 design, one custom integrated circuit and two external 8-bit SRAM devices comprise a module. It is advantageous to include all RAM on-chip but this makes fabrication more costly. The lookup table for reconfigurable connectivity as well as the pRAM weights is held in the fast SRAM.

Expansion of a pRAM net beyond 256 neurons is achieved through the use of five serial links, which enable a pRAM module to communicate with its neighbors, and this allows a cluster of up to 1536 interconnected pRAMs to be constructed. Larger nets than this may be built, but not all pRAM nodes will then be able to connect to any other node. External digital data may input to the pRAM chip in serial form using these serial links.

3
On-chip Training

The reinforcement learning rule [5] used is:

$$\Delta\alpha_u(t) = \rho\,((a - \alpha_u)r + \lambda(a - \alpha_u)p)(t) \times \delta_{u,i} \tag{1}$$

where α_u is the contents of the memory location addressed by the input vector u, a is the pRAM output (0 or 1), and ρ and λ are the reward and penalty rates and r and p are the reward and penalty signals. This rule acts to reinforce beneficial responses (i.e. increases the probability of making a similar move in the future) and to penalize other behavior.

The learning rate and decay rate used in the training algorithm are stored in pRAM-256 on-chip registers, which may be written to using the memory port. This requires the chip to be halted before the buses can be used. In this way, the learning rate can be changed as the learning process proceeds. The learning algorithm of Eq. 1 is implemented in hardware as shown in Figure 7.

A learning configuration is achieved by writing to the Connection Pointer look-up table held in SRAM, which defines the source of the reward and penalty inputs for each pRAM. External *reward* and *penalty* pins are provided on the pRAM-256 and externally computed environmental signals can be applied here and thereby broadcast to all nodes which are connected in this way. These signals are called the global reward and penalty signals. It is possible to calculate the global reinforcement signals within the pRAM-256, in which case nodes have their *reward* and *penalty* inputs connected to a pRAM output instead.

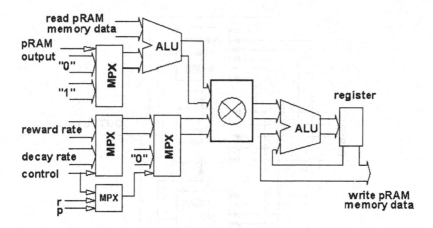

Fig. 7. The on-chip learning algorithm uses one single-cycle multiplier and implements Eq.1 in two passes.

Two other examples of training configurations are shown in Figures 8 and 9. Fig.8 shows how two pRAMs are used as *auxiliary* pRAMs to a central, learning pRAM to implement local, Hebbian learning. In this case, only 5 of the 6 inputs of the learning pRAM are used, the remaining input is permanently connected to either 0 or 1 to keep it inactive. The *auxiliary* pRAMs are non-learning and are loaded with memory weights according to the kind of actions that the learning pRAM is required to reinforce or penalize. This kind of learning is unsupervised. Each learning pRAM of this kind within a pRAM module may have a distinct behavior, which it is required to reinforce or penalize.

Fig. 9 shows how the central pRAM, when firing, may be used to penalize two other pRAMs to achieve a form of competitive learning. Where groups of neurons form mutually inhibiting or mutually exciting clusters, the activities of neighboring pRAMs are combined, using further pRAMs, into a single reward or penalty input.

Since each pRAM in a module is uncommitted, it may be used as a learning pRAM or an *auxiliary* pRAM as desired. The pRAM module may be used to build a single, multi-layer network or a number of smaller, independent networks. The reward and penalty inputs are likewise uncommitted so that different learning methods can be employed within the same module. Even if training is enabled for the pRAM-256 (TRAIN=1), nodes can be made non-learning by connecting *reward* and *penalty* inputs connected to GND.

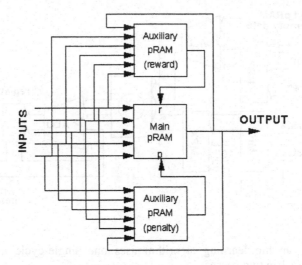

Fig. 8. Two auxiliary pRAMs (top and bottom) are used to implement local, Hebbian learning in the central pRAM.

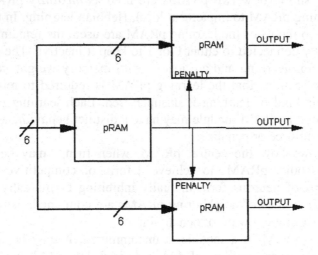

Fig. 9. An example of competitive learning where the central pRAM suppresses the firing activity of the other two pRAMs. Normally the configuration will be more complex than this, with auxiliary pRAMs combining the activities of several pRAM outputs into a single reward or penalty input.

For global reinforcement learning, the reward and penalty signals fed back to the net at time t, must coincide with the internal states of the network which caused the output at time t, so that the correct internal states or correlations are rewarded or penalized. This would be hard to achieve if the net has internal states representing t, t-1 and t-2 at the time that reinforcement is applied. For the pRAM-256 therefore, the whole network is processed, from input to output, within one pass and only the most recent state need be stored in the *Output List* and *Vector Cache* of Fig. 4. This implies that pRAMs in the input layer should have the lowest pRAM numbers and pRAMs at the output should have the highest pRAM numbers, i.e. they are processed last. This applies even if the network is spread over multiple pRAM modules, since all modules operate concurrently.

With a 33MHz clock rate, the pRAM-256 can process 4000 input vectors with training enabled and 6000 input vectors with no training. At the stated rate, all of the 256 pRAM nodes in a pRAM-256 chip will have been processed. This rate is maintained even when multiple chips are used, since data transfer between nodes in different pRAM-256 chips is synchronized.

4
Interface to a Host Computer

The pRAM-256 can operate autonomously, but interrogation by a host processor is normally required to monitor the neural network's output. In addition, training and test data will need to be downloaded to the module and the look-up tables will have to be set up. An FPGA interface has been built which allows the host computer to monitor the mean firing frequencies of selected pRAM outputs without halting the pRAM-256.

For other actions by the host, the pRAM-256 may be halted using the HALT input and the local address and data buses can used by the host processor to access the SRAM once ACK_HALT is asserted. In this way, the weight memory may be read or written to or the connection pointer table may be rewritten, so reconfiguring the network. The FPGA controls other aspects of the pRAM-256 operation, such as training. The TRAIN input is used to enable or disable training. When training is disabled, the memory update cycle is cancelled and the processing time is thereby reduced.

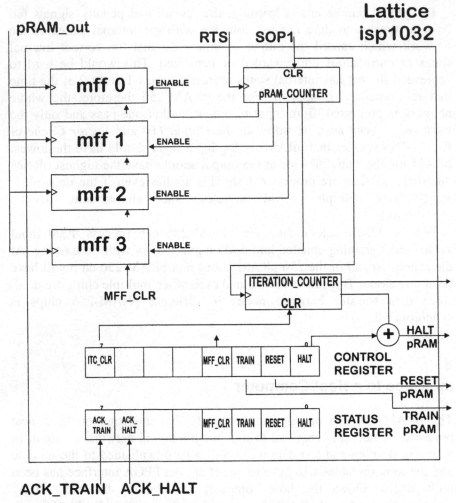

Fig. 10. One configuration of the pRAM to host in-system programmable FPGA.

The FPGA currently used (a Lattice *isp* device) can itself be reconfigured in-situ so that the whole pRAM system can be substantially modified according to the application, with no rewiring. A typical FPGA configuration is shown in Figure 10 and the whole system has been built on a PC-compatible board which can hold up to 5 pRAM-256 modules (Fig. 11).

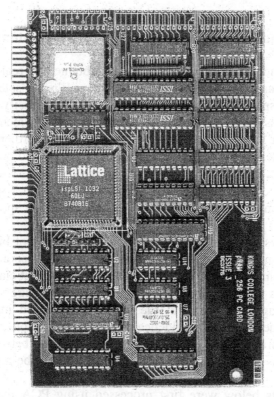

Fig. 11. Portion of the pRAM-PC board showing one pRAM-256 processor and, adjacent to its bottom-right corner, two SRAM chips for weight memory. The FPGA programmable interface to the PC is in the center-left of the picture.

5
Applications

The pRAM-256 modules have been used for image processing, pattern classification and real-valued function learning. Some applications are briefly outlined below. Those applications which require fast processing, low power or a compact processing system are explained in most detail as it is in such areas that the benefits of VLSI hardware and on-chip learning are most clearly seen.

5.1
Using Neurons in Thermal Image Processing Systems

A video sequence of infra-red images was obtained in real-time from a camera. This was first processed by a non-linear filter to select regions of interest, or hot-spots. A pRAM classifier was used to classify the hot spots in the image as either a target or clutter. Image segments that were identified as a target were then forwarded to a further system for processing. At least 25 decisions were required per second on up to 40 hot spots per frame. Each hot spot is 8 by 8 pixels square. The pRAM-256 chip is capable of real-time performance with up to 4 hot spots. Several pRAM chips can be used in parallel to process more hot spots if required [6, 7, 8, 9].

Fig. 12 shows that the images were gray-scale and not binary and the definition shown is typical of the image sequence. Notice also that some clutter is quite similar to a target. Better than 95% correct classification of single hot-spots was achieved; this improves when image sequences are used. With image sequences, a true target is classified many times in successive frames and the confidence of the classification increases with the number of frames. With clutter or noise, correlation between frames is low and misclassified clutter (i.e. as a target) tends to be rejected after a few frames.

The hot-spots below were first processed using PCA masks obtained during a pre-training process, using typical data. The pRAM network only required the first 8 PCA masks for good classification and the neural network input was the magnitude of these 8 vectors. The single neural network output was ideally 1 or 0 for a target and clutter respectively. Most hot-spots caused a network output of greater than 95% or less than 5% firing rate and these were classified respectively as targets and clutter.

Fig. 12. Examples of clutter (top row) and targets (bottom row) taken from the infra-red image.

5.2
Neural Net Object Identification

A pRAM network has to find the coordinates of a known target building within a scene. In this particular case, the training set was taken from high-resolution photographic images and the test set was from a low resolution infra-red image. Speed was important as the images were acquired at a rate of at least 4 frames per second and had to be processed within the same time period.

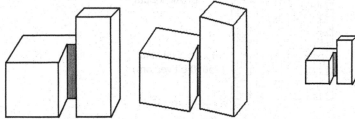

Fig. 13. A reference building (left) is derived from a high-resolution photographic image and is used to train the neural network. The network must then recognize the building in a low-resolution infra-red image from different viewpoints and at different scales (right two images).

The difficulty of this problem lies in the visible to infra-red transition. Therefore both sets of images were edge-detected before use, as the structure of the building remains constant even though certain surfaces change color between the visible and infra-red scenes. For example a black wall will appear white in the infra-red image if it is hot and emits significant infra-red radiation. This color change could confuse other methods of processing the images.

The data is taken from real gray-scale images so the building suffers from background clutter as well as shadows at certain times of day. The visible image was downsampled 4:1 to match the resolution of the infra-red image. To improve the accuracy of the classification, a multi-scale approach was used with a number of different window sizes. Ultimately, the smallest window was a 16 x 16 pixel area and this was used to train the neural network which was trained to output a 1 when the building features were presented and to output a 0 when features of other buildings were presented (Fig. 14).

The 16×16 window obtained from the training process was scanned across the infra-red image in 1 pixel increments and the point of highest correlation was expected to be the location of the building. This proved to be the case (Fig. 15).

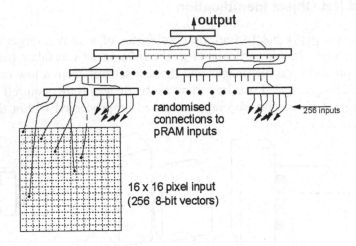

Fig. 14. Mapping the input vector onto the pRAM neural network.

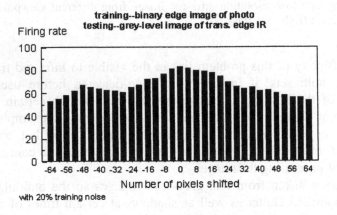

Fig. 15. Results obtained from infra-red image showing a maximum at a shift of zero pixels from the reference.

The neural network output is an indication of the degree of correlation between the image segment seen and the reference image. Fig. 15 shows the result of a horizontal scan across the image in 4 pixel increments. In practice, a 3D plot would be used to show the correlation between the learned image and the acquired image at all points. By scanning the acquired image with the field of view of the neural network, the point of highest correlation indicates the best match and defines the position of the desired object. In every case presented, all objects were correctly identified [10].

5.3
Character Recognition and the Use of Noise in Training

This was a set of pilot studies, which did not use any of the standard preprocessing techniques common in optical character recognition as the application was intended to work with random binary patterns. The original patterns were input as bitmaps to the network. This work was principally to investigate the use of noise in training to improve the classification of noisy images (Fig. 16). It was demonstrated that the pRAMs perform well with noisy data and that the internal representations were optimally separated [11, 12, 13, 14, 15]. Maximal separation of internal representations gives the best performance in the presence of white noise.

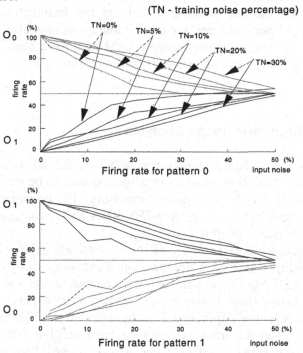

Fig. 16. Firing rates of two pRAMs at the output of the classifier, for different levels of training noise.

Fig. 16 shows the firing rate of two pRAM outputs in a network for two patterns in a character set. Pattern 0 (upper graph) has the target output of 01 for pRAM outputs O_1 and O_0 and pattern 1 (lower graph) has the target output of 10 for the same outputs. The x-axis shows the amount of noise present in the binary test images up to a maximum of 50% signal-to-noise ratio, where the probability of a bit being a 1 or 0 is 0.5. At 50% noise, the neural network cannot discern whether the bit should be 0 or 1 as each is equally likely. Therefore the pRAM network output is 0.5 as expected.

At lower levels of pattern noise, it can be seen that the network which was trained with noise-free patterns (TN=0%) degrades fairly quickly with increasing noise in the test patterns. With an output confidence margin of 20%, such a network will only be useful with less than 20% noise in the test patterns.

As the training noise increases, up to 30% (TN=30%), it can be seen that the degradation with increasing noise is much slower and the network is useful up to 45% test pattern noise, for a training noise of 30%. Typically, for a given level of training noise, the network gave a usable response with pattern noise 50% higher than the level of training noise.

This finding on the use of noise in training has implications for all RAM-based neural networks and for other implementations also. Optimal representations of class structures using pRAM nets have been achieved and this has been proved by analysis and simulation [16, 17].

5.4
Medical and Biometric Image Analysis

Whilst this does not require a real-time solution, the advantages of a dedicated hardware solution allow an intelligent device to be embedded in medical equipment for thermal image processing [18] or equipment for fingerprint detection [19]. The pRAM-256 offers the advantages of low power consumption and small size.

In this application, the symmetry of the thermal image is significant. Thus preprocessing was used which developed measures of symmetry in the patterns (Fig. 17) and these parameters were input to a neural network. The network was first trained using images labeled using expert opinion. A binary decision only was required, indicating whether an abnormality was present or not. Then the network could be used to give a preliminary decision on further images and only the images where abnormality was reported were presented to a medical expert for final diagnosis. The threshold at which the network output triggered an abnormal diagnosis was made variable and can be adjusted by the users.

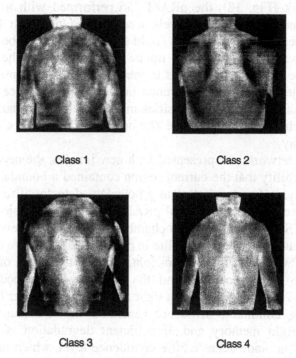

Class 1   Class 2

Class 3   Class 4

Fig. 17. Thermal images classified by a pRAM neural network

5.5
Satellite On-Board Processing

A pRAM-256 device and its SRAM memory were tested in a severe radiation environment to assess the effects of single event upsets (SEUs) on the operation of a neural network [20, 21]. Conventional processors are susceptible to radiation errors unless special and expensive measures are taken. Single-bit errors can be damaging to spacecraft control and on-board processing. It was supposed that a neural network would provide greater redundancy and therefore would perform better in this adverse environment.

A pRAM-256 neural processor was proposed for use in a satellite to allow data to be preprocessed in space and so that the downlink communications requirements would be eased. This ultimately leads to a reduction in the power budget of the satellite for two reasons; shorter transmission periods and the pRAM-256 consumes less power than a conventional microprocessor performing the same task. In the image processing task (Fig. 18), the pRAM-256 performed with no detectable errors when normal radiation levels were used. Only with levels 1000 times that experienced by satellites could some deterioration be noticed.

The task was to segment the image and to identify the land/water boundary. The neural network was trained on image segments containing such boundaries, taken from reference images. The reference images are false-color images with low intensities in the blue region (dark) and high intensities in the red region (light). The output of the network is presented in a similar way.

When this network was presented with new images, the network output was the probability that the current region contained a boundary (Fig. 19). Thus the neural network is acting as a boundary-detector. The two images in Fig. 19 were produced by a real pRAM-256 that was subject to single-event upsets (SEUs) in a radiation chamber. The radiation level was up to 1000 times that expected in a satellite in order that errors were measurable.

The image was processed left-to-right, so that at the start of processing an image, no errors occurred and the boundary is defined with high probability (>70%) and shows as a light area against a darker background. As processing continues, SEUs are generated which corrupt the neural network's weight memory and, if sufficient degradation is caused, the network's output approaches a 50% confidence level, which means „don't know" (see section 4.5.3 above). Thus an output in the *mid-range* region is produced.

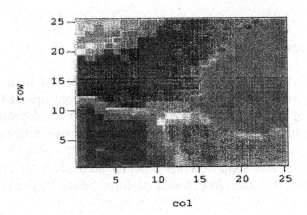

Fig. 18. Landsat image showing land/water boundaries (including a bridge in the center of the image)

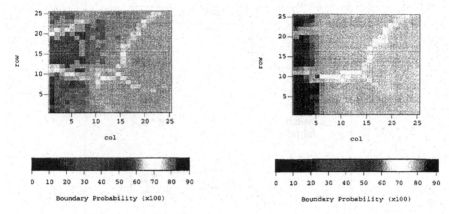

Fig. 19. Satellite images classified by a pRAM neural network subject to data corruption due to SEUs.

Even though deterioration of the output can be seen, the neural network still gives a usable and correct result. It should be repeated that the level of SEUs is considerably higher than would ever be seen in practice. Also, if such a level of single-bit errors occurred in a digital processor performing a similar task, it would be expected to crash at an early stage. Thus the inherent redundancy of a neural processor gives it a higher fault-tolerance than a conventional microprocessor system.

5.6
ATM Network Control

pRAM networks have been used to perform the admission control and policing functions in ATM telecommunications networks. They perform well with stochastic traffic and are able to learn on-line within a telecommunications switch [22, 23, 24, 25, 26, 27].

In this example, call requests are generated at a constant rate of 5 calls/sec in the high traffic state, and 0.01 calls/sec in the low traffic state. The duration of the high and low traffic states is 16 seconds, and the initial number of active connections is 20, so that the number of requests oscillates between $1/P=20$ (peak allocation) and $1/D=100$ (average allocation).

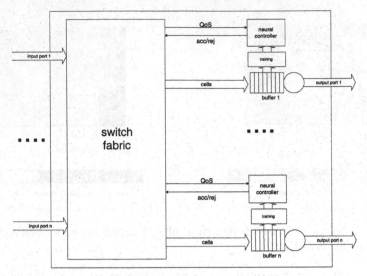

Fig. 20. Integration of a neural controller with an ATM switch.

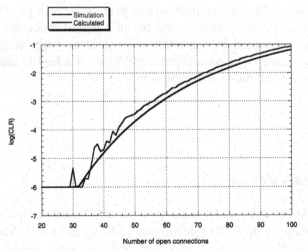

Fig. 21. Comparison of simulated and calculated cell loss rates, showing that the CLR was successfully learned.

The simulation enables us to verify the validity of our method to measure the CLR. The simulation was performed for a simulated time of 5000 seconds with a link capacity of 50 Mb/s. The measured CLR is then compared with the values obtained using an analytical computation of the CLR. The results of this comparison are shown in Fig. 21.

The graph shows that the measured CLR closely follows the analytical calculation for high values of the loss rate, becoming less accurate for lower values. The reason for this is that in order to measure very low values of the CLR we would need to run the simulation for a long time. In a real ATM network this would not be a problem, because the measure would be obtained during normal network operation.

Knowledge of the CLR can then be used in the admission control algorithm. This and many similar neural algorithms have been used and applied in the area of network control. The main advantage of neural hardware is that it allows integration of the controller into the switch hardware. Fast decisions can also be made with the hardware that will allow a given switch to handle many new calls per second.

6
Conclusions

The pRAM-256 is a VLSI processor incorporating 256 neurons with on-chip reinforcement learning. Several of these processors can be used together to form larger networks if required. Owing to a reconfigurable architecture achieved by a look-up table in RAM and a reconfigurable FPGA interface a wide range of applications can be investigated with the same hardware. A selection of applications has been presented.

Once an application has been developed by simulation or using the pRAM-256 hardware above, the delivered system will normally reengineer the pRAM module to customize the number of nodes required, pruning unused neurons and connections. This reduces in size the silicon area and speeds-up the processing by removing unused nodes. In addition, if the final system incorporates custom VLSI hardware of its own, then the pRAM may be fabricated together with the other circuitry in a single custom VLSI design.

References

[1] Aleksander I., *Microcircuit learning computers*, Mills and Boon, London, 1971.
[2] Clarkson T. G., Gorse D., Taylor J. G., Hardware-realizable models of neural processing, *Proc. of IEE International Conference on Artificial Neural Networks*, London, 242-246, 1989

[3]   Clarkson T. G., Gorse D., Taylor J. G., Ng C. K., Learning Probabilistic RAM Nets Using VLSI Structures, *IEEE Transactions on Computers*, 41(12), 1552-1561, 1992

[4]   Clarkson T. G., Ng C. K., Christodoulou C., Guan Y., The pRAM: An Adaptive VLSI Chip, *IEEE Transactions on Neural Networks, Special Issue on Neural Network Hardware*, 4(3), 408-412, 1993

[5]   Clarkson T. G., Gorse D., Taylor J. G., Biologically plausible learning in hardware realizable nets, *Proc. ICANN91 Conf.*, Helsinki, 195-199, 1991

[6]   Ramanan S., Petersen R., Clarkson T. G., Taylor J. G., pRAM nets for detection of small targets in sequences of infra-red images, *Neural Networks*, 8(7/8), 1227-1237, 1995

[7]   Clarkson T. G., Automatic Target Recognition using Neural Networks, *Neural Network World*, 6/95, 861-871, 1995

[8]   Ramanan S., Petersen R. S., Clarkson T. G., Taylor J. G., Adaptive learning rate for training pyramidal pRAM nets, *Proc. ICANN'94*, 1360-13631, 1994

[9]   Ramanan S., Clarkson T. G., Taylor J. G., An adaptive algorithm for training pRAM neural networks on unbalanced data sets, *Electronics Letters*, 34(13), 1335-1336, 1998

[10] Clarkson T. G., Automatic Target Recognition using Neural Networks, *Neural Network World*, 6/95, 861-871, 1995

[11] Guan Y., Clarkson T. G., Taylor J. G., A noisy training method for digit recognition using pRAM neural networks, *Proc. IJCNN'92 Conference*, Beijing, I-673/678, 1992

[12] Guan Y., Clarkson T. G., Aspects of pRAM training in noise, *Proc. WNNW'93 Workshop*, York, 111-116, 1993

[13] El-Mousa A., Clarkson T. G., Output Coding in Noisy-Trained pRAM Neural Networks, *Proc. ICANN'94*, 1356-1359, 1994

[14] Guan Y., Clarkson T. G., Taylor J. G., Learning transformed prototypes (LTP) - a statistical pattern classification technique of neural networks, *From Natural to Artificial Neural Computation*, Eds. Mira and Sandoval, Springer-Verlag, 441-447, 1995

[15] El Mousa A. H., Clarkson T. G., An improved hardware-realizable learning algorithm for pyramidal feed-forward pRAM-based ANNs, *Proc. ANN'95, IEE 4th International Conference on Artificial Neural Networks*, Cambridge, 495-498, 1995

[16] Clarkson T. G., Guan Y., Gorse D., Taylor J. G., Generalization in Probabilistic RAM Nets, *IEEE Transactions on Neural Networks*, 4(2), 360-364, 1993

[17] Guan Y., Clarkson T. G., Taylor J. G., Gorse D., Optimal attractor distributions and generalization in feed-forward pRAM nets, *Proc. BNNS Meeting*, Birmingham, 1993

[18] Ding Y., Guan Y., Clarkson T. G., Clark R. P., The Back Thermal Symmetry Identification by pRAM Neural Networks, *Proc. ANN'95, IEE 4th International Conference on Artificial Neural Networks*, Cambridge, 437-441, 1995

[19] Ding Y., Clarkson T. G., Extracting the directional image of fingerprints by a neural algorithm, *WNNW'95*, Canterbury, 1995

[20] Oldfield M., Underwood C. I., Clarkson T. G., Spacecraft Autonomy Via Probabilistic RAM (pRAM) Artificial Neural Networks, *Proceedings of the 12th AMSAT-UK Colloquium 1997*, University of Surrey, 102-110, 1997

[21] Oldfield M. K., Underwood C. I., Clarkson T. G., Evaluation Of The pRAM Neural Network Processor For Use In Ionizing Radiation Environments, *IEEE Radiation Effects In Electronics Components Conference*, Oxford, September 14-15, 1998

[22] Balaskas I., Jun I., Panteli P. L., Clarkson T. G., Adaptive ATM network traffic modeling using a combined source model, *Proc. ICC'98*, Atlanta, 238-242, 1998

[23] Krasniqi X., Onyiagha G., Clarkson T. G., Performance evaluation of a distributed ATM switch architecture, *International Network Conference (INC'98)*, Plymouth, 1998

[24] Jun I., Panteli P. L., Clarkson T. G., Simulation Analysis with a Measurement based Connection Admission Control on a European ATM Network, *6th IFIP workshop on performance modeling and evaluation of ATM networks* (ATM'98), Bradford, 1998

[25] Onyiagha G., Krasniqi X., Clarkson T. G., OpLIAC - Open-loop intelligent access control for interworking LAN and ATM networks, *6th IFIP workshop on performance modeling and evaluation of ATM networks* (ATM'98), Bradford, 1998

[26] Balestrieri F., Panteli P. L. et. al., ATM connection admission control using pRAM-based artificial neural networks, *6th IFIP workshop on performance modeling and evaluation of ATM networks* (ATM'98), Bradford, 1998

[27] Onyiagha G., Balestrieri F. et. al., Optimal quality of service guarantees for noisy packet data networks, *IEEE Globecom'98*, Sydney, Australia, 13-18, 1998

Part 4

Algorithms for Parallel Machines

Chapter 9

Parallel Subgraph Matching on a Hierarchical Interconnection Network

Stuart Campbell[1], Mohan Kumar[1,2], Horst Bunke[3]

[1]School of Computing, Curtin University of Technology, Perth, Australia.
[2]New address: Department of Computer Science and Engineering, The University of Texas at Arlington, Texas, USA.
[3]Institute of Computer Science and Applied Mathematics, Bern, Switzerland.

The identification of subgraph isomorphisms is a well-known problem that occurs in many application areas. An important variant of the problem occurs when there are many model graphs and a single input graph, and we wish to search for subgraph isomorphisms from any of the model graphs to the input graph. This chapter discusses the Parallel Network (PN) algorithm; a parallel, deterministic algorithm for finding subgraph isomorphisms from a database of attributed, directed model graphs to an attributed, directed input graph. The algorithm decomposes the model graphs and forms the resultant subgraphs into a number of search networks. Subgraphs common to any number of model graphs are represented only once. This approach allows rapid, parallel detection of matches of common subgraphs onto the input graph. In parallel, all mappings found for each model graph are searched to detect complete, consistent mappings, which define subgraph isomorphisms. When used on a hierarchical interconnection network, the algorithm allows local communication to be used to advantage, reducing communication overheads and improving performance.

1
Introduction

Graphs are a flexible data structure, which are used in a wide variety of disciplines and applications. Communication and transport networks, chemical compounds, economies and control processes can all be conveniently modeled using graphs. Detecting subgraph isomorphisms (subgraph matching) can be extremely useful when dealing with graph based representations. However, subgraph matching is a computationally expensive problem, which is known to be NP-complete. If practical use is to be made of subgraph matching there is a requirement for high performance algorithms, capable of dealing with large graphs. Both deterministic and non-deterministic methods have been developed; currently non-deterministic methods must be used if high performance is required on large data sets, although the quality of the result may be less than desired. The use of parallel processing is one possible way to boost the performance of deterministic methods and obtain high quality results in acceptable time.

A new parallel algorithm, the parallel network (PN) algorithm, was designed as an efficient, deterministic, parallel algorithm to detect subgraph isomorphisms from a set of model graphs to a single input graph [7]. The algorithm is irregular in nature, which can result in poor performance if mapped onto a parallel processor with an inappropriate structure. A hierarchical interconnection network allows work distribution to use local communication by preference, resorting to longer communication paths as infrequently as possible, thus saving communication time and increasing performance.

The chapter is set out as follows: Section 2 first outlines some of the many applications of subgraph matching and defines the underlying graph concepts and terminology, then discusses the subgraph isomorphism problem and some existing methods for solving it. Section 3 describes a hierarchical interconnection network, the *hierarchical cliques* (*HiC*) interconnection network. Section 4 describes the PN algorithm, discusses the forms of parallelism within the algorithm, and then considers ways that parallelism can be exploited on a parallel computer using a *HiC* interconnection network. Section 5 analyses the complexity of the algorithm. Conclusions are drawn in Section 6.

2
Subgraph Isomorphisms

2.1
Applications

A large number of applications of subgraph matching have been reported in the literature. It has long been widely used in chemistry, biochemistry and pharmacy. The structure of molecules is readily described in terms of attributed graphs, allowing many useful search and compare functions to be carried out [2], [3], [5], [24], [25]. In electronics the task of identifying subcircuits in large circuit graphs arises naturally in several contexts, such as the extraction of gates from transistor netlists for gate-level simulation, comparing netlists hierarchically, and checking for questionable circuit structures in layout. Subgraph matching presents a natural way of performing this task [19]. In the field of programming language development subgraph matching is an important tool for identifying substructures [21] [23], while in pattern recognition and machine vision some of the many applications reported are floor plan recognition [14] character recognition [16], [22] and searching for models or prototypes in images [6], [27]

2.2
Graph Definitions and Terms

In order to clearly understand both the problem and the proposed solution, it is necessary to have an unambiguous set of terms and definitions with which to describe them. The definitions and notations used here generally follow those in [4].

A graph G is an ordered triple (V(G), E(G), Φ_G) consisting of a nonempty set V(G) of *vertices*, a set E(G), disjoint from V(G), of *edges*, and an *incidence function* Φ_G of a graph that associates with each edge of G an unordered pair of (not necessarily distinct) vertices of G. The number of vertices in G is denoted by |V(G)|, and the number of edges in G by |E(G)|. An example graph is defined below, and shown diagrammatically in Figure 1:

$$H = (V(H), E(H), \Phi_H)$$

where

$$V(H) = \{v_1, v_2, v_3, v_4\}$$
$$E(H) = \{e_1, e_2, e_3, e_4, e_5, e_6\}$$

and Φ_H is defined by:

$$\Phi_H(e_1) = v_1v_2, \Phi_H(e_2) = v_2v_3, \Phi_H(e_3) = v_3v_4$$
$$\Phi_H(e_4) = v_4v_1, \Phi_H(e_5) = v_3v_1, \Phi_H(e_6) = v_4v_2$$

For a graph G, if e is an edge and μ and v are vertices such that $\Phi(e) = \mu v$, then e is said to *join* μ and v; the vertices μ and v are called the *ends* of e. The ends of an edge are said to be *incident* with the edge, and an edge is *incident* with its ends. Two vertices that are incident with a common edge are *adjacent*. An edge with identical ends is called a *loop*. A graph is *simple* if it contains no loops and no two of its edges join the same pair of vertices.

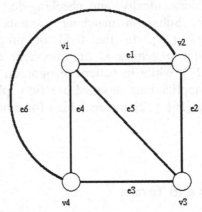

Fig. 1. Diagram of graph H

A directed graph or digraph D is an ordered triple V(D),E(D),Φ_D) consisting of a nonempty set V(D) of *vertices*, a set E(D), disjoint from V(D), of *edges*, and an *incidence function* Φ_D that associates with each edge of D an ordered pair of (not necessarily distinct) vertices of D. Thus a digraph differs from a graph in that edges incorporate an additional property, that of direction. In general, all of the concepts and properties of graphs apply equally to digraphs; however, concepts that involve the notion of orientation apply only to digraphs. An example digraph is defined below, and shown diagrammatically in Figure 2:

$$D = (V(D),E(D),\Phi_D)$$

where

$$V(D) = \{v_1,v_2,v_3,v_4\}$$
$$E(D) = \{e_1,e_2,e_3,e_4,e_5,e_6\}$$

and Φ_D is defined by:

$$\Phi_D(e_1) = (v_1,v_2), \Phi_D(e_2) = (v_2,v_3), \Phi_D(e_3) = (v_3,v_4)$$
$$\Phi_D(e_4) = (v_4,v_1), \Phi_D(e_5) = (v_3,v_1), \Phi_D(e_6) = (v_4,v_2)$$

For a digraph D, if e is an edge and μ and ν are vertices such that $\Phi_D(e) = (\mu, \nu)$, then e is said to *join* μ to ν; μ is the *tail* of e and ν is the *head*. We may say that **tail** $(e) = \mu$ and **head** $(e) = \nu$.

For a set of *attributes* A an attributed graph G is an ordered quadruple $(V(G), E(G), \Phi_G, \alpha_G)$ where α_G is a mapping function that associates with each vertex of V(G) an attribute from A. The attribute of a vertex μ is represented as $\alpha_G (\mu)$.

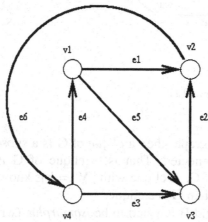

Fig. 2. Diagram of digraph D

When just one graph is under discussion it will usually be denoted by G. In this case symbols such as V(G) may be written simply as V, omitting the G which served only to identify which graph the symbol was referring to. Also, when dealing with simple graphs, it is often convenient to refer to the edge with ends μ and ν as 'the edge μν'. This results in no ambiguity since, in a simple graph, at most one edge joins any pair of vertices.

A graph H is a *subgraph* of G (written $H \subseteq G$) if $V(H) \subseteq V(G)$, $E(H) \subseteq E(G)$ and Φ_H is the restriction of Φ_G to E(H). Figure 3 shows a graph H that is a subgraph of graph G.

Suppose that V' is a nonempty subset of V. The subgraph of G whose vertex set is V' and whose edge set is the set of those edges of G that have both ends in V' is called the subgraph of G *induced* by V' and is denoted by G[V']; the subgraph G[V'] is an *induced subgraph* of G. The induced subgraph obtained from G by deleting the vertices in V' together with their incident edges is denoted by G − V'. In Figure 3, H is not an induced subgraph of G since E(H) does not contain e_1, e_3, e_5, e_6.

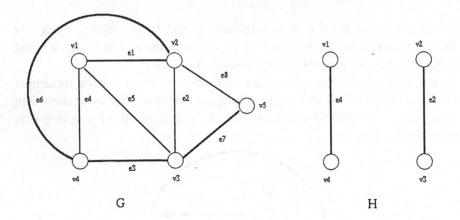

Fig. 3. Properties of G and H

If G is a simple graph, then a *clique* of G is a subset V' of V such that G [V'] is fully connected. That is, a clique of G is a fully connected induced subgraph of G. A clique with $|V'| = k$ is known as a k-clique. If G is fully connected, then G is a clique.

Two graphs G and H are said to be *isomorphic* (written G ≅ H) if there are bijections $\theta:V(G) \to V(H)$ and $\phi:E(G) \to E(H)$ such that $\Phi_G(e) = \mu\nu$ if and only if $\Phi_H(\phi(e)) = \theta(\mu)\theta(\nu)$; such a pair (θ,ϕ) of mappings is called an *isomorphism* between G and H. Figure 4 shows two graphs G and H which are isomorphic. Note that, if G and H are simple graphs, then specifying θ implies ϕ.

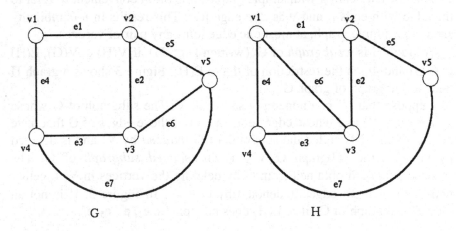

Fig. 4. Isomorphic graphs G and H

For two graphs G and H, G is said to be *subgraph isomorphic* to H if there are injections $\theta:V(G){\to}V(H)$ and $\phi:E(G){\to}E(H)$ such that $\Phi_G(e) = \mu v$ if and only if $\Phi_H(\phi(e)) = \theta(\mu)\theta(v)$; such a pair (θ,ϕ) of mappings is called a *subgraph isomorphism* between G and H. Figure 5 shows two graphs G and H where G is subgraph isomorphic to H.

For two attributed graphs G and H, G is said to be *subgraph isomorphic* to H if there are injections $\theta: V(G){\to}V(H)$ and $\phi: E(G){\to}E(H)$ such that $\alpha_G(\mu) = \alpha_H(\theta(\mu))$ and $\Phi_G(e) = \mu v$ if and only if $\Phi_H(\phi(e)) = \theta(\mu)\theta(v)$.

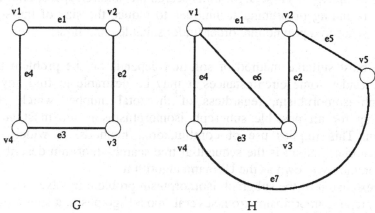

G   H

Fig. 5. Graph G Subgraph Isomorphic to graph H

2.3
Solving the Subgraph Isomorphism Problem

There are many situations where, given two graphs G and H, one may wish to answer the question, does H contain a subgraph isomorphic to G? A special case is the graph isomorphism problem; is H isomorphic to G? The graph isomorphism problem has had polynomial algorithms proposed for several special classes of graphs [8, 10, 12, 13]. Various special cases of the subgraph isomorphism problem are also known, for instance a polynomial algorithm for subgraph isomorphism when G is a tree and H is a forest was reported in [17], and another for two-connected series-parallel graphs in [15]. More recently a polynomial algorithm when G is a *bounded tree-width* graph where $|V(G)| = O(\log|V(H)|)$ was reported in [1]. However the subgraph isomorphism problem in general is known to be NP-complete [11].

Two broad categories of methods exist for solving the subgraph isomorphism problem.

1. Nondeterministic methods which use nonlinear optimization techniques (or heuristic approximations thereof) to reach approximate solutions. Programs employing these methods run in less than exponential time, but may not reach a solution with a satisfactory degree of accuracy.

2. Combinatorial algorithms which are guaranteed to yield the correct solution, but in the worst case have exponential complexity. These algorithms search the solution space, relying on bounding or pruning techniques to reduce the size of the search space to a polynomial order under suitable conditions.

The most suitable method of solution depends on the problem to be solved. Under some circumstances it may be desirable to find any one subgraph isomorphism, regardless of the total number which occur. Searching for all possible subgraph isomorphisms is the most general problem. This implies use of combinatorial methods. A widely used combinatorial method is the sequential tree-search algorithm described in [26], commonly known as the Ullmann algorithm.

An extension of the subgraph isomorphism problem involves searching for subgraph isomorphisms from several 'model' graphs to a single 'input' graph. Messmer and Bunke proposed a two part algorithm to solve this problem in [18]. An "off-line" part of the algorithm involved constructing a search network from subgraphs of all the model graphs. During the "online" portion of the algorithm the network is used to find successively larger subgraphs within the input graph until subgraph isomorphisms from entire model graphs are identified. This approach allowed them to take advantage of common elements within the model graphs, thereby reducing duplication of effort during the "online" search process.

As well as investigating improved serial algorithms, work has also been done on developing parallel algorithms, to allow large graph problems to be solved in reasonable time using powerful parallel computers. There are many avenues for parallelisation of the Ullmann algorithm. Even the original sequential algorithm packed binary vectors into a single word and used bitwise logic in order to achieve some level of parallelism in a single processor environment. This could be described as word parallelism. In a multiprocessor environment the major forms of parallelism available could be described as tree-node parallelism and branch parallelism. Tree-node parallelism uses multiple processors to speed the computation at a single tree-node of the tree. Branch parallelism examines multiple branches of the tree in parallel. Tree-node parallelism tends to result in single branches being descended more rapidly, which can result in a single solution being found faster. Branch parallelism can result in the entire search space being covered more rapidly. The results of a theoretical and experimental study of the effect on performance of the various forms of parallelism were reported in [9]. They showed that the best choice of parallelisation depended on the number of solutions required and the distribution of solutions within the search space, as well as the architecture of the machine on which the algorithm is implemented. In general, they found it preferable to be able to take advantage of all forms of parallelism as the occasion demanded.

We have developed a new parallel algorithm, the parallel network (PN) algorithm, for solving the subgraph isomorphism problem when there are many model digraphs and a single input digraph. The algorithm deals exclusively with simple, directed, attributed graphs. The principles involved could, however, be easily extended to other forms of graph, particularly weighted digraphs. The PN algorithm offers several advantages. Like the algorithm of Messmer and Bunke it has an off-line and an online stage. This allows a database of model graphs to be developed off-line, then matched against input graphs online without the overhead of the off-line stage. At an early stage of the PN algorithm a simple but effective check is performed to detect model graphs which cannot be subgraph isomorphic to the input graph, eliminating them and preventing wasted computation. In its final stage, the PN algorithm employs a tree search similar to that of the Ullmann algorithm. An advantage of the PN algorithm is that each tree-node incorporates more information than a tree-node in the Ullmann algorithm, which allows lookahead techniques to be employed more effectively. Also, in the PN algorithm the number of tree-nodes at each level of the tree is known in advance. This allows levels with the least nodes to be searched first, reducing the best case complexity of the search. The PN algorithm allows effective use of multiple forms of parallelisation and uses dynamic load distribution to achieve efficient use of resources under variable load conditions.

3
Hierarchical Cliques: A Hierarchical Interconnection Network

A factor that can greatly affect the efficiency and ease of design of a parallel algorithm is the interconnection network that provides communication between the processors. Underlying the ability of any interconnection network to be effective and efficient is its topology. The basic characteristics of any interconnection network, including minimum latency, throughput, reliability and cost, are affected by the parameters of the underlying topology. Perhaps the most important aspect of the topology of an interconnection network is the quality of the mappings it allows from problem data and algorithmic processes onto individual processors. A good quality mapping will result in processes being close to data they require, and close to other processes with which they are likely to communicate. Such a mapping means that the majority of communication required will be localized, reducing message latencies and lowering the likelihood and impact of congestion. The addressing scheme used by an interconnection network is also important, as it can affect the efficiency of routing algorithms and the ease with which message passing processes communicate. This section describes the topology, addressing scheme and message passing algorithms of *HiC*s, establishing the basic system descriptions. When describing interconnection networks the convention in the literature is to use graph theoretic terms, but to call vertices *nodes* and edges *links*.

$HiC_{(k,h)}$ is a k-ary tree of height h modified so those groups of nodes on the same level form cliques. Members of a clique are referred to as *neighbors*. The root node is at level h, and has address 0. The k children of the root node are at level $h-1$ and form a clique. They have addresses consisting of a single unique digit in the range 1 to k. In general let μ be a node at level l of $HiC_{(k,h)}$, where $(0 \leq l < h-1)$. Then μ has address M consisting of a sequence of digits $\langle M_l, ..., M_{h-1} \rangle$, where each digit is in the range 1 to k. Consider a second node ν in the same HiC as μ. If ν's address N is a proper suffix of M then ν is an ancestor of μ and μ is a descendant of ν. If M = $\langle M_l, N \rangle$ then ν is the parent of μ and μ is a child of ν. If a sequence P exists such that N = $\langle P, N_{h-1} \rangle$ and M = $\langle P, M_{h-1} \rangle$ then μ and ν are neighbors.

As an example of the structure and addressing scheme of an HiC, consider Figure 6. Figure 6 shows part of an HiC with $k = 4$ and $h = 3$. (Only one quarter of the level 0 nodes is shown). The root node has address 0 and is at level 3. The root node has four children at level 2, with addresses 1, 2, 3 and 4. The nodes at level 2 form a clique; in Figure 6 nodes of a clique are shown enclosed in a dashed line. Each level 2 node has four children at level 1. The address of a node at level 1 consists of the address of its parent node appended to a digit between 1 and 4. The digit distinguishes the level 1 node from its siblings. Thus nodes 12, 22, 32 and 42 are all children of node 2. Nodes at level 1 are neighbors if their parents are neighbors and the first digit of their address is the same; for example nodes 21, 22, 23 and 24 form a clique.

The address of a node at level 0 consists of the address of its parent node appended to a digit between 1 and 4. The digit distinguishes the level 0 node from its siblings. Thus nodes 141, 241, 341 and 441 are all children of node 41. Nodes at level 0 are neighbors if their parents are neighbors and the first digit of their address is the same; for example nodes 241, 242, 243 and 244 form a clique.

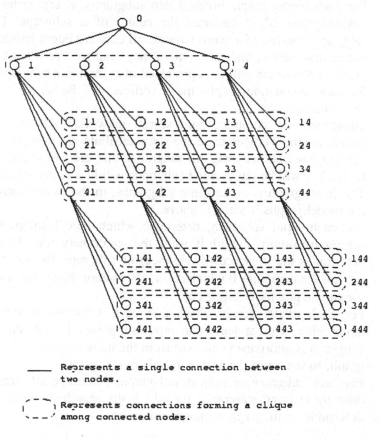

_____ Represents a single connection between two nodes.

⌐‒‒¬ Represents connections forming a clique
⌊‒‒⌋ among connected nodes.

Fig. 6 Part of a *HiC* with *k* = 4 and *h* = 3.

The topology and addressing scheme described can support several different multiprocessor configurations. The configuration being considered here employs processing elements (PEs) only at the leaf nodes and at the root node. The root processor can, if desired, act as a control processor for such things as global synchronization.

4
Algorithm Design and Implementation

For a set of attributed directed model graphs and an attributed directed input graph, we wish to identify any and all subgraph isomorphisms between any of the model graphs and the input graph. Informally, the PN algorithm can be described in the following way.

1. For each model graph, break it into subgraphs. Every vertex that has outgoing edges becomes the center of a subgraph. Every subgraph consists of a central vertex, all outward edges incident to the central vertex, and the vertices they lead to. For a connected graph every vertex will be represented in at least one subgraph and for most interesting graphs many vertices will be represented in several subgraphs.

2. Subgraphs are compiled into search networks. All subgraphs whose central vertices have the same attribute are compiled into the same search network. All subgraphs that are isomorphic with each other will be represented only once within a search network.

3. The input graph is broken into subgraphs, in the same manner as the model graphs in step (1) above.

4. For each input subgraph, determine which model subgraphs is subgraph isomorphic with it, using the search networks. This step determines the presence (or absence) of subgraph isomorphisms, but not the mappings θ which define the isomorphisms (recall that, for simple graphs, θ implies ϕ).

5. For each model graph, check that each subgraph is subgraph isomorphic with at least one input subgraph. If not, then any subgraph isomorphism can exist from the model graph to the input graph, so terminate the search for this model graph.

6. For each subgraph of each model graph, determine all mappings onto those input subgraphs for which the search networks have determined a subgraph isomorphism exists.

7. For each model graph, check for complete, consistent mappings from model subgraphs onto input subgraphs. A complete mapping contains a mapping from every model subgraph. A consistent mapping has no two vertices in the model graph mapped to a single vertex in the input graph, and no vertex in the model graph mapped to more than one vertex in the input graph. Each complete, consistent mapping determines a subgraph isomorphism between the model graph and the input graph.

The algorithm is shown more formally in Algorithms 1 to 12. At the top level, Procedure PN receives as arguments a set of attributed, directed model graphs $M = D_1,...,D_L$, a set of search networks N and an attributed, directed input graph I.

Procedure PN(M, N, I)
Call Off-line (M, N)
Call On-line (N, I)

Algorithm 1: PN algorithm

The algorithm has a pre-processing or off-line stage, comprised of steps one and two in the informal description, and a runtime or online stage, comprising steps three through seven. Maximum advantage is taken of the two stage algorithm if the same set of search networks can be used repeatedly, with many different input graphs. The top level algorithm described here deals only with a single input, but the extension to multiple inputs is trivial. The off-line stage, described in Algorithm 2, simply calls Function *MakeSubs*, described in Algorithm 3, and Procedure *MakeNetworks*, described in Algorithm 4.

4.1
The Off-line Algorithm

Procedure Off-line (M, N)
S_M = MakeSubs (M)
Call MakeNetworks (S_M, N)

Algorithm 2: Decompose model graphs into search networks

Function *MakeSubs* creates a set S_M of subgraphs from the model graphs in *M*. In Figure 7, $M = \{D,E\}$ and $S_M = \{D'_1, D'_2, D'_3, E'_1, E'_2, E'_3\}$. Each subgraph D' has a vertex known as the *central Vertex* $v_C(D')$, which is the tail of all the edges in the subgraph. All other vertices in V(D') are known as *satellite vertices*. For example, in Figure 7 subgraph D'_1 has central vertex v1 with attribute *a*. Subgraph D'_1 has v2 and v3 as satellite vertices.

Function MakeSubs (*M*)
$S = \varnothing$
for all D $\in$ *M* **do**
   for all $\mu \in$ V(D) **do**
      if e $\in$ E(D) such that **tail** (e) = μ **then**
         Construct graph D' $\subseteq$ D such that:
         $\mu \in$ V(D')
         e $\in$ E(D')$\Leftrightarrow$ e $\in$ E(D) and **tail** (e) = μ
         v $\in$ V(D')$\Leftrightarrow$ e $\in$ E(D') and **head** (e) = v
         $S = S + D'$.
Return *S*

Algorithm 3: Decompose model graphs into subgraphs

Procedure *MakeNetworks* transforms S_M into a set of search networks *N* containing zero or more search networks η_j. Each search network $\eta_j \in N$ is an attributed, directed graph which represents those subgraphs in S_M having a central vertex with attribute *j*. As an example, Figure 8 shows the search networks which represent all the subgraphs from Figure 7.

The attribute $\alpha_{\eta_j} (\mu)$ of a vertex $\mu \in$ V(η_j) is an ordered pair ($AO (\mu)$, $D'(\mu)$). With A representing the set of model and input graph vertex attributes, element $AO(\mu)$ is a set of ordered pairs. Each pair (*att*, *ord*) consists of an attribute *att* $\in$ A, and *ord*, the number of times that attribute *att* occurs at this search network vertex. The *size* of a vertex μ, given by **size**(μ), is the sum of the values of *ord* for each pair in $AO(\mu)$. Taken in conjunction with the known attribute *j* of the central vertex, and the restricted structure of the subgraphs in S_M, $AO(\mu)$ contains sufficient information to describe an entire attributed digraph. Looking at Figure 8, it can be seen that vertex v3 of η_a has $AO(v3) = \{(b,1),(c,1)\}$. Thus vertex v3 of η_a represents a graph with a central vertex with attribute *a* and two satellite vertices with attributes *b* and *c*. The second element of $\alpha_{\eta_j} (\mu)$ is

$D'(\mu)$; which is the set, possibly empty, of all subgraphs D' which are isomorphic to the graph represented by $AO(\mu)$ and j. Looking again at vertex v3 of η_a in Figure 8, we see that two subgraphs, D'_1 and E'_2, are isomorphic to the graph v3 represents.

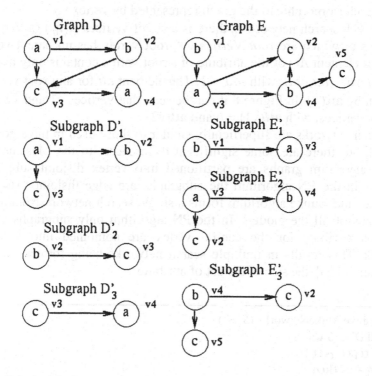

Fig. 7. Subgraphs of graphs D and E

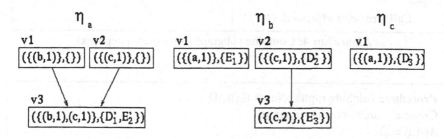

Fig. 8. Search network for model graphs D and E

The direction of the edges in $E(\eta_j)$ indicates a parent/child relationship between vertices; if edge $(\mu,\nu) \in E(\eta_j)$, then vertex μ is a parent of vertex ν in search network η_j. If μ is a parent of ν then the graph represented by the first element of $\alpha_{\eta_j}(\mu)$ is subgraph isomorphic to the graph represented by the first element of $\alpha_{\eta_j}(v)$. In Figure 8 it can be seen that vertex v1 is a parent of v3 in η_a. Vertex v1 represents a graph with a central vertex with attribute a and a satellite vertex with attribute b, which is subgraph isomorphic to the graph represented by vertex v3.

For each search network η_j there is a set of vertices $R(\eta_j) \subseteq V(\eta_j)$ the elements of which are *root* V*ertices*. A root vertex has no parent vertex. The first element AO of the attribute of a root vertex contains only a single ordered pair *(att,ord)*, with *ord* = 1. The element *att* for any root vertex μ is given by $\mathbf{att}(\mu)$. In Figure 8 it can be seen that vertices v1 and v2 of η_a are root vertices, with $\mathbf{att}(v1) = b$ and $\mathbf{att}(v2) = c$.

Search networks are superficially similar to those used in the algorithm of [18], but there are some significant differences. In the Messmer and Bunke algorithm graphs are partitioned into vertex disjoint subgraphs, whereas in the PN algorithm the subgraphs are edge disjoint. Also, the Messmer and Bunke algorithm forms a single search network from all the subgraphs of all the models. In the PN algorithm only subgraphs with a common attribute for the central vertex are combined into a search network. This results in multiple search networks being formed, up to a maximum of $|A|$, the size of the set of attributes.

Procedure MakeNetworks (S, N)
for all D' $\in S$ **do**
   $j = \alpha_{D'}(v_C(D'))$
   if $\eta_j \in N$ **then**
      Call AddToNetwork (η_j, D')
   else
      Call CreateNewNetwork (N, D')

Algorithm 4: Combine subgraphs into search networks

Procedure AddSubgraphToNetwork(η_j, D')
Create a search network vertex μ
$AO(\mu) = \varnothing$
$D'(\mu) = D'$
for all $v \in V(D')$ such that $v \neq v_C(D')$ **do**
   if $(att,ord) \in AO(\mu)$ such that $att = \alpha_{D'}(v)$ **then**
      $ord = ord + 1$
   else
      $AO(\mu) = AO(\mu) + (\alpha_{D'}(v),1)$
Call AddToNetwork (η_j, μ)

Algorithm 5: Combine subgraphs into an existing search network

---

Procedure AddToNetwork (η_j, μ)

if $\nexists$ (*att*,*ord*) $\in$ $AO(\mu)$ such that *att* = **att**(v) for any v $\in$ $R(\eta_j)$ **then**
   $V(\eta_j) = V(\eta_j) + \mu$
   Call ExpandNetwork (η_j , μ)
else
   Find v $\in$ $V(\eta_j)$ such that max (**size** (v)) and $AO(v) \subseteq AO(\mu)$.
   if size (v) = size(μ) **then**
      $D'(v) = D'(v) \cup D'(\mu)$
   else
      $V(\eta_j) = V(\eta_j) + \mu$.
      $E(\eta_j) = E(\eta_j) + (v, \mu)$
      Create a new search network vertex υ
      for all (*att*,*ord*) $\in$ $AO(\mu)$ **do**
         $AO(\upsilon) = AO(\upsilon) + (att,ord(\mu) - ord(v))$
      Call AddToNetwork2(η_j , υ, μ)

Algorithm 6: Combine search vertices into search networks: part I

Procedure AddToNetwork2(η_j,μ,ω)

if $\nexists$ (*att*,*ord*) $\in$ $AO(\mu)$ such that *att* = **att**(v) for any v $\in$ $R(\eta_j)$ **then**
   $V(\eta_j) = V(\eta_j) + \mu$
   $E(\eta_j) = E(\eta_j) + (\mu,\omega)$
   Call ExpandNetwork(η_j ,μ)
else
   Find v $\in$ $V(\eta_j)$ such that max (**size**(v)) and $AO(v) \subseteq AO(\mu)$.
   if size(v) = size(μ) **then**
      $D'(v) = D'(v) \cup D'(\mu)$
      $E(\eta_j) = E(\eta_j) + (v, \omega)$
   else
      $V(\eta_j) = V(\eta_j) + \mu$.
      $E(\eta_j) = E(\eta_j) + (\mu,\omega)$
      $E(\eta_j) = E(\eta_j) + (v,\mu)$
      Create a new search network vertex υ
      for all(*att*,*ord*) $\in$ $AO(\mu)$ **do**
         $AO(\upsilon) = AO(\upsilon) + (att,ord(\mu) - ord(v))$
      Call AddToNetwork2(η_i,υ,μ)

Algorithm 7: Combine search vertices into search networks: part 2

Procedure CreateNewNetwork (N, D')
$j = \alpha_{D'}(v_C(D'))$
Create a network η_j
$N = N + \eta_j$
Create a search network vertex μ with $AO(\mu) = \varnothing$ and $D'(\mu) = D$
for all $v \in V(D')$ such that $v \neq v_C(D')$ **do**
   if $(att, ord) \in AO(\mu)$ such that $att = \alpha_{D'}(v)$ **then**
      $ord = ord + 1$
   else
      $AO(\mu) = AO(\mu) + (\alpha_{D'}(v), 1)$
$V(\eta_j) = V(\eta_j) + \mu$
Call ExpandNetwork(η_j, μ)

Algorithm 8: Create a search network

Procedure ExpandNetwork(η_j, μ)
Given $AO(\mu) = \{(att_1, ord_1), \ldots, (att_k, ord_k)\}$
if $k > 1$ **then**
   Create a search network vertex v
   $AO(v) = \{(att_1, ord_1)\}$
   $D'(v) = \varnothing$
   $V(\eta_j) = V(\eta_j) + v$
   $E(\eta_j) = E(\eta_j) + (v, \mu)$
   Create a search network vertex υ
   $AO(\upsilon) = \{(att_2, ord_2), \ldots, (att_k, ord_k)\}$
   $D'(\upsilon) = \varnothing$
   $V(\eta_j) = V(\eta_j) + \upsilon$
   $E(\eta_j) = E(\eta_j) + (\upsilon, \mu)$
   Call ExpandNetwork(η_j, v)
   Call ExpandNetwork(η_j, υ)
else
   if $ord_1 > 1$ **then**
      Create a search network vertex v
      $AO(v) = \{(att_1, 1)\}$
      $D'(v) = \varnothing$
      $V(\eta_j) = V(\eta_j) + v$
      $E(\eta_j) = E(\eta_j) + (v, \mu)$

Algorithm 9: Expand a search network

4.2
The On-line Algorithm

The algorithm of Procedure *Online* is described in Algorithm 10 for a directed, attributed input graph I and a set of search networks N. It calls Function *MakeSubs*, described in Algorithm 3, to create a set S_I of subgraphs from the input graph. Figure 9 shows an example input graph and the subgraphs derived from it. Function *SearchNetworks*, shown in Algorithm 11, then uses the search networks in N to determine whether subgraph isomorphisms exist between any model subgraphs and the input subgraphs in S_I. Subgraph isomorphisms are searched for in search networks made up of model subgraphs with the same attribute for the central vertex. For an input subgraph I' with $\alpha_{I'}(v_C(I')) = j$, each root vertex μ of η_j is *visited* once for each satellite vertex v of I' with $\alpha_{I'}(v) = $ **att**(μ). The number of times vertex μ has been visited is given by **visit**(μ). Once all satellite vertices of I' have been considered, the search visits all vertices of η_j which are *eligible*. Two types of vertex are eligible.

1. A vertex μ where $AO(\mu)$ contains only a single ordered pair (*att,ord*) with *ord* > 1 has only a single parent, the root node v where **att**(v) = *att*. Vertex μ is cligible if *ord* ≤ **vislt**(v).
2. A vertex μ where $AO(\mu)$ contains more than one ordered pair has two parents. Vertex μ is eligible if both parents have been visited.

Procedure On-line(N,I)
S_I = MakeSubs({I})
P = SearchNetworks(S_I,N)
Call Mappings(M,S_M,P)

Algorithm 10: Determine subgraph isomorphisms from search networks

The search continues to visit eligible vertices until no more can be found. No checking for the existence of edges or vertices linking the subgraphs represented by the parent nodes is required. This means that the network can very rapidly find all model subgraphs that are subgraph isomorphic to the input subgraph. The output from Function *SearchNetworks* is a set P of ordered pairs of model subgraphs and input subgraphs to which they are subgraph isomorphic. For the example input graph shown in Figure 9 and the search networks shown in Figure 8 the result of SearchNetworks is

$$P = \{(D'_3,I'_1),(D'_3,I'_2),(D'_2,I'_3),(E'_3,I'_3),(D'_1,I'_4),(E'_2,I'_4)\}. \quad (1)$$

```
Function SearchNetworks(S,N )
P = ∅
for all I' ∈ S do
  j = α_{I'}(v_C(I'))
  if η_j ∈ N then
    for all v ∈ V(I') such that v ≠ v_C(I') do
      if ∃μ ∈ R(η_j) such that att(μ)= α_{I'}(v) then
        Visit μ
    for all μ ∈ V(η_j) do
      Given AO(μ)={(att_1,ord_1), ... ,(att_k , ord_k)}
        if k = 1 and ord_1 > 1 then
          if (v, μ ) ∈ E(η_j) and visits (v) ≥ ord_1  then
            Visit μ
    repeat
      for all μ ∈ V(η_j) do
        if (v, μ ) ∈ E(η_j) and (υ,μ) ∈ E(η_j) and visits(v) ≥ 1 and
          visits(υ) ≥ 1 then
            Visit μ
    until No new vertices visited
    for all  μ ∈ V(η_j) which are Visited do
    for all D' ∈ D'(μ) do
      P = P + (D',I')
Return P
```

Algorithm 11: Search Networks

Procedure *Mappings*, detailed in Algorithm 12, is a three step algorithm, corresponding to steps 5, 6 and 7 in the informal description. The first step determines, for each model graph D in M, whether all the subgraphs of D are subgraph isomorphic to at least one subgraph of the input graph I. If not then D cannot be subgraph isomorphic to I, so no further processing is required.

Consider the set P shown in Equation 1, which is derived from the example model graphs shown in Figure 7 and the example input graph shown in Figure 9. For model graph D, all three subgraphs D'_1, D'_2 and D'_3 are subgraph isomorphic to at least one subgraph of I. However, for model graph E subgraph E'_1 is not subgraph isomorphic to any subgraphs of the input graph, so model graph E need not be considered further.

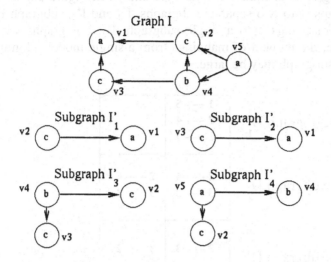

Fig. 9. Subgraphs of input graph *I*

Procedure Mappings(*M*,*S$_M$*,*P*)
for all D ∈ *M* **do**
    INCOMPLETE = FALSE
    for all D'∈ *S$_M$* such that D' ⊆ D **do**
        if ∄ (D',I') ∈ *P* **then**
            D can not be subgraph isomorphic to I
            INCOMPLETE = TRUE
        else
            for all (D',I') ∈ *P* **do**
                Determine all possible mappings from D' to I'
    if NOT INCOMPLETE **then**
        Perform a tree search of mappings to determine any which are complete
        and consistent.
        Output all complete consistent mappings found.

Algorithm 12: Create mappings between subgraphs and detect subgraph
isomorphisms

If every subgraph of D is subgraph isomorphic to at least one subgraph
of I the second stage of the algorithm is entered. The second stage
determines, for each pair of subgraphs (D',I') ∈ *P* with D' ⊆ D, all
possible mappings from D' to I'. In the example graphs, the mappings

from the subgraphs of model D onto I are shown in Figure 10. Note that, while D'$_3$ maps onto two separate subgraphs, I'$_1$ and I'$_2$, subgraph D'$_2$ has two distinct mappings onto a single subgraph, I'$_3$. For graphs with high vertex degree, the number of mappings from a single model subgraph to a single input subgraph may be large.

Subgraph D'$_1$	1 --- 5 2 --- 4 3 --- 2	
Subgraph D'$_2$	2 --- 4 3 --- 2	2 --- 4 3 --- 3
Subgraph D'$_3$	3 --- 3 4 --- 1	3 --- 2 4 --- 1

Fig. 10. Mappings of subgraphs of graph D onto input graph I

The third and final stage of the algorithm detects any and all combinations of mappings from subgraphs of model D to input subgraphs that form a single *complete* and *consistent* mapping. A complete mapping contains a mapping from every model subgraph to the input graph. A consistent mapping has no two vertices in the model graph mapped to a single vertex in the input graph, and no vertex in the model graph mapped to more than one vertex in the input graph. Each complete, consistent mapping determines a subgraph isomorphism between the model graph and the input graph. Searching for complete, consistent mappings can be done using a tree search. Each level of the tree corresponds to a single model subgraph. Each tree-node at a level represents a mapping from the model subgraph to some input subgraph. Expanding a tree-node means comparing the tree-node mapping with the mapping accumulated from previously expanded tree-nodes. If any inconsistencies occur, the branch is pruned. Otherwise the mapping is added to the accumulated mapping and the search continues down the tree. Looking at Figure 10, expanding the single node at the top level of the tree D$_1$' gives a mapping $\theta(v1) = v5, \theta(v2) = v4, \theta(v3) = v2, \theta(v4) = v1$. This mapping is consistent, but not complete. Expanding the first node at the next level of the tree D$_2$' compares the mapping $\theta(v2) = v4, \theta(v3) = v2$ with the existing mapping, revealing no inconsistencies. Proceeding to expand the first node at the bottom level of the tree D_3' reveals an inconsistency, as $\theta(v3) = v3$ conflicts with the current mapping of $(v3) = v2$. This branch is therefore pruned and we proceed to expand the next node of the bottom level. This reveals no inconsistency, and since this was a node at the bottom of the tree the mapping it produces must also be complete, since a node from every level of the tree, representing every subgraph of the model graph, has been expanded. We have therefore discovered a subgraph isomorphism from D to I, given by the mapping $\theta(v1) = v5, \theta(v2) = v4, \theta(v3) = v2$, $\theta(v4) = v1$. Since there are no further nodes at the bottom level we return to the level above and expand the second node there. An inconsistency is revealed, $\theta(v3) = v3$ conflicts with the current mapping of $(v3) = v2$. This branch is therefore pruned and the search terminates.

4.3
Parallelism within the PN Algorithm

Although designed as a parallel algorithm, the descriptions of the PN algorithm so far have included no explicit parallel statements. There are many opportunities for exploiting parallelism within the PN algorithm. In this section the major areas of potential parallelism will be described, and the circumstances under which they are most likely to be useful will be discussed. Although the off-line stage of the algorithm is not insignificant, the online stage will generally have the most impact on overall performance. This section considers the parallelisation only of the online stage of the algorithm, as shown in Algorithm 10.

Function *MakeSubs*, shown in Algorithm 3, transforms the input graph into a set of subgraphs S_I. The transformation is essentially a binning algorithm, allocating the edges in E (I) with a common originating vertex to bins. This can be done sequentially in linear time. It can also be considered an embarrassingly parallel problem, as it can readily be divided into completely separate sub-problems. For most applications, it would be expected that the number of edges $|E(I)| < 10000$, so it is likely to be effective to parallelise this part of the algorithm only with a small number of tightly coupled processors. When employing the *HiC* architecture, the processor at the root node would perform this task. If a number of input graphs were to be checked against an existing database of model graphs, the root processor could be expected to transform one input graph while the previous one was being checked by the PEs at the leaves.

Function *SearchNetworks*, shown in Algorithm 11, uses the search networks in N to determine whether subgraph isomorphisms exist between any model subgraphs and the input subgraphs in S_I. During the off-line stage, search networks are allocated to processors. Online, each input subgraph may be allocated to a separate processor with the appropriate network. Each subgraph can be processed independently of all others. Since the number of input subgraphs in S_I is less than or equal to $|V(I)|$, the maximum parallelism available is of order $|V(I)|$.

Procedure *Mappings*, detailed in Algorithm 12, involves three steps for each model graph in M. Since each model graph can be treated independently for this procedure, individual models can be allocated to separate PEs. Thus there is already parallelism of the order of $|M|$ available. The first step determines, for each model graph D in M, whether all the subgraphs of D are subgraph isomorphic to at least one subgraph of the input graph I. This step simply checks the number of input subgraphs which each model subgraph has been found subgraph isomorphic to, and can be done in linear time. The second stage determines all possible mappings from the model subgraphs onto the input subgraphs they are known to match. Since each pair of model and input subgraphs can be searched for mappings independently, this process readily offers parallelism according to the number of subgraphs in a model and the number of input subgraphs each model subgraph matches. Beyond this, however, each search is readily parallelizable, allowing this stage of the algorithm to use as many processors as the workload efficiently allows. The third stage performs a tree search of the mappings determined in the second stage to determine any complete and consistent mappings from a single model graph D to the input graph I. No more than $|M|$ tree searches are required, however it is possible to employ either branch parallelism or tree-node parallelism, or both, during this stage. As discussed earlier, it was shown in [9] that the best choice of branch or tree-node parallelisation depended on the number of solutions required and the distribution of solutions within the search space, as well as the architecture of the machine on which the algorithm is implemented.

4.4
Parallelising the PN Algorithm on the HiC

The PN algorithm is a highly irregular algorithm, as the amount of computation and communication required, within the algorithm as a whole and within individual stages, varies substantially with the size and nature of the data sets used, as well as the exact output required. Under these circumstances it is difficult to map the problem onto a parallel architecture in such a way as to match the capabilities of the architecture with the requirements of the problem, since the requirements are highly variable.

One approach to this problem is typified by the parallel depth first search method of [20], where available work is maintained on a stack and idle processors request work from the controlling processor. This has proven an effective means of dividing work in order to employ many processors without incurring prohibitive management overheads. In the PN algorithm, however, each of the major stages requires either centralization of work to a single stack, which can incur considerable communication overheads, or the use of multiple work stacks on multiple processors. In a request oriented system, if multiple work stacks are maintained a processor requiring work must determine which processor it should request work from. The hierarchical structure of the *HiC* architecture provides a natural sequence for processors to follow when requesting work. An idle processor will look for work first amongst its neighbors. The rich local connectivity allows work to be rapidly distributed at a local level, meaning the workload within a clique will be rapidly balanced. If an entire clique is idle, the processors within it will seek work from their siblings. If any processor or processors within the clique receive work, the load can quickly be balanced among the members of the clique. Proceeding in this way, work can be effectively distributed amongst all processors in a self-organizing manner that minimizes the distances over which work must be transmitted.

5
Complexity

This section analyses the worst case, complexity of the PN algorithm and makes some comparisons with existing algorithms. As in the previous section only the online part of the algorithm will be considered. It is worth noting that all combinatorial methods for solving the subgraph isomorphism problem will have worst case complexity that is at least exponential. All algorithms aim to provide acceptable average case performance, generally over as wide a range of inputs as possible. Worst case complexity analysis in this case is not useful as a means of performance comparison. Rather it can be used to predict which types of input are likely to result in poor performance.

We use the following notations:

- $|V(I)|$, the number of vertices in the input graph I.
- $|E(I)|$, the number of edges in the input graph I.
- $|A|$, the number of possible attributes of a model or input graph.

- $|M|$, the number of model graphs.
- $|S_I|$, the number of subgraphs in the input graph.
- $|S_M|$, the total number of subgraphs in all model graphs.
- $|R(\eta_j)|$, the number of root vertices in search network η_j.
- $|V(\eta_j)|$, the total number of vertices in search network η_j.
- $V_m = \max(|V(D)|)\ \forall\ D \in M$, the maximum number of vertices in any model graph.
- $Z_i = \max(|V(I')|)\ \forall\ I' \in S_I$, the maximum size of the subgraphs in S_I.
- $Z_m = \max(|V(D')|)\ \forall\ D' \in S_M$, the maximum size of the subgraphs in S_M.
- P, the number of processors used.

Function *MakeSubs*, shown in Algorithm 3, bins all the edges in I in $O(|E(I)|)$ time. The maximum number of edges $|E(I)| = O(|V(I)|^2)$, so *MakeSubs* is $O(|V(I)|^2)$.

For input subgraph I' with $\alpha_{I'}(v_C(I')) = j$, and search network η_j, Function *SearchNetworks*, shown in Algorithm 11, first searches each root vertex of η_j for each satellite vertex $\mu \in V(I')$, in time

$$O(|R(\eta_j)| \times |V(I')|).$$

In the worst case $|V(I')| = Z_i$, so this stage takes time

$$O(|R(\eta_j)| \times Z_i).$$

Next, eligible vertices are visited. A vertex is visited in constant time. The search network is checked iteratively until no eligible vertices are found during an entire pass. This process takes time

$$O((|V(\eta_j)| - |R(\eta_j)|)^2).$$

Finally, each visited vertex μ adds the set $D'(\mu)$ of model subgraphs it represents to the set P of pairs of subgraph isomorphic subgraphs. In the worst case $|S_M|$ model subgraphs will be added in $O(|S_M|)$ time.

For each I' $\in S_I$ the search is purely sequential. Therefore, for $|S_I| \leq P$, the total complexity of Function *SearchNetworks* is

$$O((|R(\eta_j)| \times |V(I')|) + (|V(\eta_j)| - |R(\eta_j)|)^2 + |S_M|).$$

For $|S_I| > P$, the total complexity of Function *SearchNetworks* is

$$O\left((|S_I|/P)((|R(\eta_j)| \times |V(I')|) + (|V(\eta_j)| - |R(\eta_j)|)^2 + |S_M|)\right).$$

For a model graph $D \in M$, the set S_M of model subgraphs, and the set P of pairs of subgraph isomorphic subgraphs, Procedure *Mappings*, shown in Algorithm 12, first checks that each subgraph $D' \subseteq D$ occurs at least once in P. Since the maximum number of subgraphs of a model graph is the number of vertices in the model, this takes $O(|V(D)|)$ time.

The second stage determines, for each pair of subgraphs $(D', I') \in P$ with $D' \subseteq D$, all possible mappings from D' to I'. Determining all mappings for a single pair of subgraphs takes time $O(|V(I')|^{|V(D')|})$. If all subgraphs of all models are to be mapped to all subgraphs of the input graph, using P processors, it will take time

$$O(|S_M| \times |S_I| \times Z_i^{Zm}/P).$$

In the worst case $|A| = 1$, all model graphs are of the same size, and both the model and input graphs are fully connected. Under these circumstances,

$$Z_m = O(|V(D)|),$$

$$V_m = O(|V(D)|),$$

$$|S_M| = O(|M| \times |V(D)|),$$

$$Z_i = O(|V(I)|)$$

$$S_I = O(|V(I)|).$$

The final worst case time complexity for the second stage is therefore

$$O(|M| \times |V(D)| \times |V(I)| \times |V(I)|^{|V(D)|}/P).$$

The third stage performs a tree search of the mappings of each subgraph of a model, searching for complete, consistent mappings from the model graph to the input graph. The complexity of tree search is given by the number of tree-nodes to expand at each level, to the power of the number of levels. The worst case conditions for stage two are also the worst case conditions for this stage. The number of levels in the search is the number of subgraphs in the model, worst case $|V(D)|$. The number of tree-nodes at a level is the number of mappings found for each subgraph in the model. Under worst case conditions the number of mappings from a single model subgraph to a single input subgraph is

$$O\left(\frac{(|V(I)|)!}{(|V(I)|-|V(D)|)!}\right),$$

and every model subgraph maps onto every input subgraph where $|V(I')|\geq|V(D')|$. The number of tree-nodes at a level is therefore

$$O\left(\frac{(|V(I)|)!\times|V(I)|}{(|V(I)|-|V(D)|)!}\right),$$

and the worst case number of tree-node expansions is

$$O\left(\left(\frac{(|V(I)|)!\times|V(I)|}{(|V(I)|-|V(D)|)!}\right)^{|V(D)|}\right).$$

Finally, the search must be performed for all models using P processors, so the final worst case complexity is

$$O\left(\frac{|M|}{P}\left(\left(\frac{(|V(I)|)!\times|V(I)|}{(|V(I)|-|V(D)|)!}\right)^{|V(D)|}\right)\right).$$

Now looking at the complexity of the entire procedure, it can be seen that the third stage dominates the first two, and the worst case complexity for the procedure is

$$O\left(\frac{|M|}{P}\left(\left(\frac{(|V(I)|)!\times|V(I)|}{(|V(I)|-|V(D)|)!}\right)^{|V(D)|}\right)\right).$$

The worst case occurs when all graphs have only one attribute, all graphs are fully connected, and all graphs are the same size.

The worst case complexity for the entire PN algorithm is determined by procedure *Mappings*. The worst case for the serial Ullmann algorithm is

$$O\left(|V(I)|^{|V(D)|}\times|V(D)|^2\times|M|\right)$$

and the worst case for the algorithm of [18] is also

$$O\left(\left|V(I)\right|^{\left|V(D)\right|}\times\left|V(D)\right|^{2}\times\left|M\right|\right).$$

Thus the worst case performance of the PN algorithm is inferior to existing methods. In particular, the algorithm can be expected to perform poorly when all graphs have only one or two attributes, and are densely or fully connected. Tree search methods generally rely on "average case" problems, where only a small fraction of the total search space needs to be visited. For such non-extremal cases the complexity appears comparable, while offering better parallelisability than the Messmer and Bunke algorithm and more efficient processing of multiple models than the Ullmann algorithm.

6
Conclusions

This chapter described the Parallel Network algorithm; a parallel, deterministic algorithm for finding subgraph isomorphisms from a database of attributed, directed model graphs to an attributed, directed input graph. The algorithm utilizes a combination of search networks and tree search to achieve a high level of parallelism. Although the algorithm can be implemented on any parallel architecture, a hierarchically structured interconnection network seems to offer particular advantages. The benefits of implementing the PN algorithm on one particular hierarchical network, the *HiC* s, have been discussed. The *HiC* s offers the low communication overheads of fully connected clusters of processors combined with the flexible structure and reasonable cost of a hierarchy.

Extension of the algorithm to work with weighted graphs and attributed relational graphs is straightforward. It is possible that a graph distance measure can be obtained by counting the number of inconsistencies found in mappings.

References

[1] Alon, N., Yuster, R., and Zwick, U. (1995): "Color-coding", *Journal of the Association of Computing Machinery*, 42 (4), 844–856.

[2] Artymiuk, P., Grindley, H., Poirrette, A., Rice, D., Ujah, E., and Willett, P. (1994): "Identification of beta-sheet motifs, of psi-loops and of patterns of acid residues in three dimensional protein structures using a subgraph isomorphism algorithm", *Journal of Chemical Information and Computer Sciences*, 34, 54–62.

[3] Benstock, J., Berndt, D., and Agarwal, K. (1988): "Graph embedding in synchem2, an expert system for organic synthesis discovery". *Discrete Applied Mathematics*, 19, 45–63.

[4] Bondy, J. and Murty, U. (1976): *"Graph Theory with Applications"*, The MacMillan Press.

[5] Bruno, L.J., Kemp, N.M., Artymiuk, P.J., and Willett, P. (1997): "Representation and searching of carbohydrate structures using graph-theoretic techniques", *Carbohydrate Research*, 304, 61—67

[6] Bunke, H. and Allermann, G. (1983): "Inexact graph matching for structural pattern recognition", *Pattern Recognition Letters*, 1, 245–253.

[7] Campbell, S. and Kumar, M. (1998): "A novel parallel algorithm for finding subgraph isomorphisms", *Proceedings of Ninth Australasian Workshop on Combinatorial Algorithms*, pages 40–51. School of Computing, Curtin University of Technology, Perth WA.

[8] Chen, L. (1996): "Graph isomorphism and identification matrices: Parallel algorithms", *IEEE Transactions on Parallel and Distributed Systems*, 7(3), 308–319.

[9] Crowl, L., Crovella, M., LeBlanc, T., and M.L.Scott (1994): "The advantages of multiple parallelizations in combinatorial search", *Journal of Parallel and Distributed Computing*, 21, 110–123.

[10] Galil, Z., Hoffmann, C., Luks, E., Schnorr, C., and Weber, A. (1987): "An $o(n^3 \log n)$ deterministic and an $o(n^3)$ las vegas isomorphism test for trivalent graphs", *Journal of the Association of Computing Machinery*, 34(3), 513–531.

[11] Garey, M. and Johnson, D. (1979): "Computers and Intractability: A Guide to the Theory of NP-Completeness", W.H. Freeman and Company.

[12] Hsu, W.-L. (1995): "$o(m\ n)$ algorithms for the recognition and isomorphism problems on circular-arc graphs", *SIAM Journal of Computing*, 24(3), 411–439.

[13] Jaja, J. and Kosaraju, S. (1988): "Parallel algorithms for planar graph isomorphism and related problems", *IEEE Transactions on Circuits and Systems*, 35(3), 304–310.

[14] Llados, J., Lopez-Krahe, J., and Martí, E. (1997): "A system to understand hand drawn floor plans using subgraph isomorphism and Hough transform" *Machine Vision and Applications*, 10(3), pp. 150-158, July

[15] Lingas, A. and Syslo, M. (1988): "*A polynomial time algorithm for subgraph isomorphism of two-connected series-parallel graphs*", Lecture Notes in Computer Science, volume 317, pages 394–409. Springer. Proceedings of the 15th International Colloquium on Automata, Languages and Programming

[16] Lu, S.W., Ren, Y. and Suen, C.Y. (1991): "Hierarchical attributed graph representation and recognition of handwritten Chinese characters", *Pattern Recognition*, Vol. 24, pp 617—632.

[17] Matula, D. (1978): "Subtree isomorphism in $o(n^{5/2})$". *Annals of Discrete Mathematics*, 2, 91–106.

[18] Messmer, B. and Bunke, H. (1993): "*A network based approach to exact and inexact graph matching*", Technical Report IAM-93-021, University of Bern, Institute for informatics and applied mathematics.

[19] Ohlrich, M., Ebeling, C., Gingting E., and Sather, L. (June 1993): "SubGemini: identifying subcircuits using a fast subgraph isomorphism algorithm", *Proceedings of the 30th IEEE/ACM Design Automation Conference.*

[20] Rao, V. and Kumar, V. (1987): "Parallel depth first search, part i: Implementation", *International Journal of Parallel Programming*, 16(6), 479–499.

[21] Rekers, J and Schurr, A (1997): "Defining and parsing visual languages with layered graph grammars", *Journal of Visual Languages and Computing*, Vol. 8, 27—55.

[22] Rocha, J. and Pavlidis, T. (1994): "A shape analysis model with applications to a character recognition system", *IEEE Trans. On Pattern Analysis and Machine Intelligence*, Vol. 16, 393—404.

[23] Rodgers, P.J. and King, P.J.H. (1997): "A graph-rewriting visual language for database programming", *Journal of Visual Languages and Computing*, Vol. 8, 641—674.

[24] Rouvray, D.H. and Balaban, A.T. (1979): "Chemical applications of graph theory", R.J. Wilson and L.W. Beineke (eds.): *Applications of Graph Theory*, 177—221, Academic Press.

[25] Truhlar, D.G., Jeffrey Howe, W., Hopfinger, A.J. Blaney, A.J. (Eds.) (1999): "*Rational Drug Design*" (The IMA Volumes in Mathematics and its Applications. Eds.: A. Friedman, R. Gulliver. Vol. 108)

[26] Ullmann, J. (1976): "An algorithm for subgraph isomorphism". *Journal of the Association for Computing Machinery*, 23(1), 31–42.

[27] Wong, E. (1992): "Model matching in robot vision by subgraph isomorphism". *Pattern Recognition*, 25(3), 287–303.

About the Editors

Horia-Nicolai L. Teodorescu has served as a professor at several universities, currently serving as Chancellor of the Department of Electronics and Communications, Technical University of Iasi, Iasi, Romania. Dr. Teodorescu received an MS degree and a Doctoral degree in Electronics, in 1975 and 1981 respectively. He served as a founding director of the Center for Fuzzy Systems and Approximate Reasoning at the Technical University of Iasi, Iasi, Romania, and as a professor at the same university from 1990. He was an invited or visiting professor in Japan (1992, 1993, 1994), Switzerland (1994, 1995, 1996, 1997, 1999) and Spain (1993, 1996). Dr. Teodorescu has written about 250 papers, authored, co-authored, edited or co-edited more than 20 volumes, and holds 21 patents. He won several gold and silver medals for his inventions in various invention exhibitions. He authored many papers on biomedical engineering and applications of fuzzy and neuro-fuzzy systems to medical engineering and holds 11 patents in the field of biomedical engineering. He won several grants for research on applying fuzzy systems in biomedical applications. He is a Senior Member of the IEEE, and holds several honorific titles, including "Eminent Scientist" of Fuzzy Logic Systems Institute, Japan, and he was awarded the Honorary Medal of the Higher Economic School in Barcelona, Spain. He has been a *correspondent member* of the Romanian Academy, from 1993. Dr. Teodorescu is a founding Chief Editor of *Fuzzy Systems & A.I.– Reports and Letters, International Journal for Chaos Theory and Applications, Iasi Polytechnic Magazine* and of *Magazine for Fuzzy Systems* and he was a founding Co-Director of *Fuzzy Economic Review* (Spain). He served as an Associate Editor to IEEE Transactions on Cybernetic and Systems – C. He is a member of the editorial boards of *Fuzzy Sets and Systems, The Journal of Grey Systems, BUSEFAL – Bulletin for Studies and Exchange of Fuzziness and its Applications, Journal of Information Sciences of Moldavia, Review for Inventions, Romanian Journal of Information Science and Technology*, and *Journal of AEDEM*. He served as a chairman or co-chairman of the scientific committees of several international conferences and was a member of the scientific committees of more than 40 international conferences.

Dr. Teodorescu is one of the Chief Editors of *Fuzzy Systems & A.I.– Reports and Letters, International Journal for Chaos Theory and Applications, Iasi Polytechnic Magazine* and of *Magazine for Fuzzy Systems* and a Co-Director of *Fuzzy Economic Review*. He is a member of the editorial boards of *Fuzzy Sets and Systems, The Journal of Grey Systems, BUSEFAL – Bulletin for Studies and Exchange of Fuzziness and its Applications, Journal of Information Sciences of Moldavia, Review for Inventions*, and *Journal of AEDEM*.

Dr. Teodorescu has been a Vice–President of SIGEF, the International Society for Fuzzy Systems in Economy and Management, and he is a Vice-President of AMSE Association for Modeling and Simulation in Enterprises, and served as President of the Balkan Union for Fuzzy Systems and of the Romanian Society for Fuzzy Systems. He served as a chairman on the scientific committees of several international conferences and was a member of the scientific committees of more than 40 international conferences.

Lakhmi C. Jain is the Director/Founder of the Knowledge-Based Intelligent Engineering Systems (KES) Centre, located in the University of South Australia. He is a fellow of the Institution of Engineers Australia. He has initiated a postgraduate stream by research in the Knowledge-based Intelligent Engineering Systems area. He has presented a number of Keynote addresses in International Conferences on Knowledge-Based Systems, Neural Networks, Fuzzy Systems and Hybrid Systems.

He served as an Associate Editor of the IEEE Transactions on Industrial Electronics. Dr Jain was the Technical chair of the ETD2000 International Conference in 1995, Publications Chair of the Australian and New Zealand Conference on Intelligent Information Systems in 1996. He also initiated the First International Conference on Knowledge-based Intelligent Electronic Systems in 1997. This is now an annual event He served as the Vice President of the Electronics Association of South Australia in 1997.

Abraham Kandel received a B.Sc. from the Technion – Israel Institute of Technology and a M.S. from the University of California, both in Electrical Engineering and a Ph.D. in Electrical Engineering and Computer Science from the University of New Mexico. Dr. Kandel, a Professor and an Endowed Eminent Scholar in Computer Science and Engineering, is the Chairman of the Department of Computer Science and Engineering at the University of South Florida. Previously he was Professor and Founding Chairman of the Computer Science Department at Florida State University as well as the Director of the Institute of Expert Systems and Robotics at

FSU and the Director of the State University System Center for Artificial Intelligence at FSU.

He is editor of the Fuzzy Track – IEEE MICRO, an Associate Editor of IEEE Transaction on Systems, Man, and Cybernetics, and a member of the editorial board of the international journals *Fuzzy Sets and Systems, Information Sciences, Expert Systems, Engineering Applications of Artificial Intelligence, The Journal of Grey Systems, Control Engineering Practice, Fuzzy Systems – Reports and Letters, IEEE Transactions on Fuzzy Systems, Book Series on Studies in Fuzzy Decision and Control, Applied Computing Review Journal, Journal of neural Network World, The Journal of Fuzzy Mathematics, and BUSEFAL – Bulletin for Studies and Exchange of Fuzziness and its Applications.*

Dr. Kandel has published over 350 research papers for numerous professional publications in Computer Science and Engineering. He is co-author of *Fuzzy Switching and Automata: Theory and Applications* (1979); author of *Fuzzy Techniques in Pattern Recognition* (1982); co-author of Discrete *Mathematics for Computer Scientists* (1983), and *Fuzzy Relational Databases – A Key to Expert Systems* (1984); co-editor of *Approximate Reasoning in Expert Systems* (1985); author of *Fuzzy Mathematical Techniques with Applications* (1986); co-editor of *Engineering Risk and Hazard Assessment* (1988); co-author of *Elements of Computer Organization* (1989), and *Real-Time Expert Systems Computer Architecture* (1991); editor of *Fuzzy Expert Systems* (1992); co-editor of *Hybrid Architectures for Intelligent Systems* (1992); co-author of *Verification and Validation of Rule-Based Fuzzy Control Systems* (1993) and *Fundamentals of Computer Numerical Analysis* (1994), co-editor of *Fuzzy Control Systems* (1994), and co-author of *Fuzzy Expert Tools* (1996). Dr. Kandel is a Fellow of the IEEE, A Fellow of the New York Academy of Sciences, a Fellow of AAAS, as well as a member of the ACM, NAFIPS, IFSA, ASEE and Sigma-Xi.

Dr. Kandel has been awarded the College of Engineering Outstanding Researcher Award, USF 1993-94, Sigma-Xi Outstanding Faculty Researcher Award, 1995, The Theodore and Venette-Askounes Ashford Distinguished Scholar Award, USF, 1995, MOISIL International Foundation Gold Medal for Lifetime Achievements, 1996 and the Distinguished Researcher Award, USF, 1997.

Index of Terms

4-input fuzzy processor, 154